This is the shocking, y[...] author. With twists, turns, highs, lows, and intrigue, it explores the common-sense of the life of one man, his devoted family, and fellow patriots whose response to government overreach parallels the lives of the lives of the Founding Fathers of this great experiment known as the United States Of America.

It's a story not yet finished in its telling. It's a story every family should read and declare in their own voice! It's a story you must decide for yourself: Is Cliven Bundy an American Terrorist or an American Patriot?

Visit us at *ClivenBundy.net*

Author
Michael Stickler

Mike is an author, radio host, ex-felon, and a highly sought after motivational speaker. His best-selling book, A Journey to Generosity, is widely acclaimed throughout the Christian community. He is the publisher of Generous Living Magazine and writes for the *Christian Post* 'Generous Life' column.

www.MikeStickler.com

CLIVEN BUNDY
American ~~Terrorist~~
PATRIOT

MICHAEL L. STICKLER

Publisher:
The Vision Group, Ltd
www.TheVisionGroupltd.com
Copyright © 2017 by Michael L. Stickler
All Rights Reserved.

ISBN: 978-0-9907441-5-3 (paperback)

Cover Art:
Cliven Bundy "Pray For America"
Artist Jon McNaughton
www.jonmcnaughton.com

Graphic Design:
KAnneDesigns

Images courtesy of The Bundy Ranch or depositphotos.com collection

Published December 2017 (hardcover)
Second edition August 2018, fully revised (hardcover & paperback)
Based on the book *Cliven Bundy: American Patriot* by Michael L. Stickler
Published by The Vision Group, Ltd.
Printed and distributed by Ingram Press

Arthur Ritter, the principle editor of this book.

My friend, mentor and the man God put in my life to make me a better writer.

From the Author:

Most people would think a book is a lonely endeavor. For me it takes a team. The help of these people have made this work a collaborative effort.

Jerry Brewer, editor
Without whose story-telling expertise and personal encouragement, I would have never made sense of all the vast information and research.

Mariah Bliss, editor
Whose professionalism I admire.

Tom Clegg, Steve Wark, Wendy Gault, & Rob Boyland
Whose invaluable critiques and suggestions I greatly needed.

Of course my wife, **Kim**, who makes my life complete. Her encouragement makes me think I can do anything.

Cliven Bundy dedicates his story to his friends and neighbors who were pushed out of the life they loved by the United States Government

Dick Reid	Von Jones	Donnie Hughes
Arther Hughes	Nephi Johnson	Chuck Simmons
Mr. Frie	Johny Jensen	Slats Jacob
Jack Hardy	Melber Jensen	Kenny Sesrell
Kent Hardy	Kelley Jensen	Munt Perkins
Charels Hardy	Omer Jensen	Jimmy Hayworth
Abe Teerlink	Andrew Jensen	Frank Taylor
Carl Wyco	Jeff Jensen	Piute Indians
Fransus Myers	Richard Jensen	3 Sodoi Brothers
Mr. Lanely	Christeen Reber	Kenny Meyers
Jim Wittmore	Danks Adams	Fay Leavitt
Denies Wittmore	Calvin Adams	Arron Leavitt
Rallen Esplin	Harmen Witwer	Kelby Hughes
Hank Rice	Merel Witwer	Dale Hunt
Paul Lewies	Melvin Hughes	Kerry Woods
Bill Pulsipher	Dan Waite	Bruce Jensen
Billie Pulsipher	Von Leavitt	Theron Jensen
Howerd Pulsipher	Duddy Leavitt	Mr. Brummery
Rex Bell	David Bundy	Howard Hughes
Alen Nay	Newl Bundy	LDS Church
Keith Nay	Mr. Longreen	John Fru
Norm Tom	Mr. Larson	Mr. Nutter
Eddy Yates	Emer Leavitt	Mr. Hartmen
Max Laitton	Lowdy Leavitt	Harley Adams
Max Hafen	Archie Hughes	Bud Hardy
Mr. Hafen	George Allen	Larry Hardy
Miss Grup	Mr. Bingum	Harmon Witwer
Mr. Akins	Daniel Benilld	Dave Fisher
Don Whitney	Dale Allen	

Table of Contents

Ryan Bundy stepped purposefully to the podium. He carried a thick, yellow legal pad with the pages folded over, writing appeared on nearly every page. He cleared his throat and fumbled about for a few seconds. Then, looking directly at the jury, began his opening statement:

"This is my ID, not my driver's license." He shows a photo of his family on the big screen behind him. *"This is who I am: a man with a family and 'I'll do whatever it takes' to provide for them.*

I want you to picture in your minds that you're out on the land. I'll take you to our ranch where you can see all the beauty of the land, the fresh air, sunsets and sunrises, the brush. You're on a horse in front of the cattle – place yourself there and feel the freedom, out of the congestion of the city – that's how I was raised. Playing in the river there, we called ourselves river rats. That is where my life began, and I hope ends.

My family has been on that land 141 years; my pioneer ancestors settled there in 1877. There was nothing there. They carved out a living; they brought a horse and wagon; some provisions.

This case, the government mentioned, is 'not about rights.' But it is. Those rights do mean something; rights are created through beneficial use. When my ancestors arrived, undoubtedly the horse would need a drink, so they lead him to the water. That is beneficial use. The horse and perhaps a cow that had been lead behind the wagon needed to eat some brush in the hills. That is beneficial use. That use established rights. The water rights are real! So real that the State of Nevada has a water rights registry, including livestock watering rights. The State of Nevada created a law to protect those rights. The water rights that my father owns were first registered in 1891 by this State. The State of Nevada is important; a sovereign state – its own unit – that entered the Union in 1864. It entered equal to the original states; it is its own entity and state laws are important.

My family and I are charged with some grievous things. They are not true and evidence will show they are not. Force, manipulation, extortion, violence – my family is not a violent family and I am not a violent man. For 20-plus years we turned to local law enforcement. Rights are real property. The fact is that 'We The People' create government to protect our rights.

To have rights you must claim, use, and defend them. Man only has rights he is willing to claim, use and defend.

There is a difference between rights and privileges.

Rights you own.

A privilege is afforded, like renting or owning a house. The Government asserts there are no rights – only privileges – and unless we pay, we can't be there. The State of Nevada says differently. These are my father's rights. Everything we have comes from the land. That is wealth, not the dollar bill. The things we use all come from the land and who controls the land, controls the wealth.

We create government to preserve and serve us. These are some of the beliefs of my family. That we have said "we will do whatever it takes" is not a threat; it is a statement. Being right here before you the jury today is part of 'doing whatever it takes.' The Founding Fathers pledged whatever it would take: their lives, their fortunes, and their sacred honor to defend rights. With the evidence you will see, that is what we were doing. There was no conspiracy to impede, to harm, but to protect our heritage that our pioneer ancestors established. We were attacked, surrounded by what appeared to be mercenaries, snipers pointed directly at me. You will hear a report from a sniper that he was keeping watch of me in my van with my wife and two of my daughters with me.

Our ranch – where children are always welcome – is a place to play, play in the river, the pond, chase or hunt rabbits, burn your toes in the hot sand in summer: always free. Never before did we feel like someone was always watching.

In early spring of 2014 we felt like someone was always watching. Our dogs were watching the hills. When you are always with a dog you get to know what they are saying with their bark. You can tell by their bark what they are seeing – surveillance cameras on one hill, but the dog looking at another and growling.

This is not what America is supposed to be. It's supposed to be a land of liberty. The Founding Fathers fought and bled so we wouldn't have to and now we find ourselves in a similar situation.

They say this issue is over grazing fees..." it's terrible, terrible, he must be a freeloader" – it's only rhetoric. I'll tell you why: You don't pay rent when you own your home! We own those rights! Not the land, I know we don't own the land, but access. You and others have rights on that land. We own water and grazing rights.

We don't pay rent for something we own.

The BLM was formed in 1960. Our rights were established in 1877, long before BLM. The original states own <u>100%</u> of their land and all states were to come in on equal footing. The crux of the issue is: Are we a state or not? They say grazing is a privilege they can revoke and charge fees. If it is only a matter of money it is no problem. In fact, Mr. Whipple," referring to his father's – Cliven Bundy – lawyer, "showed a copy of a check made out to Clark County. If the whole purpose is to show we owe a fee, then we'll pay to the proper owner of the land. That was not the only check written to Clark County, we sent several. Also, in Clark County there were 53 ranchers who owned rights. There is only a single one still out on the range. My father, Cliven Bundy.

The BLM is not gaining revenue; it's not important to them. My father could see they were there to manage him out of business. It's not about grazing fees. In the BLM office there were signs that read: No More Moo by '92 and Cattle Free by '93! If it were only about the grazing fees, the fees would have been under $100,000 over 25 years. It is rumored – it may not be seen in evidence – but it is rumored that they spent $6 million on the operation. Who spends that and court costs rumored to be over $100 million to collect $100,000?

What is this about? The court orders! They say my father had an opportunity in the courts. The court wouldn't consider states rights. They have forgotten they are servants of the people. 'We the People' are the sovereign and, ultimately, 'We the People' are the government formed to meet needs that are better met by a group than by individuals. We are not slaves; we need to remember that. I think that's forgotten. The definition of freedom is lost in America. When we have to have a license or ask permission to do everything, we are subjects to a ruler.

Back to the charges... They claimed I went to Richfield, Utah, and that the sheriff had to be called because we were causing such a ruckus – evidence will show otherwise. We boycott to influence to change ways; we protest to cause a change. These are first amendment rights! We that should be called the prohibition of government. We have freedom of speech, freedom of the press, freedom of religion, freedom of assembly. We can petition for a redress of grievances: rights we don't want the government to mess with.

A redress is to find an answer, find a solution – one way to protest. The BLM put up first amendment zones – not much bigger than this courtroom and we called them "pigpens" – and by creating that area, they were denying our right everywhere else. That's what they used to arrest my brother; he was outside the pigpens. The First Amendment has been protected over and over again in our history. There's lots of media here in the gallery today; they wouldn't be happy to have their right to free speech taken. The First Amendment was put in the Supreme Law of the land, the Constitution – they shall make no law restricting these things. As you saw in the video yesterday, my brother was not impeding, was not blocking, he was on a state road, on its right of way, simply to take pictures with his iPad of them stealing our cattle. The BLM attacked him, threw him to the ground, rubbed his face in the ground.

The American public saw this and came not to impede or do harm. They came because they felt the Spirit of the Lord, spirit of freedom and felt "we the people are not going to put up with that behavior." It was not pointed out there were snipers on the hill. I witnessed that through binoculars and the evidence will show this."

Ryan paused for several seconds and flipped back through his notes. Then continued.

"Back to Richfield, Utah... Evidence and witness testimony will show there was not a ruckus there that disrupted or shut down that auction. I called the sheriff – that's the pattern – the local law enforcement and state brand inspectors in Nevada, Arizona and Utah and I had contact with the highway patrol, county commissioners in several counties and state officials – not all face to face, but some through phone calls. Is this what a criminal does? No. We were there protecting life, liberty, property.

You saw the video of the officer hip chucking my Aunt Margaret, 50 plus years and just finished with cancer treatments, the mother of 11 children. They call these BLM guys law enforcement, but they are just BLM employees. All authority comes from 'We the People;' we delegate authority to the county sheriff, who we elect, and he hires deputies. And we then have a sheriff's department to protect our life, our liberty, our property. Choosing for yourself is freedom and we have no right to impede or harm others. That's God's law. Man-made law is to follow that. Man is supposed to be free, not controlled, serfs, or slaves. Government is to be our servant. The government went in and shut down 600,000 acres.

Not one of us ever went into their enclosed area and never impeded them. Even my brother driving into the dump truck; isn't that impediment? The court order did not allow destruction of water infrastructure. What was a dump truck doing out there? Since that was beyond the scope of the supposed court order, we had a right to know. They could have stopped and answered our questions. But no, they set out attack dogs and Tasers and threw Aunt Margaret to the ground.

Every incident they are charging us with happened on property that belonged to the State of Nevada. Even if BLM had authority to close public land, they have no authority to close State of Nevada public land. The fence was on the State of Nevada land. Except by invitation, you will not see one of us breach that fence or impede the gather of cattle. We did not violate the court order. Dave (Ryan's Brother) went over the fence by the invitation of BLM officers. And then the sheriff took over and asked for our help to take down the fence. Then the cowboys, led by sheriff's squad cars, went to release the cattle. The sheriff honored his oath and did his job.

He should have done it sooner.

I love my family. I love them. I love this land. I love freedom. I am from the State of Nevada. I'm a true Nevadan. I mentioned before that Nevada became a state on October 31ˢᵗ and we always got out of school on that day. I always thought we got out because it was my birthday. I'm a true Nevadan. I believe you are, too, and love freedom as much as I do.

Our freedom's not being lost overseas; it's lost right here at home in our backyards, our front yards. Until we are willing to "do whatever it takes," liberty will be – is being – lost.

We are not anti-government! Government has its proper place and duties to perform. I want government to do its job. Nothing more. Nothing less. When government does more or less than its job, it becomes the criminal. When government damages our rights, it becomes the criminal. When someone harms or damages another's life, liberty or property that is the definition of a criminal. Extortion, violence, pointing guns – everything we are charged with, they were doing and thousands of people came running – the world knew about this – China, Ireland (they sent us a flag), New Zealand and other countries. Why? Because America stood for freedom and has for years and the world is interested in seeing how America will deal with its freedom. The world wants to know. The American people said, 'Yes, we will stand for freedom. Government, you've gone too far and we will put a stop to it.'

The courts have a place. It is said that 'We the People' are the fourth branch of government. I say we are the first. The legislature to make laws, the executive to execute laws and the judicial to judge. All three branches are to protect your rights, our rights, freedom, liberty.

Government does not have the authority in and of itself – man creates government to fulfill and protect our rights. 'We the People' give government the authority through the Constitution. The Tenth Amendment insures state's rights.

Evidence will show my father and my brothers are innocent men. We need you to put on that paper that we are not guilty. You are the twelve to represent us: peers, equals, people ... We the People.

Guns ... lots of guns ... scary ... camo ... freedom of speech ... also, the right to bear arms, the Second Amendment ... a militia was necessary. What is a militia? It is defined in the law. U.S. Code defines militia: "all able-bodied men 17-45 years of age". How many of you are a member of the militia? State of Nevada extended that and includes men up to the age of 64. How many of you now are a member of the Nevada militia? There is the organized militia, the National Guard and the unorganized militia – everyone else.

Why did the Founding Fathers include the Second Amendment? Was it for duck hunting? No ... no! Militia is mentioned six times in the Constitution. Such a small document and few things are mentioned more than the militia; the central government of this union and yet media or whoever wants to put a bad face on militia.

Why did militia come to Bundy Ranch? To peacefully assemble, redress of grievances. No one was harmed except Davey, Ammon and Margaret. You will not see in evidence that we ever harmed anyone! They attack and we turned the other cheek. We were peaceful. Insistent? Yes! And, yes, demanding. These men, these people did not come to seek an opportunity to point guns at government. Hundreds, even thousands of people we didn't know. That's exemplary. These people came to do good: to protect me; to save my life. I had a sniper pointing at me, 200 armed men surrounding my home, my family. Ryan Payne has been portrayed as a bad man. Evidence will show otherwise. He saved my life. He saved my life. Others came. I didn't even meet most of them until I was in jail with them. May have seen them in passing, but I didn't know them until jail. I honor and thank them now! I thank all who came. We only have rights we are willing to fight for.

You'll see evidence that I was nearly always with the sheriff or a deputy – always in communication with them – I was side-by-side with (Sheriff) Lombardo.

Thank you for coming, for being here. I will still "do whatever it takes."
This is not a threat; it is a statement of <u>determination</u>.

I love my freedom. Listen to the still small voice to discern between truth and
error. The indictment and grand jury testimony is full of lies. Truth has been
blocked in previous trials. Listen closely – we will try to get you the truth.
The truth will set me free and I'm counting on you to help me see that.

I invite you to our ranch.
I recognize your right to use the land.
We want you to come and enjoy it.

I thank you for this time. Please find me not guilty and these other men not
guilty. Stand up for freedom.

Thank you."

Ryan folded his papers back neatly, smiled to the jury and walked
quietly back to his seat in the courtroom. The courtroom remained
silent and the halls of justice became hallowed halls, all due to the
words of a simple rancher's son.

Ryan Bundy's opening statement in the criminal trial of his brother Ammon, his
father Cliven, Ryan Payne and himself, Las Vegas, Nevada, 15 November 2017.
(Edited lightly for readability.)

Chapter 1

– THE AMBUSH –
Cliven Bundy's Arrest

It was a cool, clear winter day on the ranch. Cliven Bundy, farmer, rancher, (and, some would say – rabble-rouser) was bouncing down the dusty ranch road in his ol' ranch pickup.

As his cell phone rang, Cliven wrestled to pull it from his front shirt pocket, the seatbelt pinning it in his pocket as it crossed over his chest. All the while he was thinking to himself that driving, bouncing, and answering the phone was not so easy anymore for a man sixty-nine years old. Persevering through the frustration of the struggle in the lurching vehicle, he finally got the phone to his ear. The words that came through its speaker were nothing any father would ever want to hear.

"Cliven, Ryan has been shot." There's a long pause. "He's dead."

Not quite grasping what he had just heard, Cliven asked the only thing he could, "What happened?"

The voice on the other end told a tale that was like something out of a blockbuster movie. Two of his boys – and others – had taken over the Harney County Resource Center in Oregon to focus attention on the plight of two local-area ranchers who had been abused by the government. Ammon and Ryan Bundy, along with a group of others including LaVoy Finicum, Shawna Cox, Ryan Payne, and several others, decided to occupy the Center some 35 miles outside of the little town of Burns, Oregon – hoping to get both the media and the publics attention to the governmental abuses of ranchers in the west.

During the "Take Over," as the media portrayed it, Ryan and Ammon often traveled to surrounding counties to speak at various events and to local officials about this subject.

What had happened?
On the afternoon of January 26, 2016, a two-vehicle caravan departed the Harney County Resource Center and passed through the nearby

mountain range on the road to John Day, Oregon. They were headed out to meet with the local Sheriff, Glenn Palmer, and a group of about 400 citizens to speak with them about the purpose of the occupation at the resource center.

The occupants of the lead truck were Robert "LaVoy" Finicum, accompanied by Ryan Bundy, Shawna Cox, and Ryan Payne. A young woman who had just turned 18 years-old the day before, singer, Victoria Sharp, at the last minute decided to come along in LaVoy's truck. She caught a ride with LaVoy because there was an extra seat, her mom and the remainder of her family's music group having gone on ahead. The Sharp Family Singers had joined the others at the Resource Center only the day before.

As Ryan Bundy held the door for Victoria to climb into the back seat of the four-door pick-up, he noticed a plane circling above his head. He didn't give it much thought as it or some other plane had been overhead day and night since they all had moved into the Resource Center. He glanced back at the vehicle behind them; there was something not right in Ryan's spirit about the driver. He paused and wondered, then chose to ignore his intuition.

Mark McConnell drove the second vehicle, a Jeep with passengers Ammon Bundy and Bryan "Buddha" Cavalier. To the public, Mark portrayed himself as Ammon's security guard. It would turn out later that Mark was an FBI confidential informant and he had already notified his FBI handler of their route and departure time.

This FBI para-military unit's task was to preclude another 'Bundy ranch incident' from happening, an incident that, two-years prior, that had made world news, deeply humiliating the Federal Government. Still stinging from the last time, this time the FBI brought in this highly trained team of operators, determined that the embarrassment from two years ago would not be repeated. They had planned to 'cut the head off' the leadership of this unfolding Harney County Resource Center "Take Over" – Ryan and Ammon Bundy.

Ryan and Ammon were unaware of the FBI's plan. In fact, they were on relatively friendly terms with the FBI agents there, regularly speaking to them during the preceding weeks. As recently as the night before, Ammon had asked if the FBI leadership wanted to come with them to see what they were doing at their various speaking engagements.

No one had any idea whatsoever what was about to happen … except, of course, the FBI.

As the truck traveled up the winding mountain road, Ryan Bundy decided he would call ahead to advise Sheriff Palmer of their estimated time of arrival. As he lifted his cell phone to his ear … nothing. He was distracted for a moment as he looked out the left passenger window and noticed the same plane was paralleling them, miles from the Resource Center and a bit lower this time.

"Darn, I'm out of range," he uttered in frustration.

Simultaneously, LaVoy remarked, "We have company!"

As they passed an intersecting dirt road, he'd noticed a dozen black vans and trucks in a line with blacked-out windows, the only distinguishable item being the flashing red and blue lights glaring out the front grill of the engine compartment as they pulled out behind the Jeep behind LaVoy's truck.

In the Jeep, in a tone much too calm for the situation at hand, Mark added, "What should we do?"

"Pull over," Ammon simply replied.

While they talked, LaVoy's truck slowed down and stopped just in front of them in the middle of the road about 100 yards ahead of the Jeep.

As soon as LaVoy's pickup stopped, Ryan Payne put both his hands out its front passenger window showing them he had no weapon. Immediately they heard a CRACK from behind them shattering the right passenger mirror. Ryan Payne jerked his hands back inside, realizing from his military experience that he was being shot at.

LaVoy wasn't having any of it. He leaned his head out the driver's window and peered back at the ominous-looking black vehicles behind them. He began shouting at them.

"Shoot me, you shoot me. I'm going to meet the Sheriff; the Sheriff is waiting for us. So, you do as you damn well please; but, I'm not going anywhere. Here I am."

"Right there," pointing directly at the cowboy hat he was wearing. Continuing, he yelled, "Right there – put a bullet through it."

"You understand? I'm gonna go meet the Sheriff. You back down or you kill me now."

Then again, he motioned to his head, "Go ahead, put the bullet through me. I don't care."

"I'm gonna go meet the sheriff. You do as you damn well please," LaVoy hollered out again.

From a distance, a voice from behind them again shouted the command to exit their vehicle.

"What for?" Shawna questioned, somewhat indignant.

"Well I'm gonna ask them if they wanna get out," LaVoy yells back at the officers.

"What for? Why are we getting out?" Shawna franticly asked again, still not seeming to fully understand the gravity of the situation.

LaVoy turned his head back to the remaining passengers, "You want out?"

"What for?" Shawna exclaimed in frustration. "Why are we getting out?"

"Who are you?!" Ryan Bundy bellowed out the left side passenger window. "Yeah, who are you? Who are you? Who are you?!"

"Oregon State Police," was shouted back.

Well, now they knew.

"Okay, well I'm goin' over to meet the Sheriff in John Day," LaVoy snapped loudly in response. "You come along with us and you talk with us over there."

Again, the command to exit the vehicle was voiced from one of the two vehicles leading that unmarked dirty dozen now positioned on the road behind them.

Carefully, Ryan Payne opened the door to exit the truck with his hands up and started walking to the rear. Shawna looked out the rear window as Payne was arrested, "Is Ryan okay?" she mutters.

"You can go ahead and shoot me. Put the laser right there, put the bullet through the head. Okay boys? This is gonna get real. You want my blood on your hands? Get it done because we got people to see and places to go," LaVoy reiterated his position. "You're wasting oxygen, son. I'm goin' into Grant County to see the Sheriff."

Each time LaVoy or Ryan Bundy stuck their head out of the truck to communicate, a red dot from a laser-targeting weapon had appeared on their forehead.

Then Shawna proposed, "Well, if we duck and you drive what are they gonna do? Try to knock us out?"

There ensued a flurry of discussion between the occupants, and then LaVoy leaned out the window again.

"Boys! You better realize, we got people on the way. You want a blood bath, it's gonna be on your hands. You got we're gonna go see the Sheriff? Better understand how this things gonna end. Gonna be laying down here on the ground with my blood on the street or I'm gonna go see the Sheriff." LaVoy was bluffing.

Now frantic, Shawna tried to dial some numbers on her cell phone to get some help. "They know it, there's no service here," she mumbled to no avail.

"We should never have stopped. We should never have stopped." Ryan stressed to LaVoy.

"I'm gonna keep goin'." LaVoy avowed.

Shawna glanced at Victoria. "Then we're gonna have to duck, you know what I'm saying? Because of Ryan. We need to get Ryan back." "Okay. You ready?" Looking back over his right shoulder LaVoy cried out, "They gotta stop, you can't get around it. I'm gonna go. You guys ready?"

"Okay get... get down." Ryan snapped at the two women.

Ryan was concerned about his brother and the other vehicle. "But what about Ammon and those guys?"

"They can't, we can't get around them. I'm gonna go get help." LaVoy said, now fired up.

"Okay!" Ryan agreed.

"Okay. Stay down, stay down, stay down!" screamed Shawna.

LaVoy jammed the truck into gear and it lurched forward, speeding off. The black vehicles didn't follow ... at first. Instead, they opened fire, hitting the fleeing truck three or four times.

But the attempted getaway only lasted for a few seconds.

Just ahead, around a long bend in the highway, a roadblock awaited with a dozen or more of the FBI's Hostage Rescue Team (HRT) members and the Oregon State Police. Their vehicles and barricade materials blockaded the road surface, the armed HRT and State Police positioned behind and among them, forming an ambush of sorts.

Viewed from the approach, across the full width of the roadway and its shoulder to the right, stood the barricades and more black vehicles, all of which were blocking the road and its right shoulder. But this deployment left open the narrow, soft shoulder between a large snow bank on the road's left embankment and the last roadblocking vehicle on the roadway surface – a space barely wide enough for a vehicle to pass through; but, a thin path of escape.

Well to the left of that snow bank, and hidden in the tree line, were armed men in tactical dress. Shooting gun supports were set up by cutting the branches off the trees, leaving just four or five inches upon which to brace their rifles.

The trap was set. Its victims lured in. The dozen unmarked, black and windows-blacked-out vehicles revving in behind, slamming that door shut behind them.

LaVoy, however, pointed his truck at that narrow, soft shoulder on the left, figuring that he could just barely fit the truck in between the barricade and the snow bank.

"Hang on!" LaVoy shouted.

Nearly simultaneously Ryan barked, "Hey!" as he was startled by a muzzle flash from around the roadblock. Two bullets pierced the cab of the truck at the window and roof line. Others were hitting the front grill of the truck. The subsequent shots missed.

Shawna cried out, "Okay, they're shooting."

Again, LaVoy shouted, "Hang on!" as he steered the truck for the opening at the embankment, nearly missing an FBI agent momentarily flushed from his cover position.

Startled by LaVoy's truck's abrupt leap toward the barricade truck that covered his position, an agent who had been behind the barricade-truck next to the narrow shoulder had sprinted toward the snowbank, away from his cover that he feared would have soon be hit and crush him – but actually into the real path of the LaVoy's truck. LaVoy jerked the steering wheel to the left, just missing him. But instantly, his truck was buried in the snowbank, tilting to the right in response to its snap-left turn, the wheels spinning helplessly in the snow.

Bullets riddled the truck compartment. Everyone but LaVoy had dropped to their knees on the floorboards.

As the truck careened to a stop, LaVoy tried to push the driver's side door open; but the truck was buried in snow and leaning to the right. The door was heavy. It took a few seconds; but he finally jumped out the driver's door – the truck still under fire

"Go ahead and shoot me!" he yelled as he walked slowly, with his hands raised, to the middle of the snow-covered embankment between the truck and the tree line. "Go ahead and shoot me," he yelled again.

"Get on the ground!" one of the State Police commanded.

"Go ahead and shoot me," shouted back LaVoy, continuing to move away from the truck, trying to draw the fire from the truck and onto himself.

"Get on the ground!" the command repeated.

"Stay down, stay down," Shawna screamed.

LaVoy's idea had worked. The attention was now focused on LaVoy and the shooting into the truck subsided.

Shawna looked over to see that Ryan was kneeling on the floorboard next to her, trying to see out the window at what was going on outside. She begged him to stay down, and noticed a little blood oozing through his shirt.

"Go ahead and shoot me. Shoot me! You're gonna have to shoot me," LaVoy shouted one more time. And they did, rapid gunfire ensuing from many directions ... and stopped.

"Damn it! Are they shooting him? Did they shoot him?" screamed Shawna. "You a**holes!"

"Oh my God!" cried Victoria, as she began to weep.

The gunshot volley's echoing report finally ceased.

"I think he's out," said Ryan.

"Is he dead?!" asked Victoria, the young girl now resolute.

Another command for the truck's occupants to exit the vehicle was shouted.

"Don't get out!" said Shawna with the first hint of fear in her voice.

"Let me out!" Ryan said. Then, looking at Victoria, he asked, "Are you hit?"

"No!" cried Victoria.

"No, hold on, hold on, don't do it. They're shooting. Don't do anything. Where the hell is LaVoy?" Shawna screamed, now totally overcome by fear.

Ryan attempted to peer over the window frame. "I can't see." Removing his cowboy hat, like in old westerns, he spied over the window frame, he muttered, "I think they just killed LaVoy."

Looking at the right-side door, a shocked Shawna said, "I think they did enough shooting on this door." She tried to assess their situation, staring at all the bullet holes throughout the cab of the truck.

"I know. I got hit too." Ryan muttered.

Victoria asked, "Did they tell us to get out of the car?"

"No, I can't hear anything. I don't dare get out of the car," replied Shawna.

Then all hell broke loose once again. This time there were explosions with more bullets ripping though the truck.

"Oh sh*t! Quit shooting my windows!" Shawna yelled over the confusion.

"Why are they shooting us?" Victoria screamed.

"They're hitting the windows, I don't know. They're trying to break out windows!" Shawna shouted though the noise.

Victoria cried out, "God keep us safe please."

"Please, please protect us God," Shawna agreed in the melee. "Please protect us. Please protect us. Please protect us. We need help. We need help. We need help." Shawna cried, as more and more explosions jolted the truck.

It became eerily quiet again.

"Did they kill him? They killed him," cried Victoria.

"I can't see, but I can see a laser coming in," replied Shawna.

"They kill … Oh, my God, they killed him!" cried Victoria, as she came to grips with what was happening

"Ryan, are you okay?" Shawna asked, looking at her friend.

"Yeah, I'm okay." as he gingerly rubbed his arm, blood soaking through his shirt.

"I can see lasers goin' back and forth," Shawna said, still lying flat on the backseat of LaVoy's truck.

With much concern, Victoria asked, "Where did you get hit?"

Not wanting to worry Victoria, Ryan replied, "I'm okay."

"We got lasers…. I can see the laser. If you see a laser, keep it away from..." cried Shawna, referring to the many red laser dots darting throughout the cab of the truck, searching for a target.

Victoria shrieked as if seeing a snake. "There's a laser, don't let it get near me!"

Shawna, wanting it to end, cried, "Stop. I don't dare get out 'cause they'll shoot me!"

Ryan replied in agreement, "I know. I don't like being hunkered down here either."

"Me either, but I don't know what to do 'cause..." as her voice trailed off, Shawna tried to decide what to do.

"I don't know either," Ryan replied.

"They keep shooting lasers at us," a frustrated Shawna cried.

"Too many stinking lights, think things are all dandy and fine, we got too damn many lights," Ryan replied, also frustrated.

"Damn, why are they keep shooting?" Shanna rambled on.

"They're trying to take my head off is what they're trying to do," Ryan declared.

"I know but all of us?" Shanna questioned loudly.

Then Shawna screamed at the top of her voice, "Stop! Stop! Stop!"

Victoria joined in, "Please!"

Shawna yelled again, "Stop!"

"Ple…-!" shouted Victoria, then starts crying again.

"That's ridiculous. You guys are stupid. They gonna kill all of us?" Shawna muttered angrily at the overwhelming pressure watching the lasers searching over her head.

BOOM

Then a second … **BOOM**

BOOM, BOOM, BOOM, BOOM, BOOM, BOOM … sounded right outside the passenger side of the truck.

Some struck the right-side passenger window (but not breaking it); still more found their way into the front compartment onto the floor.

The explosion was deafening, the flash extinguished as the three were pinned to the floorboard of the truck. Their ears were ringing, painful, their minds confused.

Ryan yelled, "Those are gas rounds."

"I can't breathe. You okay?" Shawna asked Victoria.

"God… God, if you..." Victoria was praying again.

"Okay, they're shooting at us, again!" Ryan exclaimed as the bullets flew through the cab of the truck again.

"They got lasers still on us," Shawna shouted through the intense noises again. "They got lasers still on us. LaVoy got out; I think they've killed LaVoy. They just shot gas rounds into the car. We're hunkered down in here trying not to get shot." She tried to use all her reasoning to decide what to do.

Then again, BOOM, BOOM, BOOM, BOOM, BOOM, BOOM, BOOM, BOOM.

"They're shooting more gas rounds, the gas is getting pretty thick in here," Ryan said.

It became eerily quiet again … Everyone remained still.

A small breeze miraculously began to blow through the open driver's door and the cab quickly cleared of gas.

"Okay, the gas is dissipating," Ryan murmured.

"How do you speak to people who ambushed us on the way to see a sheriff and now they're shooting into our vehicle and we're hunkered down. We don't even have phone service at this location to call for help," Ryan was now talking aloud to himself about the situation.

Then came a command from the outside: "Come out of the left side door!"

They had had enough. They were trapped and they knew it.

Ryan climbed slowly out of the truck with hands raised. There, lifelessly lying in the snow, was LaVoy's body, face up toward the sky. "LaVoy's dead," Ryan said back to the two women still in the truck.

"Sh*t. Okay," Shawna replied, now knowing the finality of the situation.

Victoria was weeping again. "He's dead. LaVoy's dead."

After the first part – and for the rest of the ambush – LaVoy's body had lain lifeless in the snow as the flash-bang and gas grenades were launched into and around the truck to disorient its three remaining occupants.

With obvious caution, another vehicle approached this scene of utter chaos from behind the roadblock. An innocent bystander, a citizen traveler, was just passing through. They stopped a few hundred yards behind the barricade, exited their vehicle, and began to take pictures.

With their arrival, the assault ended and the three were allowed to surrender. This decision probably saved the rest of their lives.

Aftermath

Each passenger emerged without further incident and all were arrested from both vehicles and taken to a nearby rest stop.

Only one .223 bullet had found it's mark. Of the nearly 100 rounds that law enforcement fired into the truck that day, this lone bullet had hit Ryan in his arm.

Ryan Bundy was taken to a nearby medical clinic to have his bullet wound checked out.

For hours Cliven and his wife, Carol, were distraught, not able to get any details of the shooting. It wasn't until that night word came that Ryan Bundy was only injured and still alive.

Later that evening, Victoria Sharpe and Mark McConnell were released. Sharpe was determined to be just an innocent bystander in the incident. McConnell, though the only occupant of the two vehicles that was openly carrying a firearm, was released and never charged.

Once Ryan Bundy was medically cleared, he was seated in a squad car. Separated from each other, Shawna Cox, Ryan Payne, Ammon Bundy, and Bryan Cavalier were also placed in individual squad cars. Then via a very high-speed motorcade – reaching 100 miles per hour – they were all rushed to the Multnomah County Jail in Portland, Oregon, five hours away … the low-altitude plane still following overhead.

Finally, the news came to his parents that Ryan was alive. But Ryan and Ammon were under arrest. And LaVoy was dead. The two women miraculously escaped without harm.

At the hospital, Ryan refused to let the doctors remove the bullet. He reasoned that if it went into evidence it would be "lost", and the proof of what happened that day would be lost as well.

It appeared that Ryan's intuition may have been accurate.

In the ensuing investigation into LaVoy's death, one HRT officer was accused and indicted for lying to investigators, bullet casings came up missing, and the following summer some unidentified governmental agency went to the site of LaVoy's death and set fire to the area burning up any evidence that the melting snow might have revealed.

Ryan Bundy still carries the bullet fragment in his arm to this day.[1]

Just Visitin'

Fifteen days after Ryan was shot, Cliven decided to head to Portland, Oregon, to visit his boys in the Federal lockup there. He had also been invited by Nevada State Assemblywoman Michele Fiore to speak to the Coalition of Western States about the land issues he had been fighting for the last twenty years. On the 80-mile drive into Las Vegas from their ranch, Cliven planned to stop at the Mormon Temple to pray, then meet Michele at the airport.

Cliven arrived at the McCarran International Airport only to find his seat was not available due to the fact he was on the Do Not Fly list. Cliven thought that odd, since in the last twenty months he had flown almost two dozen times for various speaking engagements. But now he was forbidden to fly? The gate agent told him to be patient and they would get the error cleared up. Michele boarded their flight and went on ahead. Four hours later, he was allowed to board another flight to Portland, the mix-up presumably resolved. The short 1.5-hour flight went quickly; Cliven had become accustomed to his new-found travel schedule, so he remained relaxed, only anxious about the opportunity to see his boys and to be sure they were okay.

As the plane touched down and began to taxi off the runway, he noticed out the window that the plane didn't seem to be heading towards the terminal, instead stopping well away from the jet bridge.

Coming to a stop, the plane was suddenly surrounded by black SUVs and armed men impeccably dressed in black were exiting the vehicles. The front passenger door of the plane opened and four men walked briskly down the aisle. Cliven thought to himself, "What's all the commotion about?" As two of the men passed him the second two stopped right in front of him. Then almost instantly, Cliven realized the first two had doubled back and were right immediately behind him. Effectively, they surrounded him the best they could in the cramped space of a commercial jetliner.

---

1 http://www.oregonlive.com/oregon-standoff/2017/06/fbi_agent_indicted_accused_of.html

"Cliven Bundy?" the man directly in front of him said, looking him right in the eye. "FBI. We have a Federal warrant for your arrest. Please stand up."

Some 40 FBI agents had come for Cliven Bundy, at the same moment FBI agents all over the western United States and in New Hampshire were moving on 15 other men in a similar fashion.

It turned out that the FBI had put Cliven on the Do Not Fly list temporarily, so they could prepare in Portland for his arrival. They loaded him up into the awaiting motorcade of vehicles, motorcycle cops, and helicopter escorts. Cliven was stunned at the manpower and resources spent in arresting and transporting him to the Multnomah County Jail; every other transport he experienced since has been with the same intensity.

"It's as if they were transporting the President himself," he has said.

With that swift action by the FBI, Cliven Bundy was swept into the Federal Justice System.

His future and very life hung in the balance.

LOCK-UP

Hello. I am Michael Stickler, Inmate 47483-048. Mike, to most.

This past summer, I spent about two months with Cliven Bundy in the Southern Nevada Detention Center in Pahrump, Nevada. As we formed a deep and lasting relationship, we talked about his story – a story that has not been told in any other medium. This book chronicles our discussion – and his story.

Before I begin with what he told me, let me tell you what it was like living there – for me, for Cliven, for the other 18 "co-conspirators" (as the judge for their trial had so prejudicially characterized them), and for the other detainees incarcerated there.

It was late in the day, April 20, 2017, when I finally entered what was to be my home for the next two months – the G2 Unit of the Southern Nevada Detention Center In Pahrump, Nevada.

Pahrump is a small dusty rural town located in Nye County, a county half the size of the state of Maryland. It is just west over the Spring Mountains – about an hour and a half ride from the Lloyd D. George U.S. Federal Courthouse, in Las Vegas.

I had arrived at the Center much earlier in the day, and was treated to a remarkably arcane intake procedure that is a hallmark of America's modern Incarceration system. This was a modern facility built around a core of inefficiency that was composed of hours of waiting, punctuated by moments furious activity. We were all brought in and unshackled (hands and feet), showered, interviewed, fingerprinted, photographed, and of course, strip-searched – a dehumanizing process in which the examining correctional officer looks in every crack and crevice of your body before giving you your new outfit and kit.

My tenure in other parts of 'the system' has enabled me to see all kinds of outfits in all kinds of prisoner outfits and colors ... the worst being the black and white striped jumpsuits that some institutions perversely prefer for their extra humiliation value. Here, my new attire was a simple, royal blue uniform, the pants and shirt being similar to the scrubs you see in the medical field, oddly enough. There were also Crocks, those rubberized shoe-sandals with a comfortable foot

16

bed (unlike the color choices preferred on the outside, these Crocks were bright-orange), and socks (a fashion-match to the Crocks, these were also bright-orange). I also received a kit – a mesh laundry bag containing extra clothes – two pair of boxers, three more pairs of those bright-orange socks, and two more uniform sets – plus a towel, a blanket, a bar of soap, a weapon-proof toothbrush (a short little thing made of soft plastic so you can't heat and form it into a weapon), and a miniature tube of toothpaste.

One of the niceties is that each detainee is also given an inexpensive radio to tune-in to the local broadcast stations. Used on an individual basis, these do help control the high volume of audio noise, which is a constant nuisance, all with other annoyances and distractions they can become overwhelming at times.

The G2 Unit where I was housed is a large open room – like warehouse space, really – maybe 75' x 75', with cream-colored cinder block walls, no windows, a plain, polished concrete floor, and a 30' high ceiling held up by bare steel beam trusses stretching from wall to wall. The heating, ventilation, and air conditioning system worked way too well, something you couldn't help but instantly notice, as the temperature was a good 40 degrees cooler than Southern Nevada's sunny-but-mild, spring outdoors. That explained why I saw that virtually every single one of the ninety-four men in the unit were wearing their tan windbreakers indoors in – an attempt to stave off the arctic blast of the air conditioners.

It was an open dorm, rather than the individual-room, cell-block style I'd been expecting. Four rows of metal bunk beds occupied two thirds of the unit's space. The bunks were two and half foot-wide steel planks, supported by a steel framework that was firmly bolted to the floor. There was no ladder to climb to the top bunk; but at least, they were furnished with a 4" thick plastic mattress which actually hung over its frame at least 6" on each side, making me think someone had forgotten to measure the frames before ordering them. They appeared to be fairly new.

Along one entire wall was a row of showers, sinks, and toilets. I was relieved (please pardon the pun) to see that the toilets and showers had privacy screens, built and sufficient to shield your private parts from every eye that came in and out of the unit, whether male or female. This is not the case in all institutions. Some are completely devoid of such screens or privacy.

On the opposite side of the unit was the 'day room' area, consisting of 21 metal tables (again, bolted to the floor) with four stools affixed to each table. The tables were for dining, cards, writing, or whatever the detainees used them for during the day. Three televisions (all flat screens) were mounted on the wall above the day room – one TV for each of the major races in the unit. One was for the 'Paisas' (literally - those from a region in the northwest of Colombia, including the part of the Andes in Colombia; though, when used to refer to Mexicans from areas like northern Mexico this term is derogatory, like calling them 'indigenous,' 'ignorant,' and/or 'flamboyant.' Here, it seemed simply to be a relatively new, prison slang term for 'Hispanic'), another for the Blacks, and the third for Whites. The racial separation was mainly expressed in the programming on each TV.

Although prison politics and forced racial segregation were the reality of prison, it didn't seem as prevalent in this facility as in others, thankfully. Perhaps it was because it was a low security unit in which most of the detainees were non-violent offenders who did not want to add the polarizing effects of racial tensions to the list of stresses with which they were already coping. Nevertheless, cultural differences exist and were still quite obvious, as seen on the TV screens.

Also in the day room area, there were phones and computers with email service. Detainees had to pay for their use. Rounding out the huge list of amenities were several microwave ovens for cooking or heating up drinks.

Just outside the unit was an adjoining 30' x 30' recreation yard from which you could view the high, earthen berm that surrounded and enclosed the facility, the upper parts of the surrounding mountain ranges, and the sky. There was one pull-up bar and one dip bar, and a 30' chain-link fence topped with razor wire. It wasn't much, but at least you could get outside – to fresh air, the sky, and sunshine.

This facility is operated for the U.S. Marshal Service by a private, for-profit company, CoreCivic, formerly the Corrections Corporation of America (though, still familiarly referred to as 'CCA'). Its appointments and operations are noticeably different from the federally-operated, government employee-run prison institutions at Lompoc, California, where I'd just been. This CCA facility is modern, clean, and has a professional (and even, respectful!) staff. I wasn't used to that, nor to being addressed as "sir," nor referred to by my last name, especially spoken in a calm, respectful manner. The amenities were obvious, too, like soap being readily available, which is important. Living in such close quarters with a constant population turn-over means exposure to infection and disease is an on-going threat.

Back in Lompoc, I remember the health nurse lecturing us on the dangers of "MRSA." Also know as methicillin-resistant staphylococcus aureus, MRSA is the king of modern hospital infections – a highly contagious, and antibiotic-resistant strain of bacteria that spreads on contact and causes severe skin infection. She told us how MRSA could even be life-threatening, so we all needed to practice "good hygiene" and wash our hands with hot water and soap – often. At the end of the lecture, one of the inmates yelled out, "Can we get some soap?" (The restrooms had soap dispensers, but their soap was only replenished just prior to a 'surprise' inspection). The officer in charge standing with the nurse yelled back, "Noooo!"

Beyond soap, the CCA had forms – actual NCR forms! ... in triplicate! Forms for medical requests, forms for grievances, and forms for everything you might need, plus an actual medical staff of several doctors and nurses. This facility, by my estimation, had three times more medical staff for its 800 detainees than the Lompoc prison had for its 3000 inmates, incarcerated in its three, separate facilities. Consequently, while a doctor visit at Lompoc took months to get, here at Pahrump it only took a couple of days.

Don't get me wrong. The detention center wasn't the Ritz Carlton by any stretch of the imagination, but it was shockingly better run than any federally-operated facility I'd ever been in. However, underneath all the smooth-running operations there was still that dark, oppressive, institutional vibe, a spirit with which I was very familiar. But, what really separates Pahrump from most other prisons is, that while it is:

> A 'detention center' holding men and women facing and awaiting trial criminal charges in the Federal District of Nevada – like Cliven and his 18 fellow detainees.

> A 'repository for the Paises' or immigrants, held for

19

the Immigration Customs Enforcement Service's
(ICE's) preparation for these people's deportation.

A 'holding center for transfers' of convicted persons
being moved from one Bureau of Prisons (BOP)
facility to another, which is how I came to be housed
there.

Because of the transitory nature of its population, here we were
considered 'detainees;' rather than 'inmates' or 'convicts,' which
institutions with a more stable population prefer. In fact, most
detainees here were awaiting trial and not yet convicted of any crime.
So, in our politically correct world, instead of inmate, to describe us,
somebody latched on to this new word 'detainee'– a term invented
maybe only as far back as the late 1920s. (The Merriam-Webster
dictionary ominously notes its meaning as, "a person held in custody,
especially for political reasons.")

The nature of the population of the Pahrump Detention Center is one
of constant change. The high turn-over results in few, if any, social
connections between detainees. Detainees can go to sleep one night
and the next morning find that some – or even most – of the men they
had dinner with the night before are gone and there already is another
person in the top or bottom bunk.

Most transfer moves are done at night.

When it comes time for you to transfer (typically unannounced) you'll
be awakened by a duty officer in the middle of the night, told to 'roll-
up' (pack your things), and then you are quickly shackled hand and
foot, loaded on a bus, and sent off to 'who knows where.' You are
not told your destination because the U.S. Marshals, who coordinate
all transfers, are always concerned that if a detainee knows when and
where they are going they may try to plan an escape. That leaves
every detainee deeply insecure about their fate. It also causes families
and loved-ones tremendous worry and frustration wondering where
their loved-one has been taken. It's not unusual for families to wait for
weeks, even months, to find out where their loved one is now detained.

When I arrived at the Southern Nevada Federal Detention Center
in Pahrump I joined other detainees awaiting their fate in this

limbo. Included in this group were "The Bundy 19," as they were affectionately dubbed by the other detainees. The Bundy 19 were the nineteen men charged by the United States Justice Department with domestic terrorism. These men were stranded here at the mercy of the federal government, with their constitutional rights to a speedy trial having long ago faded away into "the way we do things." I found myself, by Divine Appointment, a fellow detainee with "The Bundy 19."

Here is the way the Federal Justice System 'does things:'

When an accused is presented before the court to hear their charges (at what is called their 'arraignment'), the accused has no idea what evidence is held against them, so, the accused pleads "NOT GUILTY" every time. At that point, if the accused asks for a speedy trial a trial held within 90 days of arraignment), as is every citizen's Constitutional right, they risk proceeding blindly. They have no idea of what, if any, evidence the prosecutor may be holding against them, which leaves them little or no ability to mount any appropriate defense.

Additionally, judges seem consistently to get angry if you force the court to rearrange its 'finely-tuned' schedule (*i.e.*, the schedule that has been coordinated, set, and is now convenient for the judge and prosecution) just to accommodate your constitutional rights. These two realities are significant hurdles the accused would have to overcome were they to establish any type of proper defense. So, most feel (and are advised) that practically, since the prosecution does not have to share its evidence with the defense before the arraignment, they have no choice but to wave their – your – Constitutional right to a speedy trial, and once they've waived that right – it is gone forever, barred from ever being asserted again as the case proceeds to trial … and then, if found guilty, to sentencing.

The consequence of waiving of this right is that the accused is now at the mercy of the system as to when they may ever see a jury (as were each of The Bundy 19 when I was there). It may take months upon months – or even years – before they get their day in court. This means that regardless of whether the accused is eventually found to be innocent in the eyes of the law, you lose your freedom while waiting for the trial date. (Actually, the accused is never found by any court to be 'innocent' of anything – just 'not guilty' of what they were accused – whether what they were accused of ever actually happened or not – or whether whatever they were accused of was actually a crime, or not!).

The Bundy 19s' situation is a good example of this institutional violation of their Constitutional right to a speedy trial. From the so-called 'Standoff' (as the Government calls it) on April 12, 2014 to their incarceration in February 2016, they remained free. For these twenty-two months, the Feds investigated them, restricted their travel, and put them on the 'no-fly' list; but, didn't pick them up or arrest them. The Bundy 19 knew they were being investigated, watched, and followed, but never fled and never committed any crime.

Once they were arrested and arraigned, the prosecutor made a very impassioned plea to the judge that (in the prosecutor's words) these accused were all a "danger to the public" and a "flight-risk." In Cliven's case, the U.S. Prosecutor, Assistant U.S. Attorney (AUSA) Steven Myhre, claimed that, "He (Cliven) has pledged to do so again in the future to keep federal law enforcement officers from enforcing the law against him …." Though Cliven has never left the country in his life, the prosecution contended that he would, *in effect*, be a "flight risk;" because he would return to his ranch and surround himself with militia establishing a refuge that "we'll never get him out of."[2]

Myhre never produced any evidence that such a fantasy would happen. But no matter, this prosecutorial myth resulted in immediate detention with no release – either on recognizance or under bond – and an open-ended period of incarceration until trial for all of The Bundy 19.

Now, this is not the practice normally inflicted by state or federal courts on even the 'worst of the worst' criminals. Rather, what determines whether pretrial release from custody (bonded or not) is granted or not, depends solely on:

> The judge's pre-knowledge of the case,
> > and (were they not to be detained before their trial)

2 Prosecutor Steven Myhre's detention memo of February 16, 2016

The judge's assessment of the physical threat the accused may
pose to the community and the threat that their flight may
pose to the ability of the case to proceed.

However, this *was* the practice for **everyone** who came afoul of the
government and was charged in this case – without exception. The
prosecution asked for immediate remand to custody until trial for each
of The Bundy 19 plus *none of The Bundy 19 was granted pretrial
release* even under the condition of a bond. All were remanded to
custody until the trial.

While I was at the Detention Center in Pahrump, I met some detainees
who had been there for years. One older detainee had been in
Pahrump for seven years only to become a walking zombie, with no
hope, beaten down, totally discouraged … and still awaiting his trial.

Another was 93 years old. He'd been free and at home leading up to
his trial. But, when the jury found him guilty, the prosecutor moved
to have him now detained until his sentencing. The judge agreed,
maybe telegraphing how he would rule on the sentence, so, there he
was, at 93, locked up, sitting in his wheel chair, confused as to what
had happened to his life. He was a war hero, and a medical doctor
for over 60 years without even one complaint, and yet, now here he
was, characterized as 'a danger to society' even though he had to be
reminded why he was there … every day … while now waiting for his
sentencing hearing.

Those years – so full of uncertainty, disruption, and danger – take a
terrible toll on a man.

So, why does our justice system work this way?

The reason why The Bundy 19's – and virtually everyone's –
constitutional right to a speedy trial has eroded away is because
detention time in lock-up, though *eventually* (albeit, uncertainly)
leading to these court events (where the prosecution's accusations
could actually be challenged), tends to make the accused <u>pliable</u> and
more willing to take a deal – a plea-deal, that is – rather than fight
their case out in court. That is what the Federal Government wants of
its citizens (whether really guilty or not) – *pliability* – so the feds can
maintain its prosecutors' 97% conviction rate.[3]

3 "United States Attorneys' Annual Statistical Report for Fiscal Year 2012" (PDF). United States
Department of Justice. Retrieved 2014-10-28.

In practice, this institutional erosion of your constitutional right to a speedy trial means that nearly every accused person takes a plea-deal and pleads guilty, regardless of their intent to 'commit' (or lack thereof), the 'crime' (if, indeed, a crime was even committed), and tragically, regardless of however innocent the accused may be.

The prosecution clearly wanted to take the fight out of Cliven Bundy and The Bundy 19, just as they want to do with every other accused person, and so here they sit.

Now you have a taste of the atmosphere in which I met Cliven. I was privileged to be trusted enough by him to hear his story, here we go…

The day I first met Cliven, it was his birthday. He had turned 72 years old. By then, he had been locked up for more than fourteen (14) months.

One of the detainees excitedly pointed him out to me, "There he is, have you heard about him and his boys?"

"I have, and I'd love to meet him," I responded.

"He's real friendly; go talk to him," he urged.

I decided to wait for the right time.

The next day, after reflecting on that morning's news and after a time of prayer, I decided to break the ice with Cliven. I approached his bunk where he sat reading and said, "Mr. Bundy, I just want you to know there are thousands of folks praying for you."

At that, Cliven's eyes lit up, and a big 'cowboy grin' swept across his face.

Let me try to describe this 'cowboy grin' for you,

'cuz I've seen it a thousand times before, in California, Nevada, and Oregon. It's a smile that is genuine and spreads across a man's entire face, ear to ear; but, there's more. It communicates – in an intelligent, knowing, simple way – an interest that is so gracious, so concerned for *your* well-being, that it makes you feel like you are the best thing of his whole day; and it is so inviting; it welcomes you in to sit.

And that's just what Cliven did, saying, "Thank you, why don't you have a seat? Just sit right there on that bunk. It's my boy, Davey's, bunk. He's gone for a bit."

There we sat, across from one another in our silly royal blue uniforms, our bright-orange Crocs, and our bright-orange socks. Cliven had been in the G2 Unit long enough to have gotten one of the coveted, end bunks against the wall – which have more privacy. He sat there with his back against a stack of pillows, blankets, and whatever other soft, cushiony things he could find to lean on.

He sat up and adjusted his padding while sharing, "Being able to lean against the wall is nice, but it's so cold it gives a man a chill."

Around him were three or four plastic footlockers, some belonging to his son, David. Normally, a detainee only gets one footlocker; but, The Bundy 19 needed extras to accommodate the volumes of their legal paperwork, court documents, and such, to prepare for their trial. Across the length of Cliven's bunk, against the wall, are a dozen photos of his family, grandkids, and the Ranch. As he turns back to look at me with his piercing, steely gray eyes, I noticed a pocket-sized copy of the U.S. Constitution in the left breast pocket of his royal blue uniform. I glanced around the bunk and scoped out a Bible, a Book of Mormon, an almanac, and a notepad with some scribbles and hand drawings.

He said to me, "Tell me about yourself," and smiled.

I realized that he actually meant it, it was not just a conversation starter. So, I did, thinking to myself, where do I begin? I decided to start where I left off, telling him about the many people and churches and prayer groups who I knew were praying over the volatile events that transpired in the lives of The Bundy 19.

He soon interjected, "Well, I thank you, and we sure can feel all 'em prayers … without 'em we couldn't 'of made it this far."

He took a moment to make eye contact, smiled, then said, "But tell me about *you*."

So, I did. I told him about my cowboy and ranching experience, my attending California Polytechnic State University to study animal science and then transferring to the University of Colorado in Fort Collins to learn about artificial insemination and embryo transfer. I told him about my years of training cutting horses and even the two years I had only recently spent in a sustainable agriculture program at Lompoc. I told him about my family, grandkids, my travels, and writings. I told him about how I had gotten in trouble with the Feds, as had he and The Bundy19. I just kept going on and on.

Cliven never broke eye contact, and never stopped smiling. He was like a border collie attentively studying a flock of sheep. By the time I was done, more than an hour had passed.

We were then interrupted by the 'call-for-count' (every three hours the entire Pahrump detention center comes to a complete stop as the detainees all return to their bunks while the officers in charge 'count' every inmate to be sure none have escaped.)

And just like that, awkwardly, but matter-of-fact like, we concluded our first meeting and I walked back to my bunk on the other side of the unit. As I lay down on my bunk, I began to reflect on the past hour or so, thinking, "Why did I just tell him all that?" I know better, I'm in prison for heaven's sake. 'Dumping my bucket' is not something I do. But with this guy, with Cliven, I did. There was something about him, it was like visiting with my grandpa and getting him all up-to-date with my life. Oddly enough, Cliven seemed to actually listen and care. But, I really didn't know him well enough at that point to know just how genuine he is ... not then, anyway.

You see, in prison you meet all kinds of characters and various types of people, from a wide range of lifestyles, cultures, and countries. Most of them fall into at least one of five general categories. Except for God's grace, they will stay as they are. Some can hurt you.

With the first two, you have the CRIMINALS and the CON ARTISTS.

These are the guys who should definitely be behind bars, because they're out to take advantage of anyone and everyone who crosses their path, in any way possible. These sociopaths may actually be innocent of the specific crime for which they are doing the time – but without a doubt, are guilty of other, maybe even more serious offenses, known to the justice system or not. I stay clear of these guys.

Then, there are the *whack-a-doos*. Mostly, they are the whacked-out conspiracy theorist that wear tin foil hats and swear the Government is out to steal their secrets and kill them, but there are others just as nuts. Clinically, some of these whack-jobs are mentally disabled, having taken too much meth, crystal, oxycodone, … or whatever. Some were just born that way. Like the first category, these guys also get a wide berth for the same reasons, but also deserve understanding and grace, in my opinion. Nevertheless, for your own safety, you also have to discern the whack-a-doos from the others.

Then, there are the *deniers*. These are the self-deceived, self-proclaimed, 'innocent victims' – of someone else, of their circumstances, or both. They refuse to look at their own role in how they got into trouble and into prison. They have long, complex, anguishing stories that extinguish or at least, minimize, their taking any responsibility for their actions, their affiliations, their omissions, or their lifestyle. No genuine, honest accounting is visible or forthcoming. These folks are doomed to failure and a return to prison if and when they are ever released. They just don't get it, but they also share the need for a wide berth for the same reasons as above.

Lastly, there are those actually *innocent* – who fall into two camps:

> Those who made some bad choices; but, *had no intent to do anything wrong*, and
> Those who *actually did nothing wrong*, either because someone else committed the crime, or because no crime was ever committed.

This last realization should shock all Americans, as it did me.

We have become so sure of ourselves, so arrogant, (or have just bought into so much of what is on the TV detective shows), that we think our justice system doesn't make mistakes.

27

The truth of the matter is this: At least a third (33%) of the currently-estimated 2 million people incarcerated in the U.S. falls into one of these two camps of *innocent*. That is, perhaps, as many as 5-700,000 Americans who are actually <u>innocent</u> of the crime of which they were accused, who are held in custody, every day, in prison.[4] What a current-day tragedy.

As I lay there waiting for 'count-time' to end, I was wondering into which category did detainee Cliven Bundy fit. To be honest, I was musing that he could possibly be a whack-a-doo. After all, he was taking on the Federal Government of the United States of America.

If so, he certainly was a *likeable* one.

Still, at this point, I had no real basis even to guess.

Time will tell, I thought.

4 www.law.umich.edu/special/exoneration/.../Exonerations_in_2014_report.pdf

Chapter 2

- THE REAL DEAL -
Domestic Terrorist or American Patriot

The next day I was sitting at one of those metal tables in the day room, trying to catch up on the news, when Cliven came over and sat down. "I've got a problem, maybe you can help me," he says.

"Okay, shoot," I reply, thinking, *here it comes, his whack-a-doo story.*

Almost everyone in the detention center is in the midst of fighting their court case, so it's natural to see them struggling mentally and emotionally with what is happening to them, their families, their career, and their future. Some are in deep depression, while others are fighting mad as they try to get their mind wrapped around their disastrous circumstances. Why would Cliven be any different? Even more so, his case is by far the most publicly publicized I've ever seen. If the government gets its way, he'll never see the light of day, but will be in prison for years and years. That kind of thing weighs on a man.

So, as I was thinking this, he began ...

"You know, I got these F1 cattle on my ranch, and I can't get the pregnancy rates with 'em I want ... I'm wonderin' if you can give me some idees? I've never been to Ag school, maybe I'm miss'n sumpin'? A few years ago, I rented some Hereford cows and bred 'em back to this big Brahma Bull, which gave me some nice brindle heifers. Then, I bought some nice Red Angus Bulls and bred 'em F1 heifers, which gave me the nicest baby calves you'd ever seen. The kind the buyers want."

Cliven laid this out with so true and plain a curiosity and concern that I had to try very hard to keep my neck from snapping as my brain shifted gears to keep up. So now I'm thinking, *he's been here in prison 14 months, and now he wants to talk about ranching!? Oh boy, this is worse than I'd thought ... he's living at the ranch in his head.* (By the way, the F1 tigerstripe female is a superior cow for the Southwest. 'Tigerstripe' is a term used to describe the F1 cross of Hereford and Brahman because of the animal's tiger-like striped brindle hair).

He went on. "But you know, I graze 'em on the open range down here in southern Nevada and it's wild, arid, harsh land, where the water is spread out. In the spring, the grass grows up nice and tall, 'em cows will graze right around the water, but in time they need to move further and further away from the water. 'Cuz, they have that Brahma in 'em, they get to traveling, maybe 10 or more miles away from the water. Then at night, they'll bed down 'em calves and head back to the water. You know, they'll even leave a babysitter with 'em babies, to protect 'em. I've rode out a daybreak many a time to see one lone cow brooding over as many as ten calves. They seem to be just right for my ranch."

"So, what do you think the problem is?" I asked, finally catching back up with him.

"Well, those darn Red bulls can't keep up. They just hang around the water trough and cover those cows when they come in for water. My cows, they're more like wild animals than domesticated beeves (cattle), more like an elk. The Red Angus bulls are too domesticated and all that walking wears their feet sore. I just don't get the pregnancy rate I should. I'd like to breed some of my cows for fall calving; but, that means that they need a breedin' in the middle of winter when the cows are furthest out."

"Can you feed lot them?" I inquired further.

"Nah. These cows are uniquely acclimated to my ranch and know how to survive in that unique environment. I spent years breedin' 'em to thrive there. If I bring 'em off the range they'll get lazy and end up not traveling like they should. Besides, they're so wild they'd just jump out."

For the next few hours, we discussed all kinds of ideas, various options and methods to approach the issues, including other ranching philosophies used in different parts of the country. In the end, to be honest, my experience and book learning didn't much help to him at all.

Over our weeks together we would return to the subject and hash it over again and again. In these talks it became quite obvious that Cliven's ranching methods were unique. In response to the harsh climate, extreme environment, specific water-source layout, land contours, and foliage cycles, Cliven and his neighboring Southern Nevada ranches must adjust procedures to meet and succeed under these severe conditions. The goal for the herds that graze this land is not just to succeed but thrive. As far as I know, this distinctive area has not been researched, taught, or even footnoted. As a result, the area is at best misunderstood. But it is more likely simply unknown, because ranching methods are distinctive to this small region's specific conditions.

And they sure aren't at all like the better-known, more widely practiced, ranching styles *that simply don't work here* and may not work at all *except* in the climates, environments, and water-source layout, land contours, and foliage cycle conditions where they were developed.

It would be just as inappropriate – *just as foolish* – perhaps even *just as dangerous* – as the tragic 'Dust Bowl' period of failed dry-farming policies of the 1930s – to extend any regional resource management policy that is based on the more widely practiced and academically understood ranching (or agricultural) conditions to this or any other unique situation that may be not so widely understood. It is perhaps *just as foolish* – and – *just as dangerous* – to formulate permanent water management policy during an extended wet-year period of the climate cycle. The policy-makers are simply trapped in 'what we know is the way it is, so this must be the way it will always be'!

Federal government resource management policies don't exactly get a passing grade on much of its 'service to the nation and its citizens' across the West – or here, in Southern Nevada.

Sadly, but predictably, policies fail when applied to where their makers have never been, because **... they don't know what they don't know**.

In glaring contrast, Cliven learned well from the generations of his family's practical ranching and breeding experience – gained the hard way – in Northern Arizona and Southern Nevada's desert climate. In our discussions, Cliven clearly knew far more than I did and I learned far more than he did.

During those weeks we were together, he also taught me about his techniques on farming melons and alfalfa with _half the water use_ of conventional techniques I had come to know. This interested me greatly, because I had just spent two years learning about modern, main-stream sustainable farming, which had helped update my views from what I'd known before or had been taught way back in Ag school. But now, Cliven was refining my understanding in even this – along with so many different areas that I'd never considered before.

This region is indeed unique. It demands unique responses across the whole agricultural and ranching spectrum. It demands resource management policies that are equally sensitive and appropriate to its uniqueness.

During this time, I was privileged to see Cliven open up and hear him share his life story with me. His story goes a long way in explaining his character, honesty, values, and credibility; for me, at least. For you too? Judge for yourself. As I recall, it went something like this:

Cliven grew up on the farm. As a boy, he often struggled with health issues. "I had bad kidneys, the tubes were too small, which made my white blood count high," he mumbled one day, as a commercial ran on the day room TV.

I couldn't tell if it was something he saw on the TV screen that reminded him of his youth or he was just in a mood to share. In lock-up, emotional swings and seemingly-random conversational triggers are fairly common. Sometimes you can be affected by news from home, or maybe some nonsense with your bunkie (your upper or lower bunk occupant). Cliven seldom watched TV, but I often did. Maybe he just wanted to connect. It's hard to say.

He continued. "I had about three months of doctorin' and stretchin' the tubes 'til I was 14. Then, I started gettin' better. It's what kept me outta Vietnam or I'd gone for sure. I was one of the first in the draft." Cliven was now looking down from the screen of the TV mounted high on the wall above.

"After high school, I just went to farmin' … didn't really like school, so college never entered my mind. I like running equipment," he stated with conviction.

"At four years old, my dad got a new Ford tractor. When it was delivered, I want to be the one to drive it off the trailer, in fact I insisted. Now, that's a big deal for an adult, let alone a little kid. He set up 'em ramps on the lowboy trailer and said 'get up there, then!' so I did. I back that brand-new tractor right off 'a there! Right down them ramps! By eight, I was drivin' it alone, using both feet to press down the clutch. I was still a little guy and I didn't have enough strength to push down the clutch with one leg. So, I'd swing my other leg over on the left side and just stand on the clutch with both feet. Shift the gears, then hop back up onto the seat. My momma, worr'in' like mommas do, asked me one day; 'What if you get into trouble?' 'I just turn off the key,' I told her with great confidence.

"When I was ten, I learn't to repair the banks of irrigation ditches. The gophers would dig their holes and tunnels all through 'em, and they'd begin to leak. These wern't little berms like you'd think. They were big

embankments that held back allot of water, 'em darn gophers would really get to digging and moving dirt around. Sometime the holes would go down ten feet or more. If I didn't fix 'em, then, in short order, they'd start to wash away. So, my dad stuck me on a tractor and I figured out what to do. All I had was a blade on that tractor. So, it took some real doing and I basically developed my own technique to getting 'er done.

"My dad often worked to town in those days. So, it was up to my mom and me to do the farm'n. On the weekend, me and dad would discuss what needed to get done. Then, he would set up the implements of the tractor, 'cuz I was too small to hook 'em up. Then dur'n the week, I just go about farm'n after school. In those years, I built up my skills; but, more importantly, my confidence in operating equipment. I developed a reputation as a 'good operator' by my neighbors, my community. So, by twelve, my neighbors would hire me to clean out their irrigation ponds. I grew up fast on the farm."

He stopped and considered his next story with a smile.

"One summer, the neighbors adopted a couple of babies, two weeks old. The adopting parents were kind'a hard cases. Didn't talk much all about farming and ranching. In their late 50s maybe even their 60s. When they brought these brand new little babies home – they were just a few days old – they didn't know what to do with 'em! I mean feed 'em, wash 'em, diaper 'em – nuttin'!" He said with a laugh. "But, they were proud new parents.

"So, they got hold of my mother and ask for help. Mom sent me to their place. Their place was over the hill from our place … *60 miles* over the hill! While usually this would be somethin' my sisters would do, but I got sent. When I got there, the husband just put on his hat and walked out the door and went up to a cabin they had some 35 miles away. He left me and the wife there to take care of those babies. I ended up staying several weeks until she could do it alone. I mean I was showing her everything, they didn't have any electricity; but, they did have water to the house. So, I'd show her how to make bottles, how to change diapers, the whole kit and caboodle. They had an old washing machine that was run by a small gas motor. But, I could never git'er to work for me. So, I washed diapers by hand. She was as much of a hard case as he was. But, she loved those babies and sure appreciated the help."

And, with that, Cliven just smiled from ear to ear.

By the time Cliven reached eighteen, he'd already become a talented dirt-work equipment operator. He was registered with the Union as a Journeyman and would get called to work all over the west, working even as far away as Los Angeles, driving a paddle scraper to level land for building pads. While working there in 1965, the fella he was working for "kinda went bankrupt" so, the John Deere manager came to him and asked if Cliven wanted to take over the payments on the equipment and continue working. He agreed, thinking that it seemed to be a good opportunity.

One of his jobs was on the south side of Los Angeles. He positioned his equipment at the job site and checked into a nearby hotel so he could just walk to work. He had left his car back in Long Beach, figuring that once he was done with his current job, he would just move to another job.

That first night, the Watts Riots broke out. Cliven was watching it all on TV. As the *Breaking News!* alerted America's watching public about the fires that were inflaming the city, he realized that the news feed looked very familiar, he stood up and walked to the window of his high-rise hotel to see the very scene that was playing on his hotel television. Cliven told me he looked out the window, and then looked back at the TV. "I think the news crew was filming from the same floor I was on, I was that close! I didn't know it; but that night, I was witnessing history."

As the next few days passed, Cliven was stuck in that hotel room, he couldn't work and was running out of money. His scraper was in the middle of it all and the job site was closed down. He didn't know anyone in Southern California except two Mormon Missionaries, who were willing to try to come and get him. With the glowing fires in the streets and the surrounding buildings in flames the missionaries decided to make a rescue attempt. The missionaries picked up Cliven's car and headed north, way north of Cliven's location, where he had 'hunkered down' waiting for his rescuers. Most of the direct roads into the area had been closed by the National Guard, so the missionaries had to take a circuitous route into the area. By the time they made it to the hotel, Cliven's car was running low on fuel and nobody had any money left for gas, even if a gas station was open, which "they wasn't." As he tried to leave the area, he kept running into crowds of people and burning vehicles.

"I just decided I needed to make a run for it right down the Harbor freeway, so I drove through all the chaos and fires, got on the freeway and headed south."

Confused and somewhat lost, he wasn't sure where he could go. The confusion was compounded by the sheer desolation on the freeway. "There wasn't a car to be seen on the freeway that night, on either side of it! The *ONLY* vehicles we saw were National Guard trucks on the overpasses.

"Then out of nowhere, two cars of black boys came along side of me.

38

It scared us to death. Were they gonna shoot at us, drive us off the road? They ended up right alongside us for nearly an hour, until I got to familiar territory, Long Beach, right in the area where I worked my last job. So, I sped up in front of them and quickly took the off ramp. It was a night I'll never forget."

He paused.

Then the story turned a corner I didn't expect.

"For fifty years I have always thought those men wanted to harm us, but, now I've come to realize those men escorted me down that freeway and kept up the escort until I was safe. I felt like they became my guardian angels."

"So, what happened to your scraper?" I asked.

"I stayed with the missionaries until things quieted down. Then I went back and got my equipment, it seemed to be untouched by all the rioters."

"So, you just drove your big, giant scraper down the freeway?" I asked.

"Yep, that's how I got it around Los Angeles."

"You never even got a ticket?" I asked, incredulously.

"No. I got pulled over one time though. I was coming from church in my suit and tie and needed to move my scraper to the next job," he paused, now grinning, "when the cop sees me in the suit, he pulled me over. Guess it looked a little weird!" He laughed.

"How did you get back to Nevada?" I asked.

"I drove 'er, Mike. I'm just a country boy and, after the riots, I wanted out of there."

Cliven finished his jobs in Southern California and headed back to Nevada, just stopping for fuel and necessities. Before he left Long

Beach, he washed the tires of his scraper in the Pacific Ocean, threw his bag behind the seat and headed to the ranch near Bunkerville, Nevada, and on to his next job site, a trip of about 500 miles up the highway, a highway that lead on through Arizona City (Arizona) and eventually on to Salt Lake City.

It was winter. When he made his way through the 4,728' mountain pass on the California-Nevada border, the scraper's tires started to slide as he was descending from the summit. But, as experienced an operator as he was even in his late teens, he scooped up a load of snow for some extra traction to get his tires back to the pavement. He was successful in negotiating the slippery roads to and through Las Vegas (crowded with traffic) and even got into North Las Vegas, still with his load of snow! Seeing a group of kids playing in the nearby field, he pulled in and, to the delight of the little ones there, he dropped that load of snow right there. As he drove off, he could see the snowballs flying in his rear-view mirror. He stayed that night at the ranch and then drove on to Bunkerville for the new job in the morning.

Eventually, Cliven got his contractor's license and completed some work on the Mesquite Airport and also built the City Sewer Lagoons, as well as many other prestigious projects. By his late 20s, Cliven had the "most irrigated farm land in Nevada."

He had evolved his hay-bailing business into a new category of feed packaging: hay cubes. John Deere proclaimed Bundy's operations as "the best cubing outfit in America." He was even exporting his hay cubes to Hawaii and Japan in the early 70's.

"I had modern equipment, coordinatin' trucks, trains, and shipping containers to get my boxes of cubes to Japan," he reflected. He'd pioneered a new box container for hay cubes and that packaging made his cubes even more desirable for exporting.

" 'Em Japanese would put 'em on their backs and hike up the mountains to the animals!" chuckling over this reminiscence as he said it. "Eventually, they fed fish and even made human supplements for 'em Japanese with Nevada alfalfa," he recounted proudly.

"So, what happened?" I asked.

"In those days, I was farmin' along Lake Mead. When they changed the way the river was damned and the water was held, Lake Mead backed-up and overtook my land. My new modern equipment was financed and I couldn't work it out with the bankers, plus at the time, my family was strugglin', with my first wife and me, her young, ambitious husband, having troubles that led to our eventually divorcin'. I spent the next ten years raising my family by myself." He broke down, as if reliving the pain from the events of that time.

"I'm sorry." Again, after a long pause: "I'm sorry." He gathered himself together. "That was a hard, hard part of my life."

By 1973, Cliven had shifted into cattle – and in a big way. He had purchased some 1400 head of cattle from Mexico and brought them to his ranch, the one that was under so much dispute.

"I think of myself as a farmer; but, I make a better livin' with the cattle."

The Mexican cattle purchase drew national attention from both *Newsweek Magazine* and CBS Broadcast News.

Cliven's personal life stabilized when he married the love of his life, Carol, in 1990. She brought four of her daughters into the family. Together, they had three more.

"All my kids wanted a mom," Cliven smiled. "Carol has been a good little heifer." Then, he proudly showed me a recent photo, saying, "We went together to the (Mormon) Temple and sealed as one family," referring to the family ceremony in the Church of the Latter-Day Saints.

He stopped and abruptly walked away.

Later that night, he came back to my bunk and sat down. This time he didn't ask for permission. I could tell he had something real serious on his mind.

"You know, Mike, as far as Carol and me are concerned we're all one family. There is no 'her kids' and 'my kids' – we are just one family. You ask any one of 'em kids of ours and they'll tell you. Carol's our mom!" He seemed a bit irritated.

"Okay, why are you telling me this?" I asked.

" 'Cuz, I don't want you t' give anyone that there is any division in our family. We are one and that's all there is to it. If you say otherwise... well, God help you."

I had never seen him quite so serious. But then, he seemed to move on from the intensity.

"I remember when it all clicked as a family for Carol and me – we were always frustrated trying to match socks during laundry time. One day, we went to Costco and bought the same socks for everybody. We knew we were a family then!" chuckling. "We were a farming family, involved in church, school, farm, and ranch life, brandin', ropin', farmin', weed'n, irrigatin', and pickin' melons. We did it all together. It was a traditional, farm-family life."

Later on, I asked Cliven's son, Mel, about the family life, the years of being without a mom and then having a whole new set of sisters and a Mother in the family enter into the house on the ranch. "Mike, as far as were all concerned Carol *is* our mother. No one ever speaks any other way." I saw something in his reply that I have seen in my own children. A deep abiding respect and love for their mother. It was then that I realized that I'd misread Cliven's irritation. It wasn't with me; it was with himself. His 'second thoughts' were about what he'd said and were not directed at me. But, it was his heart's desire to protect Carol's feelings and to not even let the thought of his and the children's commitment to her appear to waiver. What he didn't realize was that his that protective love was what made him endearing as a husband and father.

One time I asked Cliven a sort of test question. Feigning curiosity, I asked, "Cliven, do you and your boys think of yourselves as buckaroos or cowboys?"

To understand this test, you have to know that buckaroos are a type of cowboy known for their short chaps (the leather leg coverings known as 'chinks' – which are worn over pants when riding horses), their use of the long *'reata,'* (sometimes spelled *riata* – a braided or twisted rawhide rope), and their flat-brimmed hats. They are especially known for their horsemanship and refusal to use mechanical techniques for handling cattle, like all-terrain vehicles (ATVs) or helicopters, stubbornly holding on to their traditional roots of the Old Spanish and Mexican horseman of a hundred years ago, or more. It was a subtle; but very telling, question. If Cliven were full of horse apples, I would know it by his answer.

"Nah," says Cliven, "we're cowboys. The buckaroos are up north. My family and tradition come from east of the ranch. Arizona really."

That was the right answer. The buckaroos are mostly found in northern Nevada, parts of Oregon, and California. Only someone **who really knew** the cowboy culture would know that. And, while they might argue the strengths of their tradition over another's, they would never claim one for themselves that wasn't theirs.

Cliven, though, went on: "But, I think of myself as a farmer, mostly. I make more money with cattle than farming; but, I like to grow things!" He said it all with that big grin of his.

"You know, I got my start in the cattle business when I was just six years old. I was out helping my grandfather gather cattle down along the Virgin River that crosses our ranch. We came across a couple of dopey calves (wobbly orphans needing their mothers' milk) that were hid'n in the thicket. My grandfather told me I could have 'em if I could catch 'em (rope them). I spend a good part of the day gett'n 'em; but I did. I bottle raised 'em. Then I was able to trade 'em for some heifers – the bloodline of my ranch."

Cliven went on sharing stories of ol' cowboys he had ridden with, fences that he had built, and how in the heat of a summer day they would shade up under the rock over-hang and swap tales of days long gone – of the cattle drives and huge brand'ns (brandings). They were stories Louis L'Amour would have envied. I tried to respond with some of my own tales; but, in comparison to his sixty-six years of farmin', ranchin', and cowboy'n, mine were just shadows in the mist.

I found, though, that if you really want to see the pride well up in Cliven's heart, just ask him about his family. And, like the proud father and grandfather he is, out will come the pictures!

One day, after he had just received a new batch for his birthday, photos printed on 8 ½ by 11 printer paper (The detention center limits the number of photos allowed that are on professional photo stock; but, not those printed on standard paper). We started with the new batch. He smiled as he showed me pictures of each of his 14 children and their families. As he went through each of them, he told me what they did for a living, where they lived, how proud he was of them, and, of course, how smart his grandchildren were. I noticed he could name off all the kids and grandkids with ease – each and every one of them!

And yes, he had a photo of the entire family together, less the five there in lock-up. I was astonished at the size of the family in this photo, so I asked Cliven, "How many family members do you have altogether?"

"Well, there's 63 grandkids ... and with their spouses, there's 24 kids ... and then, there's Carol, my wife, making 88." Plus Cliven, too, of course.

I sat there stunned at the implications of the 84 loved ones in that one photo (the five at Pahrump missing from it, of course). In the picture, they were holding up a bright red banner that said: "SEND OUR DADDIES HOME." That touched me deeply.

By then, I'd been working on the outside for justice reform and serving both prisoners and ex-prisoners and their families for some 25 years. I had seen first-hand, and personally experienced, the hardships families

All we want for CHRISTMAS is our GRANDPA and DADS home!

face when a spouse or family member is locked up. It is a tremendous strain on the family, the community, and the taxpayers. It's a lose-lose-lose for everyone on the outside, too.

And sitting there with Cliven, even though married, a father of two adult boys, and grandfather of three more young ones (one of whom I had not yet seen), I could only begin to know the pain of the members of this close-knit, extended family whose picture was held in Cliven's hand.

My heart ached at the pain and anguish this family was going through. I grieved for the children growing up without their fathers, for the wives, and the financial hardship of losing the families' breadwinners. I knew how the worry of the future loomed over every member of those families, not sure when, how, or even whether the nightmare would ever end.

The whole thing made me think about the various studies I'd read – reports of how an estimated 80% of incarcerated people will return to prison[1], and children who have an incarcerated parent are about three times as likely to be adversely involved with the justice system.[2] Looking at those precious little faces in this family photo made

1 https://www.nij.gov/topics/corrections/recidivism/Pages/welcome.aspx
2 https://www.ccsu.edu/imrp/Publicatons/Files/CIP_Seven_Out_of_Ten_Not_Even_Close.pdf

me wonder, what will become of this family when this is all over? Whatever 'all over' may mean for them.

A few weeks later I was sitting with Cliven, Mel, and Davey Bundy as the boys reported to their dad how their families were doing on the outside. Each day these three would call home to check in. One family had been forced to move to another rental property, while one wife was looking for a new mini-van, because the old one had taken its last breath and died. Carol, Cliven's wife, was constantly having to deal with well-wishers, the media, and attorneys while running the ranch, not to mention overseeing all the children and grandkids as only a mom-grandmother can do. You could see the anguish on these men's faces. How they wished they could be there to help their families and loved ones.

And that's where they should be.

At one point, I asked Cliven, "What's the hardest part of all this?" thinking he might say the 'unfairness of it all,' or maybe, the 'feeling of entrapment,' or 'being caged in lock-up.'

But instead, his reply surprised me. He said, "You know, I've had my life, and I've made my bed, but these families – the families of the other men locked-up in here because of me – they have wives and babies who need their daddies home. We gotta figure a way to get 'em home."

He continued. "Some of THE 19 locked up here, I don't even know. Oh, I might have met 'em, shook hands with 'em once or twice; but I hardly ever talked to 'em. All they did was come to stand with me to support me. They each had their own reasons they come. But, they didn't bargain for this. They need to get home to their families."

That night I lay on my bunk thinking about all we'd talked about. One thing kept swirling around – out of place, like a puzzle piece that you couldn't find a place for. It centered on that last picture among his recent birthday photos Cliven showed me of his cows.

"Look at 'em," Cliven had said, "they're all fat, slick (winter coat now shed), and greasy (shiny). My wife and son-in-law are doing a pretty good job."

And I remember asking him, "Wait a minute, your cows are still on the range? I thought the Feds took them?"

"Nah," Cliven responds, still looking down at the photo of his cows, "The government gave up trying to take 'em, they've a been grazin' on their home range ever since the Protest in April 2014. They haven't even seen a Federal Government man on the property ever since."

It turns out that under the civil impound order to seize the cattle in dispute over grazing on government land back in April 2014 (before the Protest), the government had rounded up and killed about 50 head of cows, and then released the remaining cattle back to Cliven to return to the land whose grazing rights had been in Cliven's family for over a hundred years.

"But, I thought this whole thing was about trespassing cows?" I pressed further.

"Naw, it's about controlling the land that they have no right to," he says, while still studying that picture of the cows, never looking up.

"You mean, that for the last three years, your cows and calves have been allowed to stay on your ranch and range?" I asked, now confused.

"Yep," he says without moving. "They couldn't take 'em, 'cuz they got no jurisdiction or policing power. Once we made the Sheriff (of Clark County) do his job to rightfully protect my life, liberty, and property, the Feds gave up and left, leaving my cows, too."

I just sat there in stunned silence. Cliven never even looked up from studying that same picture. His comments were so matter-of-fact, like everybody knew what had happened.

"Darn," he exclaimed in pride. "Don't those cows look fat?! We sure musta had good grass this year!"

And that was the moment of clarity; the puzzle piece fit and the penny dropped. Lying there on my back on my bunk at the Southern Nevada Detention Center, I realized something.

Cliven Bundy is truly "THE REAL DEAL."

A true, live, American Patriot.

Chapter 3

– THE STAKES –
Today's America vs. An American Republic

E arly the next day I met with Cliven.

I addressed him directly. "What everyone wants to understand is, why are you in lock-up? Let me interview you, and write it down so I can pass the word along for the rest of the country, and even the world, to tell the true story of what went on here, with you and The Bundy 19. What do you say?"

He thought for a moment, lifted up his head with that country-wide grin, and said, "Okay, Mike, let's do it. But if you're goin' to write it down, why don't you put it in a book? I'm not goin' to write the book – you should. You're the author." he said with a grin.

And with that, I entered the world of constitutionalists, militiamen, and a story – of which, the more I uncovered, the more unfathomable it revealed itself to be.

We dove right in…

"Cliven, I think the most obvious question is what seems to be the most controversial. Why did the Federal Government's agents back down from your ranch back in 2014?" I asked.

He jumped right on it. "Because they weren't allowed to take us, they had no jurisdiction and no policing power on Nevada land. Only the Nevada County Sheriff does. He told them to leave."

"Back in 2014, then-U. S. Senator Harry Reid called you a Domestic Terrorist, while today, there are many people, perhaps, tens of thousands, who call you a patriot. Were you in the right to take on the Federal Agencies toe-to-toe? And why?" That was my next logical question.

"I'm a constitutionalist, Mike. I not only believe in the strict interpretation of the U.S. Constitution, but, I believe it was divinely inspired, and worth fightin' for. If the Federal Government would be willin' to be controlled by the Constitution, then we would comply, but, they will not. Many of 'em do not care about the Constitution any more, nor the laws the Constitution establishes. That's the reason I don't feel I can back down and give up, even though I'm in prison, it's my purpose on this earth, and it's my salvation."

"Some think that's crazy, Cliven," I paused a moment, "taking on the U.S. Federal Government – I know I do." With that question, I tested his temper.

Cliven pondered a moment before answering. "I don't believe we should overthrow our government, quite the contrary, but, I believe that our Government is so far off course of what the framers of the Constitution envisioned, that the only hope is for the people to stand up with conviction and moral authority, risking it all, to set the Constitution back on its rightful course."

That was not the answer I expected; but, I wanted to understand more about the backstory in how this all could have come about. "Tell me about the history of the Federal Department of the Interior's Bureau of Land Management (BLM), and why they are, in your opinion, abusing their power and corrupting the Constitutional rights of the American citizens, especially here in Nevada."

Cliven put on his 'teachers hat' – something that surprised me about him. He has spent nearly a lifetime researching this subject and he had a cogent argument:

"When a U.S. Territory becomes a State, the Federal Government disposes of its authority over the public lands within this new State's borders, turning all these public lands over to this new State as the land-owner, and the State becomes responsible as to their management, ownership, and disposition.

"Back when the early settlers were coming out west, it was said that all you needed was 40 acres and a mule; but, what they found was that they, the farmer and ranchers, constantly needed more and more acreage because land itself was becoming more and more arid and less and less fertile.

"So, what took 40 acres back east, soon took 340 acres moving westward, and so on, and, eventually, the western model for ranching became that a family would settle a homestead then graze their herds on the 'open range' where these settlers would establish 'beneficial use' of this open, public land. 'Beneficial use' is determined when the settler first uses any part of the virgin land for his benefit. Grazing his cows, digging a well, all of it is considered 'beneficial use.' As the west was settled and as the 1934 Taylor Grazing Act was established, these first settlers were given 'preemptive rights' on the range, because of their established 'beneficial use.'

"The Taylor Grazing Act was enacted to counter-act the many range wars that were breaking out all over the west. Ranchers were in-fighting and killing each other over need for more land, more open range. Under this Act, a local board of ranchers was established to adjudicate disputes, and authorize preemptive rights. The Federal Government would survey, and map, and keep records of the adjudicated grazing rights.

"Eventually, the Federal Government was invited in to manage the entire process. It made sense at the time to the ranchers; because, many of those ranches were extensive, crossing over state lines.

"Now remember, this (surveying, mapping, record keeping, even managing the process) was, at the time, services that the Federal Government provided to the ranchers. Services that the ranchers desired."

Cliven spoke on like the teacher he is, driving home his point.

"Over time; however, the Government also wanted to establish and manage range improvements. The ranchers agreed to this and were willing to pay a fee[1] for these needed services. AMU[2] was the measurement to establish how much the rancher

---

1 Author's notes: a *Fee* (as used in its transactional sense) is payment for professional services performed. A fee is not a tax and it is not rent.
2 Actually, the term is Animal Unit Months (AUMs). In a grazing area, it is calculated by multiplying the number of animal units by the number of months of grazing.

would pay based on how many animals he grazed on the range for this service."

It's important to note here that a rancher's property includes both his homestead and all of the rights that attach to the ownership of the homesteaded land and the rights to certain exclusive uses over public (or open) land related to the ranch's business purpose – provided these homestead and its rights and the exclusive use rights are properly established and recorded. The rancher exclusively owns the homestead and all of its inherent rights once he has established its claim and recorded its deed. The rancher exclusively owns the rights of use (for water, grazing, forage, right-of-way, etc.) on public land (or 'open range') once he has applied for and received the necessary permit(s) for access to the previously unencumbered public land for the purpose of developing it to the intended use, established the boundaries of such use, fulfilled the developments' necessary improvement requirements – and – the government has surveyed, mapped, and recorded the boundaries of these developed, exclusive-use rights. Of course, he can also inherit such owned rights from their legal holder, or he can purchase such owned rights from their legal holder.

Cliven and most ranchers almost always refer to their property (the combination of all of the inherent rights attached to their homestead **plus** all the specific, exclusive use rights which they own over the open range, as described above) as their 'ranch.' He used this term throughout this interview and our conversations.

Government agencies, on the other hand, seem always to use the term 'allotment' to mean that portion of open range upon which the rancher has the exclusive right for its use (grazing, water, right-of-way, etc., as described above) – perhaps just as habitually as the ranchers use the term 'ranch' for their property. Allotment is a term that (in the Federal Government's modern use) ranchers **despise** as it usually comes with some kind of regulation that they never agreed to and that erodes their historic and still legal, exclusive-use rights.

Cliven continued:

"By the 1960s, the Bureau of Land Management (BLM)[3] began to evolve into more of a control board, telling ranchers what they could and could not do. By 1976, they had become managers of all concerns regarding public land-use beyond just ranches, to include recreation, mining, environmental, and more. And so, with this new-found power, the BLM, began to dictate the amount of animal units (which quickly translates into the size of the herd) that could be grazed on each rancher's allotment, often cutting AMU by 40% or more, which cut the BLM's revenues down. So, in response, the BLM raised their AMU fees to 100 times what they were when they began.[4]

"Now remember, this fee thing was done originally because the ranchers wanted – and agreed to pay for – the services the Federal Government had offered: their adjudication, range improvement, and record keeping. But now, with all the new controlling factors the BLM introduced, the ranchers began to push back. So, in response their push back, the Federal Government began to require contracts for all ranchers, inserting 'small print' (clauses) that gave the Federal Government the ultimate power over the ranchers' ranches.

"That is when we (the Bundys) became the last ranch left. We simply stopped signing any contracts with the Federal Government, putting the BLM on notice that we no longer needed their 'services.'

"But by then, the BLM was under the impression (and gave the impression – strongly) that they owned the land. Like squatters, who had settled in; but nobody (in authority) could do anything about it, because no one (of the neighbors) was complaining. Everyone

---

3 (Author's note:) Cliven uses the terms 'BLM' and the 'Federal Government' somewhat interchangeably, similar to the way he refers to 'Federal agents,' 'Federal Government agents,' 'government agents,' 'BLM agents,' – as the 'Feds' or 'feds.' Again, Cliven's uses of the terms are preserved as they occurred in the interview.
4 And, as Cliven told me later, hit with these new costs in such a slim-margin industry, the ranchers in Clark County – almost every family – began to sell out, or even, just pull out.

had forgotten who owned the land in the first place, the way I see it, because they'd been there for so long. Not even the State Government, nor the common rancher. Operating their own ranches, they came to believe they were *leasing* the land from the Federal Government to graze their cattle on – thinking they were *buying the grass!*

"But we knew better. We knew that the Land belonged to the State of Nevada, and that the Constitution does not allow the Federal Government to own land, except for the District of Columbia in Washington, for military uses, and for "certain buildings," like post offices, administration buildings, *etc.*, because the framers of our Constitution never intended for the Federal Government to lay claim over this much land, as in the case of the Bureau of Land Management has done here, laying claim to approximately 85% of the entire State of Nevada! The Constitution requires the Federal Government to pay for whatever land they do own."

Here, Cliven opens his pocket Constitution to Article 1, Section 8, item 17 of its list of 18 items.

"Here, read this, right here...," as he points me into this little book:

> The Congress shall have the power: ... (a list of several powers, the next in its midst)
> To exercise exclusive legislation in all cases whatsoever, over such district (not exceeding ten miles square) as may, by cession of particular states, and the acceptance of Congress, become the seat of the government of the United States, and to exercise like authority over all places **purchased** by the consent of the legislature of the state in which the same shall be, for the erection of forts, magazines, arsenals, dock-yards, and other needful buildings: ... (the list continues to its end).
> U.S. Constitution Article 1, Section 8, Item 17 (Emphasis added.)

"So, did the Federal Government pay for the State of Nevada?" Cliven rhetorically demanded, "Did they pay for California? Or how much of Oregon did they pay for? What about the rest of the Western United States? How much did they pay for those States' land?"

I quickly pressed on, fumbling, somewhat, to avoid giving or allowing an answer to these questions. "Now, Cliven, ah, is it true that you've refused to acknowledge any Federal Government claims over Nevada public land ... and that since 1998 you've just ignored the Federal Government ... um, ... insisting that the Clark County Sheriff, elected by the citizens of Nevada in Clark County, is in the rightful position to be your protector for your life, your ranch, your property, and your Constitutional rights and from any efforts of the BLM to force you to sign a public lands use contract to use those lands by virtue of the use-rights that you exclusively own, right?"

Cliven waited patiently – to see if I'd clumsily found my way to some sort of finished question.

He responded, "Yes. Every time since 1998, when I would have an encounter with the BLM Federal Agents, I would just call the local sheriff out and that would settle the problem. The local sheriff's department wrote up a memorandum of understanding between the Sheriff's Department and the BLM regarding the procedures of the BLM to gain access to my ranch."

"So, Cliven, in your opinion, who is the problem here?" I began to see his point of view.

"Clearly, the States are. As they should be, exercising their rights to the lands that they own. And then, there's the ranchers, too. They should be willing to stop signing 'em contracts, which give the Government the power over 'em, for without those contracts, the Federal Government would have no power at all," Cliven said forcefully.

Out came his pocket Constitution again. "Here, read that," pointing to:

> No State shall enter into any Treaty, Alliance, or Confederation; grant Letters of Marque and Reprisal; coin Money; emit Bills of Credit; make any Thing but gold and silver Coin a Tender in Payment of Debts; pass any Bill of Attainder, ex post facto Law, or Law impairing the Obligation of Contracts, or grant any Title of Nobility.
>
> – Article I, section 10, Clause 1 (Emphasis added)

Cliven went on:

"Let me explain. When the rancher signs one of 'em contracts with the Government, he is giving away his property rights to come instead, under the terms of their use that the contract with the Government decides and allows. But, even if I spent the rest of my life traveling all over America speaking to groups about this solution, I reckon only a few hundred ranchers, at best, would dare to refuse to sign 'em contracts, because the Federal Government has them all scared. And they should be ... they might think ol' Bundy's right, but look how he has fared? He's in prison! If you sign one of 'em contracts, your through, ... even the State can't help you. They'll use it to take away your livelihood.

"But what needs to happen is the Feds need to get out of our land. They need to cancel all of 'em contracts and send the ranchers a letter telling them that they are actually responsible for the management of their own land."

At this point, I started to realize I needed to mentally digest all of this. "So, 'bottom line' this for me. Just tell me more about why you feel the United States Constitution supports your position and its plain reading exposes the Federal Governments' usurping of the State's land rights and the ranchers' land-use rights, and the citizens civil rights, jeopardizing the freedoms, liberty, and independence of the American people, and particularly, the citizens of Nevada."

"Basically," Cliven responded, without missing a beat – by beginning a series of applications of the Constitution to the issue at hand – "under Article I, Section 8 of the United States Constitution, the Federal Government is given right to own 10 square miles, known as Washington D.C. (the District of Columbia), and also, with **consent** of the State legislature, to **purchase** land for military use, and other needful buildings."

> To exercise exclusive Legislation in all Cases whatsoever, over such **District (not exceeding ten Miles square) as may, by Cession of particular States, and the acceptance**

of Congress, become the Seat of the Government of the United States, and to exercise like Authority over all Places **purchased** by the **Consent of the Legislature of the State in which the Same shall be**, for the Erection of **Forts, Magazines, Arsenals, dock-Yards, and other needful Buildings**; ...

– Article I, Section 8 (Emphasis added)

"Article IV, Section 3, of the U.S. Constitution" Cliven notes, "allows the Federal Government to own or possess land as a territory, acquired by Treaty, or acquisition. The Federal Government has complete power over those lands, to make rules, regulations, and to dispose of those territories. But, as each territory becomes a State of its own, the Federal Government is to 'dispose' of the territorial land forming the state, and all titles cleared and given to the Sovereign State, who now becomes the owner of all lands not privately owned."

New states may be admitted by the Congress into this union; but no new states shall be formed or erected within the jurisdiction of any other state; nor any state be formed by the junction of two or more states, or parts of states, without the consent of the legislatures of the states concerned as well as of the Congress.

The Congress shall have power to dispose of and make all needful rules and regulations respecting the territory or other property belonging to the United States; and nothing in this Constitution shall be so construed as to prejudice any claims of the United States, or of any particular state.

– Article IV, Section 3 (Emphasis added)

"However, if the Federal Government was ever to become an owner or possessor of any land again after its formation as a State, then the Federal Government would need to *purchase it* from the State, with the consent of the owner, and for the purposes as stated in Article I, Section 8," Cliven reminded me.

To exercise exclusive Legislation in all Cases whatsoever, over such District (not exceeding ten Miles square) as may, by

59

Cession of particular States, and the acceptance of Congress, become the Seat of the Government of the United States, and to exercise like Authority over all Places **purchased by the Consent of the Legislature of the State in which the Same shall be**, for the Erection of Forts, Magazines, Arsenals, dock-Yards, and other needful Buildings; ...

– Article I, Section 8 (Emphasis added)

Moving to judicial power, he noted: "Article III, Section 2 provides and allows for judicial Federal power to be extended over disputes and controversies to which the United States is a clear party ... as with them BLM contracts, where *all of the signers **also** become a party.*"

> **The judicial power shall extend to all cases, in law and equity, arising under this Constitution, the laws of the United States, and treaties made, or which shall be made, under their authority;**--to all cases affecting ambassadors, other public ministers and consuls;--to all cases of admiralty and maritime jurisdiction;--**to controversies to which the United States shall be a party**;--to controversies between two or more states;--between a state and citizens of another state;--between citizens of different states;--between citizens of the same state claiming lands under grants of different states, and between a state, or the citizens thereof, and foreign states, citizens or subjects.
>
> ...

– Article III, Section 2 (Emphasis added)

Which is clarified by Amendment 11:

> **The Judicial power of the United States shall <u>not be construed to extend</u> to any suit in law or equity,** commenced or prosecuted against one of the United States by Citizens of another State, or by Citizens or Subjects of any Foreign State.
>
> – Amendment 11 to the Constitution (Emphasis added)

"In my case it (this Amendment 11 clarification of Article III, Section 2)," said Cliven, "don't make too much difference, but (it does) like some of these cases where these guys have come from Idaho down into Nevada." After a pause, he continued, "The Federal Court wouldn't have jurisdiction over them. Normally they do not have jurisdiction over them. The state has jurisdiction, not the Feds. Even where I thought the Feds had jurisdiction, they don't."

Turning to the importance of the Constitution, Cliven pointed to Article VI of the U.S. Constitution, which … "makes the Constitution *the supreme law of the land.*"

> **This Constitution**, and **the laws of the United States** which shall be made in pursuance thereof; **and all treaties made, or which shall be made**, under the authority of the United States, **shall be the supreme law of the land**; and the judges in every state shall be bound thereby, anything in the Constitution or laws of any State to the contrary notwithstanding. …
> – Article VI (Emphasis added)

And finishing by addressing The Tenth (10th) Amendment to the United States Constitution, he asserted that it protects the Sovereign States' rights because it stipulates that all "… powers not delegated to the United States (Federal Government) by the Constitution, are reserved to the states, or to the people of the United States."

> The **powers not delegated to the United States by the Constitution, nor prohibited by it to the states, are reserved to the states respectively, or to the people.**
> – the United States Constitution, Amendment 10 (Emphasis added)

I thought maybe I was starting to see what this was all about, so I said, "It would appear, Cliven, that you stand aligned with the United States Constitution, which is the supreme law of this United States, and that Article I, Section 8 was written expressly to prevent this very situation that now exists within the State of Nevada – as the Federal Government has asserted ownership of the public land in the State of Nevada (and it is a lot of land!). This ownership is without its purchase or approval by the State, entered into trades of this land within Nevada without this State's approval, is exercising unlimited authority over this State's public lands without this State's approval, and sometimes (rare as this may be) makes whatever purchases of land it desires without this State's approval. That was the public land that belongs(ed) to the people of Nevada, and was just taken by the Federal

Government, without purchase and without any State Governor's or State Legislature's doing anything about it!"

"Yes," Cliven answered, "That pretty much sums it up. However, this has caused some troubles, because the Constitution wasn't written to protect the Government, or the majority; but rather, to protect the rights of We the People – as individuals.

"It cannot be more clearly stated, than in New York v. United States, when the court said,

> The Constitution divides authority between the Federal and State Governments for the protection of its individuals.

"So, State Sovereignty is not just an end in itself; rather, Federalism secures to citizens the liberties that derive from the diffusion of sovereign power.

"See, the fight here is not just about me and my cows, and it's not just about the ranchers in Nevada, or the entire West for that matter; but, it's about the rights of all American citizens. Because if the Federal Government overreach in Nevada is allowed to continue, then it sets the precedent to allow the Federal Government's overreach to prevail everywhere, in every State in the Union, and destroy the division of powers as afforded by the United States Constitution and by the founders who envisioned a divided and balanced governmental approach to ensure

the people's rights. It was quite an idee they had." He ended with a big, satisfied smile across his face.

Then, he laid out this shocker:

"As it stands now, the citizens of Nevada are being deprived of their right to local self-government. In Nevada, the State's citizens have practically *no say* in the laws of 85% of their State's land, resources, and development." This was, perhaps, demonstrated on April 12, 2014, when Federal Agents conducted a military operation at the ranch, while local Sheriff and State Troopers were ordered to stand by and watch. It was only after pressure from the demonstrators re-asserting the Constitutional limits to Federal power over the State's land that, as Cliven concluded: "The local Sheriff broke ranks and negotiated a stand-down with the BLM, saving lives and my property (the Bundy's ranch)."

"OK, Cliven, then what do you think should be done to get America back on track? ... I'm thinking as a citizen now."

"Mike, here's six questions that should be asked of the American people. Because it's the American people who need to stand with me, and say, 'No—Enough' to our Federal Government." He dug through his gray box, then another, until he found what he was looking for. He handed me a well-used, typed document (by typewriter) with scribbles all over it. It said:

How can it be, that the Constitution of the United States allows the Federal Government the authority to exercise jurisdiction within an admitted State of the Union, which has been declared without limitations; and which deprives citizens living therein of their constitutionally protected rights when we know that the primary purpose for writing the Constitution was for the protection of individual rights ... or are we to believe otherwise?

How can it be, that the Federal Government can claim to own 85% of the lands within an admitted State of the Union, when it was so clearly stated by the delegates to the constitutional convention that one of the greatest fears was that should the Federal Government ever be permitted to own vast amounts of land within an admitted State of the Union, that it would awe the State into an undue obedience to the Federal Government?

How can it be, that the Federal Government can exercise jurisdiction within an admitted State of the Union, which allows the Federal Government to act both as State Government and Federal Government, when the Supreme Court of the United State has declared that such a denial of the citizens' rights (to be protected by divisions of powers doctrine) might be pronounced the very definition of tyranny?

How can it be, that the Federal Government can exercise jurisdiction, which has been declared without limitation, within a territory that was acquired pursuant to the treaty of Guadalupe Hidalgo, one hundred and fifty-three (153) years ago (author's note – as of when Cliven's document was typed, nearly two decades ago), after which a State was carved out of said treaty – that the inhabitants of the ceded land shall be incorporated in the Union of the United States, and admitted to the enjoyment of all rights, advantages, and immunities of citizens of the United States.

How can it be, that the Courts have long upheld the notion that such lands that lay beneath navigable rivers pass to a respective State upon Statehood, yet assume that the open and unappropriated lands do not?

How can it be, that the Courts have come to accept the notion that it is Constitutional for the Federal Government to exercise jurisdiction within an admitted State of the Union which deprives citizens of the right to local self-government; the right to be tried by one's peers; and, the right to have property interests recognized and protected by state, local and common law?

It was a long and exhausting interview. And it wasn't over for me when we were done for that day! Cliven generously shared with me many of the documents from his boxes, as well as pointers to other resources that kept me busy for many days, then, and since. Some of what I learned from these sources I've shared with you as inserts above – and some of which I'll share with you in the coming chapters.

With all of what was said in the interview as background, Cliven Bundy's position for the past three decades has remained the same.

The "Standoff" (as the Media call it) of April 12, 2014 was NOT a 'force-of-arms' resistance or even a protest against the Federal Government, the BLM, the US Park Service, or the individual agents who came armed for combat on that fateful day.

… so, what WAS it?

His defense in 1998, 2012, that day and every day since remains the same.

… so, what IS it?

Chapter 4

– THE FIFTEEN SECOND DEFENSE –
The Feds have No Jurisdiction on My Ranch

"It's real simple," Cliven said. "In fact, I have a 15-second defense," as he gives his big cowboy grin. And with a zest of anticipation he asks, "Are you ready?"

"Sure, fire away," I responded.

"In April 2014, *we were protesting to the Sheriff* for not protecting my life, liberty, and property from the Federal Government."

He paused.

"I graze my cattle only on Clark County, Nevada land and I have no contract with the Federal Government."

He paused, again.

"The Federal Government has no jurisdiction on my ranch."

With a chuckle, he said, "I think I still have a few seconds left!"

Why The One-Sentence Summary?
Cliven believes the Federal Government has taken possession of the public lands in Nevada and much of the western states erroneously, illegally, or better still, unconstitutionally.

This is a bold claim for a simple rancher with little formal education.

But, before we dismiss his argument with a mere wave of the hand (as the Federal Courts often do) let's give his position a fair hearing.

Who owns the public lands of Nevada and the other western states?
In 1792, James Madison wrote,

> "Government is instituted to protect property of every sort;
> as well that which lies in the various rights of individuals, as
> that which the term particularly expresses. This being the
> end of Government, that alone is a just government, which
> impartially secures to every man, whatever is his own."[1]

> An unjust government; one which fails to secure the property
> of its citizens, is one "where property which a man has ... is
> violated by arbitrary seizures of one class of citizens for the
> service of the rest."[2]

Fixed in American law before the Constitution was even written, the
Congress at the end of the Revolutionary War, was to dispose public
lands in the territories. It was to be ceded to settlers who would make
the land productive, or to newly created states and from them to its
settlers. More recently in the West, the Federal Government was
invited to manage range use agreements made among ranchers as the
ranches sometimes crossed state lines. These early laws – as did their
following laws – rested on the role of Federal 'stewardship' of the
public lands, both as these became parts of States at their formation
and as their uses involved more than one state.

We, the average citizens, assume that the Government protects
property and the rights of the individuals, yet the Federal Government
is termed by many to be the "largest landlord in Nevada ..."[3, 4] But,
tiring of providing mere stewardship of the States' public lands
for their citizens late in the last century, the Feds simply asserted
these lands' ownership. By doing so, overturned American law and
judicial precedent dating back to the Constitution itself, to before the
Constitution was even written, and to the basic concepts of public land
ownership rooted among the reasons for the American Revolution.

---

1 See "Property", by James Madison (1792) http:press-pubsuchidago.edu/founders/documents/
vlch1616523.html
2 Id.
3 Special Feature: Who OWNS Nevada? An Introduction to Public Lands, 20 Nevada Lawyer
12, 12
4 The U.S. Government claims to own over sixty Million Acres in the State of Nevada. That
represents 84.9% of the total of the approximately 70,762,880 Acres of land within the State of
Nevada.

Many see this assertion of ownership to be what it was – a simple land-grab, and what a land-grab it was! As trumpeted on many occasions, the Federal Government lays claim to 85% of the entire State of Nevada, and makes ownership claims to varying amounts of the public lands in other Western States. Though the official Federal land-ownership claim is 'only' 79.6% of all of the land in the State of Nevada (*per* the most recent Congressional Research report of March 2017[5]), what's a few million acres among bureaucrats? For the purposes of this book, we'll stay with the generally accepted figure of 85%.

As if that wasn't bad enough, this self-asserted 'landlord' charges fees and rents from Nevada ranchers for their use of their own property, often putting these same ranchers out of business by regulating their use of their own exclusive rights to use their own property. All while they conduct land swaps, land sales, and land trades to favor "one class of citizens for the service of the rest" – in this case is (supposedly) for the furtherance of the 'public' interest; but, without the Constitutionally-required approval of the States that got ripped off.

We assume that a landlord would provide its tenants with a quiet and safe enjoyment of the land. But, as the self-styled 'benevolent landlord' of 85% of the State of Nevada, the Feds have used (and misused) Nevada's public land, turning it into a nuclear testing ground,[6] which has, according to reports, resulted in the death of some Nevada citizens.[7] The Federal Government– against the will of the people of Nevada and without their, or their Legislature's, approval – in fact, over the ***continuous objection*** of the Nevada State Government, has also developed the Nation's Nuclear Waste Dump at Yucca Mountain, which, thanks only to the Nevada Congressional delegation's strenuous, unrelenting, bi-partisan, and unanimous opposition in Congress, has yet to open.

If this sounds like a conflict of either 'landlord' or 'stewardship' interest, it's because there has been indisputable harm, damage, and loss perpetuated by the Federal Government to Nevadans, not only in recent years; but also to past generations – as the Federal Government

---

5 Federal Land Ownership Overview p.8 https://fas.org/sgp/crs/misc/R42346.pdf
6 Prescott V. United States, 523 F. Supp. 918, 921-22 (1981)
7 http:/commondrains.org "50 years later, the Tragedy of Nevada Nuclear Testing."

has increasingly presented itself as a 'benevolent landlord,' managing the public land as National Domain for the 'benefit of all the people of the Nation.'

However, if anyone (like Cliven Bundy, for example) challenges or confronts the Feds as to their claim to be the owner of America's public lands, they are met with asserted enforcement 'powers' and an inexhaustible arsenal of weaponry employed in military-like response (as Cliven was in his case), declaring and labeling any challengers as *dissenters, domestic terrorists, enemies of the state*, and, of course, *outlaws*.

To understand how we as a nation got into this mess, we must first review the details of the underlying principles of the founding framers of America and their property, land, and ownership concepts. That's what I have done here. I've researched the papers Cliven shared with me, the pointers he gave to other documents, and additional sources to find the answers I put in this book, **We** need to understand *what happened* and *why*.

Let's start at the beginning…

Forming the Country

America's land ownership concepts were formed in the American Colonial experience by both those who had been sent to develop the newly-found lands across the sea – and – by those who came on their own. They were fleeing oppressive monarchial governments with their centuries-old population control and oppression systems. These systems revolved around monarchy-centered land ownership. Predominant in Western Europe, these systems were the mainstay of the monarchies who funded the exploration of the New World and who granted to private companies both large tracts of the New World's lands (which the monarchs claimed to own by right of discovery) and broad powers to develop them for these monarchial owners' economic and political gain.

Foremost among these monarchies (as far as what would become today's United States of America was concerned) were the British, the Spanish, and the French who projected into this New World development both their European political squabbles and their predominant, monarchy-centered land ownership concept – feudalism. This would have continued unchallenged in the New World but for the advent of the Age of Enlightenment and its new political ideas that questioned the appropriateness of everything.[8]

Let's examine how that worked out.

In 1774, Thomas Jefferson observed that…

> William the Conqueror, upon his successful invasion of England first introduced feudal land ownership to Britain by claiming ownership for himself of the lands "which belonged to those who fell (died) in the Battle of Hastings (1066)," and the subsequent insurrections against his reign. That land formed a considerable portion of the entire Kingdom.[9]

> In earlier ages of the Saxon settlement, feudal holdings were certainly altogether unbeknown; and very few, if any, had been introduced at the time of the Norman Conquest. Our Saxon ancestors held their lands, as their personal property, in absolute dominion, disencumbered with any superior,

8 http://www.history.com/topics/enlightenment
9 Thomas Jefferson "A Summary View of the Rights of British (1774) America" Avalon Project. Yale Law School

answering merely to the nature of those possessions, which the feudalist termed allodial.[10, 11]

That was how nationwide institutional Feudalism was introduced to England's Saxon settlements – by the complete, military conquest of a foreign power. Even though the people had been used to a very different land-ownership concept, that concept was lost to that of the victor. And just as Feudalism was imposed by the new monarchy, English society, power, and influence realigned to the new political reality, with no ability to continue living by the old customs, let alone, any former land-ownership concepts. In war, the winners get the spoils.

Jefferson continues to observe that "America was not conquered by William, the Norman, nor its lands surrendered to him," and that, therefore, land was to be held "undoubtedly (in) the allodial nature."[12] In his view, the lands of America were not 'owned' by any government or King, as the occupants of the lands who had worked it to productivity were not feudal tenants; but rather, were the actual and sole owners of the land.

He based this shocking concept on the work of John Locke, who, at the dawning of the Age of Enlightenment nearly a century before, had written:

> *As much Land* as a Man Tills, Plants, Improves, Cultivates, and can use the Product of, so much is his *Property.* He by his Labour does, as it were, inclose it from the Common. Nor will it invalidate his right to say, Everybody else has an equal Title to it; and, therefore, he cannot appropriate, he cannot inclose, without the Consent of all his Fellow-Commoners, all Mankind. God, when he gave the World in common to all Mankind, commanded Man also to labour, and the penury of his Condition required it of him. God and his Reason commanded him to subdue the Earth, *i.e.* improve it for the benefit of Life, and therein lay out something upon it that was his own, his labour. He that in Obedience to this Command of

---

10 *Ibid.*
11 Author's note: **Allodial** title constitutes ownership of real property (land, buildings, and fixtures) that is independent of any superior landlord.
12 *Ibid.*

God, subdued, tilled and sowed any part of it, thereby annexed to it something that was his *Property,* which another had no Title to, nor could without injury take from him. Nor was this *appropriation* of any parcel of *Land,* by improving it, any prejudice to any other Man, since there was still enough, and as good left; and more than the yet unprovided could use. So that in effect, there was never the less left for others because of his inclosure for himself. For he that leaves as much as another can make use of, does as good as take nothing at all.

John Locke, Second Treatise,

Chap. V. Of Property. §§ 32-33. 1689

Jefferson also observed, however, that colonial Americans "were farmers and not lawyers" and were easily fooled into believing the principle of all lands belonged to the King and thus, allowing themselves to utilize their own land as tenants rather than owners, via their "grant ... from the crown."[13] At first, the crown would rent the land to colonial Americans for small sums, generally leaving them alone, the majesty later doubled the price and rendered the acquisition of lands"[14] difficult. Cliven noted that this is the "same situat'n the ranchers have gotten em'selves into – by being fooled into this relationship by the BLM – with even the same of deception: those darn contracts to rent the use of the same rights that they already owned!"

This was a key feature of the American Revolution – throwing off the crown's governmental tyranny (including its onerous concept of feudal land ownership) and not substituting another feudal owner (the American Government) in the King's place; but rather, to put aside feudal land ownership, and embrace in its place, John Locke's principle of appropriation by homesteading, expressed as Jefferson's notion of allodial land ownership – free from "superior landlords."[15]

Leading up to the American Revolution, Jefferson privately instructed the Virginia delegation to the First Continental Congress (but, by these instructions' printing as an unauthorized; but, widely distributed pamphlet, instructed the colonies, and thus, this Congress itself) to "lay matters before his majesty, and declare that he has no right to grant lands to himself."[16]

---

13 *Ibid.*

14 *Ibid.*

15 *Ibid.*

16 The meaning that the King has NO right to grant privileged title to land by his mere decree.

This led this First Continental Congress to petition the King essentially as the pamphlet read. Jefferson continued in it,

> From the nature and purpose of civil institutions, all the lands within the limits which any particular society had circumscribed around itself are assumed by that society, and subject to their allotment only.[17]

As the word 'allotment,' as used here, means to 'distribute or parcel out,' and in its conceptual context, it also means that this must be done by the local society, collectively, or by their legislature. However:

> ... if (the lands) are allotted in neither of these ways, each individual of the society may appropriate to himself such lands as he finds vacant, and occupancy will give him title.[18]

The American colonists rejected the idea of large masses of land owned by mere assertion or decree, refusing the crown's ownership that caused the lands to be owned by landlords rather than the locals, the actual producers upon the land. The fundamental understanding of the tyranny that the early Americans had thrown off must be understood to include that the allotment and distribution of land holding is not achieved by the Government merely declaring itself the owner of large swaths of virgin land, and declaring it has distributed and allotted the land unto itself, now and forever. In fact, the mere idea that a central government would declare for itself such absolute power, from and to itself, or to a class of citizens it privileges, is precisely the tyranny Jefferson and his American collaborators brought "before his majesty ... to declare that he has no right to grant lands to himself."[19]

Of course, the Americans won their revolution and went about forming a constitutional government, enshrining Jefferson's ideals into Article 1 Section 8 Paragraph 17:

> ... to exercise exclusive legislation in all cases whatsoever over such District (not exceeding ten miles square) as may be cession of particular states, and acceptance of congress, become the seat of Government of the United States, and to

---

17 Article: The Constitutional Underpinnings of Homelessness, 40 Hous. L. Rev. 211, 225-226
18 Author's Note: In other words, the allotment of land is to be localized.
19 Thomas Jefferson "A Summary View of Rights of British (1774) America" Avalon Project. Yale Law School

exercise like authority over all places purchased by consent of the legislature of the state in which the same shall be, for the erection of Forts, Magazines, Arsenals, Dock-yards and other needful buildings;

Further, in Article IV Section 3,

The Congress shall have power to dispose of and make all needful Rules and Regulations respecting the territory or other property*[20] belonging to the United States; and nothing in this Constitution shall be so construed as to prejudice claims of the United States, or any particular state.

With a fundamental understanding of the context of the lives our founding fathers lived, it becomes clear that:

Our forefathers had no intention that the Federal Government, which they formed, would be feudal owners or 'Landlords' of the land. Indeed, the central Government was to only own land for what we now know as Washington DC, and properties for military uses and other necessary buildings, like a post office. However, ... such land must be purchased from the Sovereign State which owns it, with the approval of that State's legislature. The rest of the land was to be disposed of to its citizens and to be developed by them for its economic use.

Territories, which may contain privately-held, government-owned, and public lands, may be obtained by treaties or purchase, and while those territories are to be under the full and complete authority of the U.S. Congress, the land ownership therein respected *per* the terms of the treaty or purchase. Any public lands therein are disposed of to the state – once such territories are formed as Sovereign States. Most of these territories have since been given over to the various fifty American States as they entered into the Union. At the time of such admission to the Union, the territory becomes a Sovereign State (again, respecting and

---

20 *Note: As we reviewed my developing manuscript, Cliven wanted to clarify what "other property' – marked above with the asterisk (*) in Article VI, Section 3 – is. His said, "In the Constitution (Article VI, Section 3), it says 'other property;' but, what they're referring to is Article 1 Section 8 Paragraph 17 property. 'Other property' is this Article 1 Section 8 Paragraph 17 property. That's the only 'other property' the government owns. (You'd think) it could be referred to something like an airplane or a building or something but when you're talking about land or any jurisdiction, it would have to go back to Article 1 Section 8 Paragraph 17. That's the only place (in the Constitution) that gives you the direction on property."

preserving such private and government land ownership as exists and transferring public land ownership to the newly-created Sovereign State), under the authority of its citizens, and legislated through a representative form of government.

And most importantly, that the powers not delegated to the United States (Federal) Government by the Constitution, nor prohibited by it (in this case, *critically*, powers over public land ownership, management, and disposition), **are reserved to the States respectively, or to the people**.

And there it is: In this last statement, you have the Tenth Amendment to the Constitution of the United States of America.

The powers not delegated to the United States by the Constitution, nor prohibited by it to the states, are reserved to the states respectively, or to the people.
– the United States Constitution, Amendment 10

According to the Cornell Law School's Legal Information Institute, the

Tenth Amendment helps to define the concept of federalism, the relationship between Federal and state governments. As Federal activity has increased, so too has the problem of reconciling state and national interests as they apply to the Federal powers to tax, to police, and to regulations such as wage and hour law, disclosure of personal information in recordkeeping systems, and laws related to strip-mining" and other land rights issues.[21]

In war, the winners get the spoils. But, the outcome may depend not only on **what** they do with these spoils (and concepts that underlie such action) – but, **how** they do it.

Two Degrees Off Course
If you've ever attempted to navigate by compass, you'll be well aware of the fact that if you're just one or two degrees off course, the further you travel, the farther you'll be off course. Eventually, you will miss your destination altogether.

---

21 https://www.law.cornell.edu/constitution/tenth_amendment

Soon after the birth of our new nation, the Americans were presented with the dual question of

How individuals would settle the land ceded to it by the British – west of the original 13 states in an orderly manner;

and

How this new nation would pay off its war debt from the Revolution while preserving a government which had minimal powers of taxation.

It was here, in the practicality of answering these questions, that the Federal Government got 'Two Degrees Off Course,' and began straying from The Founders' view of land ownership. Out of the apparent necessity of arbitrating the 13 original states' claims to these lands to their west ceded by Britain at the close of the Revolutionary War, the Second Continental Congress persuaded the States to allow for a centralized allotment of western lands and codified the agreement in the Northwest Ordnance of 1787 to this purpose, so that, this Congress could parcel out land to new settlers, at a price which would go to help pay off the war debt.

This system has been characterized as falling within property rights as the early Americans understood them. They understood that they, the people, were bound together with this war debt, and being there was no other practical way to pay that debt off as there was no Federal income tax at that time,[22] and so, the only alternative asset presented was this: that the Western lands would be allotted to settlers for payment, as representing the settlers' proportional responsibility for the nation's debt.

This system was grudgingly accepted as the early Americans were well aware of this 'off course' deviation from what the Forefathers intended. It was only accepted out of necessity and with the genuine belief that this Congress would act in good faith regarding the land, and dispose of it to the States, so that thereafter, the land could be owned by local residents, and open to ordinary functions of occupancy, homesteading, and allodial title.

---

22 Income Tax was established, February 3, 1913

Astounded, Thomas Jefferson vehemently rejected this system, writing:

> ... has it not been practice of all other nations to hold their lands as their personal estates in absolute dominion? Are we not the better for what we have hitherto abolished of feudal system? Has not every restitution of ancient Saxon laws (of ownership) by actual occupiers of the (lands) had happy effects? Is it not better now that we return at once into that happy system of our ancestors, the wisest and most perfect ever yet devised by wit of man, as it stood before the eighth century?[23]

Jefferson thought this proposed system was so absurd, observing that centralized allotment was met with "such determined opposition" by Americans themselves, that he mistakenly concluded, "The idea of Congress selling out (unallocated lands) ... will never be proposed." He understood that the centralized allocation system was another form of that same system lorded over the colonies by the English Crown.

Jefferson, himself a highly educated man and a wealthy plantation owner, was fascinated, as were many of the educated revolutionaries, by Locke's notion of individuals simply appropriating land, mixing with it their labor, and by this, creating ownership thereof, that he wrote to Edmund Pendleton that he was "against selling the lands to all," observing "by selling the lands to them, you will disgust them, and cause aversion of them, from the common union. They will settle the lands in spite of everybody."

Jefferson's contemporaries; however, didn't listen to his warnings – a failure due to their optimism and belief that this Second Congress (by now, termed by some, *'The Confederation Congress'*), having written, and the states having ratified *The Articles of Confederation of the United States* (actually more of a treaty among these states than a constitution establishing any real governing body with any Federal power to compel any state action), would act honorably and in good faith, and never go beyond its limited power, and just paying back the war debt. Although its governance weaknesses were soon to be corrected by the Third Continental Congress (which wrote and got the states to ratify the Constitution of the United States of America –

---

23 Thomas Jefferson, letter to Edmund Pendleton, August 13, 1776 Avalon Project. Yale Law School

which got the principles right), this mistaken belief in how land would be handled *in practice* continued for more than a century.

And, in fact, even well into the late 1900s, the idea that Congress would do anything <u>but</u> dispose of land to settlers, or to the states, and keep only small portions of military and "other buildings" as necessary, was the common or 'accepted understanding' and the underlying principles of the implementing public land law. Anything otherwise would be considered an unrealistic expectation (even possibly un-American) that could or should never be ascribed to the benevolent American Congress, who would never exceed its limited power. Or at least that's what the majority of Americans perceived as would be true.

Even the opinion of Supreme Court Justice Brewer in *Stearns v. Minnesota* (1900) criticized the Supreme Court of Minnesota for the Court's "imagination" regarding the intentions of the Federal Congress. Justice Brewer observed that nothing in the Constitution explicitly prohibited Congress from attempting to "keep withdrawn a large area of land out of local use and thus beyond the State's jurisdiction of taxation."

Justice Brewer found that even though the Federal Government could theoretically "withdraw all the public lands of Minnesota from private entry or public grant ... no such possibility of wrong conduct on the part of Congress can be entered into consideration," because at that time, it was the nationwide assumption that Congress *would not engage in 'wrong conduct.'* Writing that, "it cannot be imputed to Congress that it would discriminate against (a state) or pass any legislation detrimental to its interest."[24]

In other words, the Federal Government *could* withhold the land within the sovereign state of Minnesota, but it *just wouldn't.* And even thinking that such withholding might be a realistic possibility was ridiculous. Justice Brewer found the idea that the Government would overstep its boundaries, simply outside of his realm of possibility. It was simply outside Justice Brewer's (and most Americans') moral paradigm to think the Government would withhold lands within one of

---

24 Meaning that Congress can be assumed to act subserviently in the management of public lands within Minnesota for the benefits of local residents of the State and not to injure them

the sovereign states, or engage in "wrong conduct."

But, Justice Brewer is not alone. Two and a half centuries of remarkably consistent commentary on the Northwest Ordinance conclude:

In 1845, the U.S. Supreme Court had noted this understanding of the terms in which the original states granted the Federal Government powers over western lands,

> … taking legislative acts of the United States, and the states of Virginia and Georgia, and their deeds of cession to the United States, and giving each, separately, and to all jointly, a fair interpretation, we must come to the conclusion that *it was the intention* of the parties *to invest the United States with temporary government and to hold it in trust for the performance of the stipulations and conditions expressed in the deed of cession and the legislative acts connected with them.* [25] (Emphasis added.)

Then, in 1988, an historical commenter noted:

> More importantly, it (the Northwest Ordinance) established that the United States would not act as a colonizing agent of new lands but would extend to those territories (after an orderly development of social, legal and political institutions) an invitation to join as *equal partners in the Union.*" [26]

Again, the 1845 finding of the Court was that:

> … the goal of this ordinance, and its proceeding generations, was to create an "empire of liberty" inviting all peoples of its lands and territories into the Union of States. First, converting the lands into monies for the payment of the war debt, then, secondly, to cede them to the new states created from the territories. Once these two purposes were accomplished, the power of the United States to govern over these lands *as their own property* was to cease. [27]

---

25 Pollard V. Hagan, 44 U.S. (1845)
26 Article: Property and Republicanism in the NorthWest Ordinance, 45 Ariz. St. L.J. 409, 462
27 Pollard V. Hagan, 44 U.S. (3 How.) 212, 224 (1845)

And as late as 2015, the Utah Commission for the Stewardship of Public Lands contended that the Northwest Ordinance was intended to remove:

> ... the last vestiges of feudal ownership of land as a matter of national policy, and provide for regular and prompt disposal of unoccupied and unappropriated land under United States (Governmental] control.[28]

It becomes clear the Federal Government was first, to temporarily manage lands as part of the "national domain" in order to convert the land into revenue to pay off the war debt, and then eventually to cede the unconverted public lands within their borders to the newly-created states as they joined the union. Once these lands were 'disposed of' to the states or individually owned by citizens, the Federal Government no longer had any interest or control of owning public lands with the exception of Washington DC, military purposes and "other needful buildings," which Congress purchased, with the assent of the State legislature.

Unfortunately, U.S. Supreme Court Justice Brewer was incorrect in his thinking when he chastised the Supreme Court of Minnesota for their "imagination" that Congress might do something "injurious" and discriminatory to the new state as to hold the majority of its lands permanently for itself, and refuse to dispose of it back to the state or sell it to individual citizens. Because the Federal Government began doing just that – in 1850 with California and all states west of the 'Federal Faultline' defined by the western borders of the Dakotas, Nebraska, Kansas, Oklahoma, and Texas through Alaska in 1959 as they were admitted into the Union from the Territories gained at the end of the Mexican war and later (more about this later). (This was not the first time the states had to challenge the Feds for their own land: Illinois, Missouri, Louisiana and their neighboring states had to band together to compel Congress to transfer the nearly 90% of their lands controlled by the federal government for decades, too. These states; however, actually won their lands back -- not by the courts' actions – rather in the Congress -- with a political solution.). [29]

---

28 Legal Analysis of the Legal Consulting Team Prepared for the Utah Commission for the Stewardship of Public Lands, December 9, 2015 at p.34

29 http://www.americanlandscouncil.org/u_of_u_legal_analysis_ignores_stubborn_facts_on_the_transfer_of_public_lands_movement

The Federal Government now sits on 85% of Nevada State lands, and a majority of the lands of the Western United States. The Federal Government literally uses the dubious claim to own the land in Nevada, *just as William the Conqueror did.* Then make it into a nuclear test range, killing numerous Nevada citizens, while making a nuclear waste dump out of Yucca Mountain, and, forcing ranchers and others to leave or pay rents and fees if they wish to remain on their own rightful ranches and work them.

Recently the Federal Government has added physical "injury" to Nevada citizens to their list of atrocities and unconstitutional violations against the people it is supposed to protect. It now acts as a feudal landlord, holding nearly all the lands, enacting heavy regulations, extracting rents, all while they have no right to do so. But more disturbing is that the Federal Government sits on its throne in Washington DC, functioning as the Lord of the states (especially Nevada), granting lands to itself – **just as the British Crown formerly granted lands to itself**.

Cruising along two degrees off-course, the Federal Government got to the forefathers' unintended destination as the policy formally slid from 'holding in *stewardship*' to 'holding in *ownership*' with the passage of The Federal Land Policy and Management Act of 1976. In it this new public policy is stated:

Sec. 102. [43 U.S.C. 1701] (a) The Congress declares that it is the policy of the United States that –

> (1) the public lands be retained in Federal **ownership, <u>unless</u>** as a result of the land use planning procedure provided for in this Act, it is determined that **disposal** of a particular parcel will serve the national interest; ... (Emphasis added.)

It is easy to see where the BLM, *et al.*, get the idea that they own the public land – and easy for them to conveniently ignore or bully those with existing rights on, over, or under that land into thinking that they don't own them anymore.

This radical departure from the historic, public lands policy of the United States; however, has a safety net provision in Section 7 of the act:

Sec. 701. [43 U.S.C. 1701 note] (a) Nothing in this Act, or in any amendment made by this Act, shall be construed as terminating any valid lease, permit, patent, right-of-way, or other land use right or authorization existing on the date of approval of this Act.

Ranchers who also ignore this section will lose everything. Those who understand it *should* find business as usual – pre-1976 – but in fact and practice, at what price?

As Thomas Jefferson once declared his rights and argued for their recognition "before the crown," Cliven Bundy has for two decades argued the very same rights, declaring that Federal dominion over the public lands within the State of Nevada, including his ranch, to be contrary to every precept of law known to the American people. After a lifetime of ranching, all the while watching his friends and neighbors' demise as they lose their ranches and their hope under the oppressive hand of the Federal Government's unlawful and unconstitutional actions as Lord of the public lands in the State of Nevada, he says "enough!" And has put all he possesses, his very life, on the line in order to end this tyranny that the Federal Government is authorizing, enacting and executing over "WE THE PEOPLE."

Nevada State History

As I noted previously, though the 'interview' session was exhausting, it was an enjoyable role-play for both Cliven and me. After we finished it (or it finished us!), we had called it a day and agreed to meet in the morning.

As I laid on my bunk reflecting on the day's events I began to thank God for men like Cliven Bundy, who were willing to stand up for what they believed – regardless of the consequences – come what may.

Maybe that's what life's all about: finding those opportunities to stand in the gap, protecting those who can't "in for themselves" as Cliven put it, making a difference for good. Making one's life count for more than just one's self.

Heck, maybe every generation is called upon to make this same stand as the original forefathers made, if we are to keep this freedom alive. We have a great history of those who have kept the light of freedom lit, and we need to follow their example, lest we lose it.

I decided then to ask Cliven more about the Nevada history and the Feds land-grab he had touched upon earlier, next time we met up. I'd had a long day, and fell asleep quickly.

The next morning I headed off to make a cup of coffee and start the new day. While walking, I saw the Bundy boys and said, "Hey boys" while smiling and lifting up my cup like a cowboy tips his Stetson in greeting friends. Cliven, Mel, and David were just finishing up their daily family 'check-in' and the boys were leaving to do errands while saying, "See ya later, Mike."

"So, how's your night, Mike?" Cliven greeted me.

"Okay, Cliven — thanks for asking, and you?"

"You know me, I can sleep through anything!" chuckling as he lifted his cup of tea for a sip.

"How are the boys, and all the family doing?" I asked, bracing myself for his response.

"It's a challenge, you know that, but, we're dealin' with it, day by day – and you?" he said with his steely gray eyes piercing me straight through.

"Good, but I've got some questions about the historical Nevada land grab you discussed about yesterday, and wondered if you'd give me some more input on that issue."

"Sure, you know these diversions away from the present legal and family worries do me good. Where do you want me to begin?"

"I remember you said that it's widely accepted that the Feds own 85% of Nevada State."

"Oh, yeah, well you know, that places the folks who live on and work

84

the land, like us Bundys, in serious jeopardy. It positions the Feds in the role of 'Lord over the entire state' and our land-lord to boot, where they, the Feds, now control the vast majority of Nevada State's land, resources, policies and politics, all jeopardizing the freedom, liberty and independence of the sovereign state's constitutional right to self-govern themselves."

The Interdepartmental Committee for the Study of Jurisdiction over Federal Areas Within the States, concluded in June, 1957: 'That there appears to be no question but that the requirement (referring to the United States Constitution's Article 1, Section 8, Clause 17) was added simply to foreclose the possibility that a state might be destroyed by the Federal Government's purchase of all the property within the state.' And its final report, subsequent to that one, drove home the point even more – stating: 'This power might enslave any particular state by buying up its territory, and that the strongholds would be a means of awing the state into undue obedience to the general (Federal) government."

Our forefathers established the Constitution with these issues in mind. Article 1, Section 8, Clause 17, specifically addresses this very situation that, nevertheless, exists within the State of Nevada. Because our founding fathers *knew* it has always been the practice for national governments, including the newly formed United States Federal Government, to do as they please.

History proves Cliven right. All you need to do is a simple Google search and you'll find endless abuses, including, but not limited to: entering into land trades within Nevada without State approval; to make whatever purchases of land they desire within Nevada without State approval; and to exercise unlimited authority, even policing power, without State approval, nor the approval of Congress, nor the approval of the American people.

"According to the Elko Daily Free Press," Cliven continued, "the Federal land claims increased between 1964 and 1993 with the majority increase being in Nevada, totaling 3.7 million acres of land. It was land that belonged to the people of Nevada, and **nobody in State leadership has done anything about it**. How can anyone **not** conclude that the Feds are controlling the policies of the State of Nevada?

WHO OWNS THE WEST?

Federal Land as a Percentage of Total State Land Area

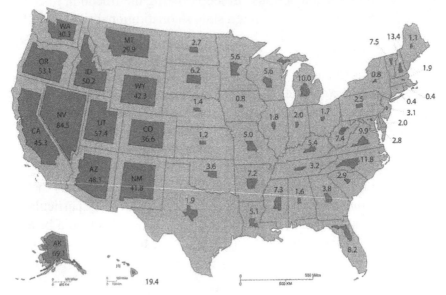

Data source: U.S. General Services Administrataion, *Federal Real Property Profile 2004,* excludes trust properties.

"These are God-given rights of the people of Nevada bein' usurped by the Feds. These rights are protected under the United States Constitution. The Supreme Court has upheld this truth and the Constitution from its very beginnings, and still does, yet the Feds continue their 'lock-up scare tactics' to deprive their own citizens of what is rightfully theirs," Cliven said with frustration.

"This is real troublin' for all Americans. If the Feds can do this in Nevada, and get away with it ... next, they'll be doing it in New York, Massachusetts, or anywhere they can," he said slowly shaking his head.

"But what about the environmental concerns, like mining, horses, water, and recreational use?" I interjected. "It needs some regulation, order, and supervision...."

"Yep," said Cliven, "but, from those locally who understand the real issues, and NOT from those idiot bureaucrats hundreds or thousands of miles away!" His steel gray eyes started to look fiery. "If you've ever driven from Las Vegas to Reno, all you'll see on that seven-hour drive through Nevada are ghost towns, junk yards, run-down building, old cars and broken-down people. The only new building you'll see out there are the BLM's. There's no more mining, no more ranchin', and no more ranchers! No more nothin'. People used to thrive in our state, but now, heck, it's sad.

"If the Feds left those new buildings, they could be used for the county, for schools, for the people who live there. Okay, this is really the concept. We talk about getting rid of BLM because of the contracts. We want to get rid of the contracts, and that's going to basically eliminate the tie between the Federal Government and the rancher. Of course, the ranchers only have certain rights on that land; but, there's many resources.

"So what my thinking is that these offices – these BLM offices and Forest Service offices – also belong to the federal government, but, what we need to do there is turn those over to county governments. Instead of making a school out of them in a general sense, let's make county resource centers out of them … and then, educate, not regulate … use those resource centers to do that.

"In other words, if you're in a timber industry, we're going to do some education there, for employment, … or research, or anything that would sustain and uphold and better use that resource.

"That's sort of my idea for it. I'm serious about that."

I sat in silence, letting it all sink in.

Cliven Bundy truly loves Nevada, its people, and its land, and yes, its history, too. He only wants what's best for them all, despite how he's portrayed by people like Senator Harry Reid, he's not out looking to gain anything for himself, unlike the Feds. He's looking out for the people of this country and for what's rightfully theirs, while trying to stop the Feds hurting, destroying, criminalizing its own citizens, and even locking them up to get their agenda accomplished. I began to see Cliven's heart, his passion, and his fire.

Again, it had been a good time of learning for me, and after a few words, I left for my bunk, as it was already lunchtime. As I sat back on my bunk, I began to think about some of the Nevada issues I'd been involved with over the years, which took me back to when the Feds would corral the wild horses and mustangs, keeping them stored in feedlots at great cost and expense to the taxpayers. Their actions have never indicated they are interested in reaching a "sustainable solution." The Feds never address the source of the problem, never properly dealing with either the increased population of the wild horses, nor with the problem that these horses' overgrazing creates for the range. It was common knowledge that the BLM would round the horses up, warehousing them in Northern Nevada, where I live.

The Feds even had these programs, like "Adopt a Wild Mustang," to lure unsuspecting, good-hearted folks into adopting one of these wild animals, either a horse or a burro, and taking them home. However, most of these nice people had no idea how to tame, train, or provide needed veterinary care for the horse in order to ride them, let alone what to feed them so they'd stay alive! Many times, these nice-but-ignorant owners of the horses would free them in order to let them 'run wild and roam the range.' But most of these horses would die, now being on unfamiliar land, or being unable to find their own herd. These new owners just didn't know that a horse from Oregon couldn't survive in Nevada – or a horse from Northern Nevada couldn't survive in Southern Nevada. As Cliven explained, his  cattle herd, once bred to adapt to his range's environment, couldn't survive somewhere else, either.

I remember discussing this wild horse problem with Christine Lund years ago, while on a flight from LA to Reno (in Northern Nevada). At the time, Christine was a Los Angeles news anchor reporting on the wild mustang round up by the BLM at the time.

She was traveling with her crew to their Northern Nevada warehousing site. She had a stereotypical urban understanding of 'the Wild Horse issue,' which completely lacked the local rancher's (like me) first-hand knowledge and perspective. So, I had the opportunity to explain to her that it wasn't about letting the 'wild horses run free.' Rather, it was about the over-grazing of the range by these horses who were multiplying far too fast, and destroying the grazing the ranchers needed for their cattle, their livelihood. She was surprised, because I'll bet she'd never met a rancher before, well, certainly not one from Northern Nevada!

It's easy to confuse the political unrest that the Feds cause by squatting on the land of others, from the real issues of farmers, ranchers, and the land usage itself. It's true that by squatting on the land, the Feds have over-reached their authority; but, when they charge money to the true landowners for the use of their own sovereign land – that's just criminal!

That's what fired Cliven up, and me, too! But, with that, I nodded off for a quick nap.

Chapter 5

– JURISDICTION –

The Federal Government Lacks Jurisdiction on State Land

Cliven Bundy, and the 18 others of The Bundy 19, sat in federal lock-up because they were accused of interfering with a federal agent, or conspiring to interfere with a federal agent. These accusations all stemmed from the April 12, 2014 BLM round-up, impound, and subsequent sell-off or killing of Cliven's cattle. The Feds also accused Cliven of refusing to pay the grazing fees that he claims are unlawful and unconstitutional. His federal indictment presupposes that the federal government owns the land and therefor can charge fees for grazing rights. On two different occasions, the Federal Court in Las Vegas, Nevada, ordered Bundy to pay the fees, or his cows would be seized and impounded.

It's important to note here that BLM agents had no authority to sell or to destroy (kill) the animals. Their only authority was to impound them. Even more noteworthy, in the author's opinion, keeping all the events that have transpired in their proper perspective, the entire issue at hand is simply about **400 cows**, or that's what the feds would have you believe.

"A large number of the trespass cattle on the federal lands are feral cattle that can pose a threat to members of the public recreating or traveling over the federal lands. The trespass cattle have also caused damage to private property, as well as to the federal lands and natural resources …" as the BLM stated in a now-closed web page on their website. This web page also stated damages and complaints including, a cow being hit by a car, an Overton Refuge employee being attacked by "one of Bundy's Bulls", and Cliven's cattle damaging gardens, property, and even a Mesquite Nevada Golf course.

400 cows?

To put a different focus on this picture, there is the nagging issue of the funding. Ah, the funding – somewhere between $560 thousand, to as much as $2 Billion – the BLM would have received. Not from the federal budget; but via various environmental groups, some of which has been delayed, because of the trespass cattle. And of course, from yet a different perspective, the biggest concern of all was the mitigation plan for solar power facilities.

> Non-Governmental Organizations have expressed concern that the regional mitigation strategy for the Dry Lake Solar Energy Zone utilizes Gold Butte as the location for offsite mitigation for impacts from solar development, and that those restoration activities are not durable with the presence of trespass cattle.[1]

This last statement became the "crack in the dam," as to why this is all happening to the Bundys; but, I will address it in a later chapter. For now, let's look at the other assertions.

The BLM even claimed that Cliven's cows used a bulldozer to make two unauthorized reservoirs. Which I am sure (I hope, anyway) was just a typo. But, the BLM also readily admits that they have no idea how many cows there are or to whom they belong. That is why they consider them feral (i.e., living 'in a wild state, especially after escape from captivity or domestication.' – Oxford Dictionary) or "trespass cattle" to use their term.

Remembering Cliven's earlier comments to me about his cattle being like "wild animals," I asked him about the population of grazing cattle in his ranch.

"There are a lot of cattle out there that are not mine, many are the progeny (of the herds of) the other ranchers that the Government ran off over the years. When they (those ranchers) left, they either couldn't find them, or just walked away in dismay after what happened to 'em."

I pressed further, "Could they be yours?"

"No, my cattle have my brand on them. It would be illegal to lay my brand on cows that don't belong to me." He paused. "Mike, I have been listening to this for years. Apparently, my cattle are to blame for every problem the BLM and Park Service has ever, or will ever, have. Sometimes those problems are miles and miles away. They (BLM)

---

1 http://www.blm.gov/nv/st/en/fo/lvfo/blm_programs/more/trespass_cattle/cattle_trespass_impacts.html is Google's cache of the page as it appeared on Apr 3, 2014 11:23:19 GMT.

are actually accusing me of letting my cows defecate and urinate in the springs me and my family developed over the years! And, my goodness, cattle get hit by cars all over the west! It's just an excuse."

The excuses added up as to why the U.S. taxpayers paid an unprecedented $200 million dollars to impound 400 cattle from Bundy's ranch and their aborted attempt to try The Bundy 19. Let us not forget these 19 lives, each with families, reputations, and careers – all destroyed so the Government could have its way with 400 head of cattle and the livelihood of The Bundy 19's families. Along with the indicted The Bundy 19, we must now include the shattered lives of the children growing up without their fathers and wives without their husbands.

Had the Federal agents and their confidential informants (CIs) been successful in trying to incite the crowd gathered for the April 12, 2014, protest to actively threaten the Federal agents with physical harm, there would have been bloodshed and a death toll added to this unnecessary and outrageously wrongful Government action against its own people.

Cliven's Heritage
It was about 9:15 PM. I couldn't sleep. I was still thinking about all the things Cliven had shared with me over the past few weeks, and I had begun to look at the bigger picture, the deeper meaning of all this, like what Cliven had said many times during the history lesson – wanting me to understand that it was a fight for more than just land, or property, or even control. This conflict, he had said, was a spiritual battle.

Cliven comes from a long Mormon heritage, handed down for generations. His ancestors followed the original Mormon missionaries to what is now Bunkerville, Nevada in 1847, still under Mexican rule. He's well aware of the plight, suffering, and prejudice his people have known, and what they've undergone to carve out their religious freedoms, particularly relocating to the Utah territory in order to practice their faith without persecution.

Actually, the present-day Bundy family is originally from Bunkerville, Nevada. Cliven Bundy's father first rented, and then bought the rights to the ranch from his family and neighbors in 1954, when Cliven was eight years old. "My dad came back to the Bunkerville area in 1940," Cliven told me one afternoon in June of 2017. "He drove his herd of cattle across the range from the Arizona Strip to our ranch."

Cliven's father, David Ammon Bundy, had relocated the family to Nevada sometime after the 1940 census. This particular branch of the Bundy family has their roots in the Arizona Strip, a stretch of rugged land in the northern part of the state that had extended west to California as the strip just south of the 1864 statehood boundary of Nevada before it was added to Nevada in 1866, as noted above.

In the late 1910s, Cliven's great-grandfather, Abraham Bundy, a *bona fide* Mormon pioneer, helped establish the Mount Trumbull community, a settlement also known as Bundyville, in a remote corner of Arizona just north of the Grand Canyon on the Shivwits Plateau. Abraham and his five sons, including Cliven's grandfather Roy, filed homestead claims there under the Stock-Raising Homestead Act (1916). Between 1925 and 1940, the family brought close to 4,000 acres into private ownership in the area and raised cattle.

But, for his ancestral rights to graze on Gold Butte rangeland, Cliven Bundy points to two of his maternal great-great-grandfathers who were among the original 1877 settlers of Bunkerville – Dudley Leavitt and Myron Abbott – who are both well-documented settlers of the Bunkerville and Mesquite, Nevada areas. Cliven's maternal great-grandfather, William Elias Abbott, grew up in Bunkerville and later became one of the founding pioneers of Mesquite. A bronze statue of Abbott erected in Mesquite says in its biographical inscription that in his youth:

He raised melons, picked cotton, cared for animals, and

made molasses. Later, he delivered mail pony express style, peddled produce to mining camps, hauled salt from St. Thomas to Silver Reef mine, and herded three thousand steer from Arizona to Utah.

Claims of ancestral rights to graze in Gold Butte could not have been documented until 1936, at least under Federal law. That is when the federal government began regulating grazing on land in Southern Nevada under the Taylor Grazing Act of 1934. Yet Cliven's maternal family had been grazing and farming the area for dozens of years, thus establishing preemptive rights.

The Bundys' move from Mount Trumbull, Arizona, to Bunkerville, Nevada, was probably predicated on family relationships. Mormon families in the area move seamlessly between St. George, Utah, the Arizona Strip, and eastern Nevada. This tri-state area is fundamentally and culturally interconnected irrespective of state or county lines.

The Cliven Bundy family purchased their 160-acre ranch in Bunkerville to make a fresh start, taking advantage of the opportunities southern Nevada offered in the 1950s. Along with the ranch, Cliven secured ground water rights through the Nevada State Engineer's Office by partnering with his now-deceased neighbor Keith Allen Nay.

Also a pioneer Mormon family, Nay's father, Allen Herbert Nay, had homesteaded 160 acres prior to grazing district organization and his grandfather, Ormus Calvin Nay, had helped settle the town of St. Thomas, which has since been submerged by / re-emerged from Lake Mead twice, as the Colorado River levels rose over it and subsided behind the Hoover Dam. Nevada water records indicate that the Nay family held the original water rights, all of which were used for stock watering purposes. The purchase of this base property along with the water rights is what allowed the BLM to permit the Bundys access to develop grazing rights on the Gold Butte Range. By Nay's death in November of 1997, he and Cliven had vested (secured in perpetuity) their water rights at a dozen springs and were permitted to water at least 100 cattle at each and up to 250 at some.

Cliven's Mormon heritage lays deep in his soul and provides the basis of his strong conviction of our Constitutional rights. Cliven had quoted Joseph Smith, the founder of the Latter-Day Saints (LDS) church, when he said that the "Constitution of the United States is a glorious standard, and is founded on the wisdom of God." And, "It is a heavenly banner." Also, he had cited LDS Doctrine A, Covenants 77-80 of the church's teaching that the United States Constitution is "divinely inspired," and that every LDS church member should "befriend it." Additionally, Cliven explained that his LDS church teaches that only under the American Constitution could the church be restored, giving credit to God for His foreordaining or predestining the putting together of the United States Constitution with the express purpose of establishing the restored church (the LDS church). Thus, Cliven felt a responsibility to see to it that those God-given, Constitutionally-protected rights that we now enjoy are perpetuated to our posterity – our children and to their children in the future.

It is these convictions that make it obvious to anyone who knows him, that Cliven would rather die than sell out his Mormon heritage and American civil rights to those who would threaten the future of America and its people, as the Feds are doing. This is what makes Cliven more than a mere patriot. It makes him a man of character and conviction. That's why he is bold in his stand that he will not be controlled by those corrupted officials who themselves will not submit to the laws of the land or to the United States Constitution; because to Cliven's thinking, it's the Feds who are the law-breakers here.

As an evangelical Christian, I relate to Cliven's deep, faith-based conviction. For my faith, too, has a long history of persecution, suffering, and martyrdom, where men and women have given their lives for their faith in Jesus. I'm honored to be a part of that heritage of the saints, as I follow Jesus.

Cliven and the courageous Bundy 19 believe God is on their side. But the Feds apparently feel that 'might makes right'; that Cliven is crazy to think he can live without bowing down to their authority. No matter how counterfeit it may be and no matter how misplaced or inappropriate their actions may be, they are still the most powerful Government in the world.

And with that thought, I heard the call for count time – and the reality of another day down in federal custody at Pahrump Detention Center sinks in.

Cliven Bundy's Argument
In essence, Cliven has five jurisdictional arguments to defend his actions:

1. The Federal Government lacks jurisdiction ...
                              ... because they NEVER owned the land.

The legislature of the State of Nevada has never consented to let the Federal Government "own" 85% of the state – *i.e.,* the public lands within the boundaries of the State of Nevada. Although the territorial legislature consented (or better, *recognized* the fact or federal ownership or its territories, as one would expect being that at the time they were a territory), the State of Nevada legislature did NOT. The fact is, only the *state* legislature has the power to make such a consent.

Recalling our review of Article 3, Section 8, item 17 of its list of 18 items:

> The Congress shall have the power to: ... (continues with a list of several powers, the next text is the seventeenth power on within its midst).
> To exercise exclusive legislation in all cases whatsoever, over such district (not exceeding ten miles square) as may, by cession of particular states, and the acceptance of Congress, become the seat of the government of the United States, and

to exercise like authority over all places purchased *by the consent of the legislature of the state* in which the same shall be, for the erection of forts, magazines, arsenals, dock-yards, and other needful buildings: ... (the list continues to its end). (Emphasis added.)

Thus, the *territorial* legislature, frankly, has no vote on this matter of federal ownership of public land according to the Constitution – only the state legislature does. In fact, the Nevada State Legislature expressly repudiated federal ownership in 1979, as more and more private citizens rejected the Federal Government's overreach of their land. The Nevada State Legislature enacted a set of statutes, declaring State ownership, control, and jurisdiction over "**all public lands**" within Nevada. Specifically, the Nevada Revised Statutes (NRS) 321.596 through 321.599. These facts preclude the claim – which Federal Agents have made – that the Nevada public lands ownership rest upon "consent."

One could even argue that although the Federal Government did declare ownership over the public lands when Nevada was a territory; but then, their title was transferred to the State of Nevada when Nevada became a state, just as a title to privately owned land would have been retained and protected under the Treaty of Guadalupe Hidalgo for a private citizen-land owner. But, the Federal Government argues ownership of Nevada lands alleging the treaty of Guadalupe Hidalgo entitles them.

The Federal Government has justified itself in its claims of ownership by pointing to the fact that the land was originally acquired from Mexico "following the Mexican-American War, and pursuant to the Treaty of Guadalupe Hidalgo, 9 Stat. 922." Mexico ceded lands, including the area comprising present-day Nevada, to the United States.

On March 2, 1861, Congress passed an ACT OF CONGRESS (1861) ORGANIZING THE TERRITORY OF NEVADA, (the Nevada Territory 'Organizing Act') That all that part of the territory of the United States, included within the following limits, (listed therein) be, and the same is hereby, erected into a temporary government by the name of the Territory of Nevada: *Provided* (several political jurisdictions agree) and *Provided, further,* That nothing in this act contained shall be construed to inhibit the Government of the United States from dividing said Territory into two or more Territories, in such manner and at such times as Congress shall deem convenient and proper, or from attaching any portion thereof to any other Territory or State.

And thusly *un*inhibited, the Government of the United States attached *to,* … and attached *to,* … and attached *to:*

>The eastern boundary of Nevada Territory had been defined as the 116th meridian; but, when gold discoveries were made to the east the Nevada territorial delegation to Congress requested the boundary moved to the 115th meridian, which Congress granted in 1862.

>The border was shifted further east, to the 114th meridian, in 1866, in part due to the discovery of more gold deposits.

These eastward shifts took land away from the then-Utah Territory.

On March 21, 1864, the Congress of the United States enacted the ACT OF CONGRESS (1864) ENABLING THE PEOPLE OF NEVADA TO FORM A CONSTITUTION AND STATE GOVERNMENT, 13 Stat. 30 (1864) – the State of Nevada 'Enabling Act,' authorizing a convention to draft a State Constitution for ratification by the residents of the Nevada Territory – in order to become a State of the Union, which they did.

… but, to round-off the State of Nevada's border story:

>The southern border of Nevada Territory – and then the State of Nevada – had been defined as the 37th parallel; but, in 1866, the State of Nevada asked Congress to move the border again, this time *south* to the Colorado River, which they did.

This last action brought the lands into the State of Nevada from the Arizona Territory – lands that would later become Clark County – which held what would become the Bundy Ranch.

Later, Cliven returned to my bunk to stress the importance of the events on this part of the timeline. He pulled up my property box and slowly lowered himself on to it.

"Ya know, Mike, I've been thinking.

"Bundy's Ranch didn't become part of the state of Nevada until 1866,"
Cliven said. "Bundy's Ranch was part of the Arizona Territory. Never
was part of Nevada Territory and so Bundy Ranch was part of Arizona
Territory and Congress, through an act in 1866, transferred, disposed
of ... let's use the proper language here ... they *disposed of* part of the
territory of Arizona and made it, attached it to the State of Nevada.
From the Territory of Arizona to the State of Nevada and that didn't
happen until 1866.

"That's a big deal. Makes me and my ranch and most of Clark County
totally different than the rest of the state. We wasn't transferred from
the State of ... We wasn't made a state ... or the Territory of Nevada.
We was made part of the State of Nevada from the Territory of
Arizona in 1866 by Congressional Act."

"I see. So why does that bring significance to your fight?" I asked.

Cliven responded, "Well, one thing it does, it takes all the Enabling
Act out of it."

"Oh, okay." I said somewhat uncertainly, not quite getting his point.

"Okay?" Cliven questioned. "That's what they've – the Federal
Government – argued all of these years – ''Cause the Enabling Act
says this and...' Well, the Enabling Act has nothing to do with Bundy's
Ranch!

"It was actually admitted from the Territory of Arizona into the State
of Nevada. Not into the Territory of Nevada; but, into the State of
Nevada. Nevada was already a state in 1864. It was already a state in
1866.

"Then there are some other things that was interesting there. That act
had some qualifications for Nevada to accept it, and actually, they
was never met until 1982. If you can believe it or not, Nevada never

actually totally admitted it – The Bundy Ranch area – into statehood until ... *19* (not **18**) *19...82!*"

"Right." I responded politely, still not grasping its significance.

"That's a pretty important part of this document, Mike; because now, we're talking about jurisdiction. We're talking about it (jurisdiction) having nothing to do with the Enabling Act. It has nothing to do with statehood. It has to do with Bundy Ranch being admitted by Congress from the Territory of Arizona into (by-then, the already *established*) *statehood*."

And right then its importance dawned on me.

I continued Cliven's thread on my own: "... of the State of Nevada – so the condition that the Territory of Nevada faced and agreed to when it became a state in 1864 (the declaim of ownership of the public lands in the Territory of Nevada to the Federal Government) simply was not raised by Congress in 1866 as a condition of attachment and thus, did not apply to this part of the Territory of Arizona as it was attached to the State of Nevada by Congress in 1866 and finalized by the vote of the citizens of Nevada in 1982, and does not apply to this part of the State of Nevada ever since it was attached."

Cliven's ever-engaging cowboy smile broadened across his face.

Even with all of these actions, however, the title of the lands of Nevada State rely 100% upon the Treaty of Guadalupe Hidalgo.[2] This treaty is easily viewed online, and only four portions deal with the land.

Its Article V basically redefines the boundary between the two nations post-war – thus ceding the territory Mexico lost in this redefinition to the United States.

Article VIII defines that the rights of individual owners of the ceded land as of the date of the Treaty shall be continuously respected into the future – whether these owners elect to remain citizens of Mexico or become citizens of the United States.

As Cliven and I reviewed my developing manuscript, he pointed out

2 https://www.archives.gov/education/lessons/guadalupe-hidalgo

here, "Interestingly, since the U.S. Constitution's Article VI makes treaties like this also the "supreme Law of the Land,' their language has considerable importance ...[3]

"... when you get to treaties, you'll find out that this Treaty took away Congress' unlimited power. Only left Congress some power. ... They didn't have no choice whether it was going to become a state or not. The Treaty said it was going to become a state and be admitted into the Union and it also said that the only paid certain. ... Took away Congress' rights to deal with freedom, property and religion. Freedom, property, and religion. Congress don't have unlimited power here. That's the point I want to bring out. It only left Congress with limited power, not _un_limited power."

More importantly, "In consideration of the extension acquired by the boundaries of the United States" (the Treaty's Article XII), the United States agreed to pay some $15 million to Mexico, making it the new steward of the public lands, and as one would expect...

> With Article V having redefined the international boundaries between the United States and the Republic of Mexico, thus making the ceded territory (which includes the now State of Nevada and other Western States), within the territorial stewardship of the United States,

> With Article VIII all the while protecting the individual landowners and the inhabitants who elect to move back to Mexico or stay and become American citizens, guaranteeing these "present owners, their heirs of these, and all Mexicans who may hereafter acquire property by contract, shall enjoy with respect to its guarantees equally ample as if the same belonged to citizens of the United States,"

> And with Article IX all the while protecting the rights of Mexican citizens who are residing on the land as the treaty is signed on February 2, 1848 "... shall be maintained and

---

3 This Constitution, and the Laws of the United States which shall be made in Pursuance thereof; and **all Treaties made, or which shall be made, under the Authority of the United States, shall be the supreme Law of the Land**; and the Judges in every State shall be bound thereby, any Thing in the Constitution or Laws of any State to the Contrary notwithstanding. U.S. Constitution, Article VI, Section 2 (Emphasis added)

protected in the free enjoyment of their liberty and property, and secured in the free exercise of their religion without; restriction."

... enfolding all of this ceded land and its inhabitants into the then (*i.e.*, 1848 – the date of the Treaty) – Utah Territory.

Considering that Cliven's ancestors followed the Mormon Missionaries in 1847 to what is now Nevada and settled the very property that Cliven's ranch now resides, all while it was still under Mexican rule – *i.e.*, neither ceded to the United States yet, nor made a U.S. Territory yet – their land ownership (and all other rights) shall certainly continue and shall certainly be respected and protected by this 1848 Treaty of Guadalupe Hidalgo – and by the Constitution of the United States of America.

Cliven likes to point out, "It is Article VI of the U.S. Constitution that allows the Federal Government to sign such a treaty."

> ... all Treaties made, **or which shall be made, under the Authority of the United States, shall be the supreme Law of the Land; and the Judges in every State shall be bound thereby, any Thing in the Constitution or Laws of any State to the Contrary notwithstanding**.
> – Article VI (Emphasis added)

"That same Article is what allows me to stay put!" Cliven states with finality. It seems clear that even the 1848 Treaty of Guadalupe Hidalgo – a solemn agreement between the United States and the Republic of Mexico – entitles the Bundy family to stay right where they are without interference and with full (State <u>and</u> Federal) protection of their land ownership and property rights.

The area that Mexico ceded to the United States in 1848 consisted of today's U.S. states of California, Nevada, Utah, most of Arizona, about half of New Mexico, about a quarter of Colorado, and a small section of Wyoming. As had the territory west of the original 13 colonies that was gained in the Revolutionary War been managed under the Northwest Ordinance of 1787, this area was duly divided (and re-divided several times) by Congress into organized incorporated territories of the United States.

As developed above, the Constitutional requirement that the legislature of the *State* of Nevada must consent to let the Federal Government 'own' public lands within its borders was not met by the State Legislature – only by the Territorial Legislature, which was desperately seeking statehood. In its findings regarding public lands ownership (NRS 321.596, par 1(a)), the 1979 Nevada State Legislature noted that statehood, itself, was held hostage to the 1864 U.S. Congress' unconstitutional insistence that the Territory of Nevada be "admitted to statehood on the condition that it forever disclaim all right and title to unappropriated public land within its boundaries." And although the territorial legislature 'consented' – with this gun to their head – we might note that, neither having yet been elected nor seated, the State of Nevada's Legislature did *NOT*.

Nor has any State of Nevada Legislature to date so consented.

In fact, following the Federal Land Policy Management Act of 1976 (FLPMA), which phased out homesteading in the United States by repealing the pre-existing Homestead Acts, recognized the value of the public lands, and declared that these lands would remain in public ownership, the Nevada State Legislature specifically and expressly repudiated federal ownership claims to public land in Nevada in 1979, as more and more private citizens rejected the Federal Government's overreach of their land claims in the state. The Nevada Legislature enacted a statute declaring *State* ownership, control, and jurisdiction over "all public lands" within Nevada (Nevada Revised Statute 321.596 - 321.599) and codified its public policy regarding return of the public lands within the borders of the state to state ownership:

> NRS 321.00051 Legislative declaration: Acquisition of lands retained by Federal Government. The Legislature hereby declares that the public policy of this State is to continue to seek the acquisition of lands retained by the Federal Government within the borders of this State.

These facts certainly disrupt the claim that Federal Agents have made that the Nevada lands ownership rest upon "consent."
One could argue that although the Federal Government declared ownership over the lands when Nevada was a territory, then

title should have been transferred to the State of Nevada when it became a state. Correspondingly, transfer of a land title would have been protected for a private citizen-land owner. But, the Federal Government now argues ownership of Nevada lands alleging the 1848 Treaty of Guadalupe Hidalgo entitles them – conveniently ignoring the Constitution, the territorial land management law in effect when Nevada was admitted to statehood, and the clear language of the 1848 Treaty of Guadalupe Hidalgo, itself!

Article IV, Section 3, of the U.S. Constitution allows the Federal Government to own or possess land as a territory, acquired by Treaty, or acquisition. The Federal Government has complete power over those lands, to make rules, regulations, and to dispose of those territories becomes a State of its own, the Federal Government is to "dispose" of the territorial land forming the state, and all titles cleared and given to the Sovereign State, who now becomes the owner of all lands not privately owned.

However, if the Federal Government was ever to become an owner or possessor of any land again after its formation as a State, then the Federal Government would need to *purchase it* from the State, with the consent of its owner, and for compliance with Article I, Section 8, the consent of the Legislature. Has anyone seen the canceled check for Nevada's public land? *<smile>*

2. The Federal Government lacks jurisdiction ...

        ... because, Constitutionally, the Federal relationship is "Stewardship Until Statehood."

Regardless of the egregious unconstitutional statehood admittance condition of the 1864 U.S. Congress and the current, erroneous claims by the Federal Government, it is clear through reviewing the historical documents referenced herein, and as written into the Constitution, that, at most, the Territory – and land that now constitutes the State of Nevada – was under Federal Government's "stewardship" control for and on behalf of the American people ... until statehood occurs. That would be the date when Nevada would become an equal sovereign state of the Union, ("equal" to all of the other states – back to the original 13 states of the union) which was October 31, 1864, proclaimed by President Abraham Lincoln. The President mentioned this concept of *'equal footing'* twice in his proclamation:

> WHEREAS the congress of the United States passed an act, which was approved on the 21st day of March last, entitled "An act to enable the people of Nevada to form a constitution and state government, and **for the admission of such state into the Union on an equal footing with the original states;"**
>
> And whereas ...
>
> Now, therefore, be it known, that I, ABRAHAM LINCOLN, President of the United States, in accordance with the duty imposed upon me by the act of congress aforesaid, do hereby declare and proclaim that the said **State of Nevada is admitted into the Union on an equal footing with the original states.**

Any other idea of Federal ownership would be disingenuous, ignoring both history and the founding principles upon which our country was formed.

3. The Federal Government lacks jurisdiction ...

... because federal ownership of state land is diametrically opposed to the Constitution and to what American freedom from government tyranny stands for.

Never mind the fact that the Federal Government is claiming ownership of 85% of Nevada's land, and whatever percentage it claims of other states, for that matter, as it becomes the *de facto* landlord of nearly an entire state, there is only one clear understanding here. That understanding is that this is completely and totally contrary to what the framers of our country envisioned when they wrote the Constitution, including those principles of property rights and ownership that were fundamental to this nation's founding.

Americans fought a war to stop this type of Government tyranny. Now it is supposed to be okay? But it's not okay, as Cliven Bundy – and the thousands of other Americans who stood by him – would argue. When we look at the historical context of property ownership, land transfer, and title, it should not, and cannot, be interpreted to produce or conclude (as the Government has erroneously asserted), such an outlandish and wildly different assertion that indeed the Federal Government owns this land, rather than the American people!

This is totally un-American by any stretch of the imagination and smacks of William, the Conqueror's feudalism – establishing a totalitarian state and occupying lands by force.

4. The Federal Government lacks jurisdiction ...
... otherwise it would make the State of Nevada, along with the other Western States, **_unequal_** to the original 13 States.

The original framers of the American Government and Constitution were diligent to make certain every state became a "sovereign" state of the Union, with "equal footing" to every other state. It was important that each group within each state had equal representation, as best as possible, and each state had equal protection under the law. If indeed the Federal Government is correct in their assertion that they do own Nevada State's public land, then Nevada would be left without representation for 85% of their state. And, if the public lands of the Nevada Territory were not transferred to the State as they were to other states, Nevada would have been admitted into the Union on an unequal footing with respect to the other states. As such, the state would be "unequal" and discriminated against with prejudice.

5. The Federal Government lacks jurisdiction ...
... otherwise, *if* the Feds are the rightful owner as they claim to be, *then* the Constitution and The People are NOT the highest law of America.

In order for the United States Government to supposedly receive title of what is now the State of Nevada, the Nation of Mexico would have had to 'own' a clear title to the land in order to transfer it through their Treaty of Guadalupe Hidalgo. Here again we must consider this as The Framer's historical perspective of feudal ownership, as was discussed earlier. The Framers of the Constitution rejected land ownership through imperial decree, as Spain asserted before their subjects rose up and established their own freedom and independence in founding the nation of Mexico. Mexico thereafter claimed its ownership over the

107

Spanish titled lands of Nevada until the United States invaded those lands, resulting in the treaty transfer and the establishment of new international boundaries.

The Federal Government's claim on Cliven Bundy's land, the impounding of his property and his cattle, and the arrest of The Bundy 19 are based on the dubious claim that the Government 'owns' the land by title originating from Spanish imperial decree. They ignore and dismiss all the people who have lived and worked on the lands in Nevada to homestead or develop their exclusive use rights. At the same time, they force upon them rents, regulations, and abuse, as a condition for the use of the land. It's clear that the Federal Government not only lacks jurisdiction on the land in question but was indeed trespassing on Cliven Bundy's property on April 12, 2014. Our Government has drifted significantly off its intended course... and the repercussions will be felt around the world, as the world has lost its greatest hope for freedom from tyranny.

Legal Precedents
Cliven makes an outstanding argument.

But, was he right?

I decided to reach out to a man who would know: Mervin Davis. Now retired, Mervin has been a constitutional lawyer for over twenty years and has been admitted to practice before the U.S. Supreme Court. I had enough money on my detainee calling card so I rang him up. This was our telephone conversation:

I asked Mervin what he thought about Cliven's situation. "Mike, I've been told all about the case, and as a constitutional lawyer, I have been following the Bundy case," Mervin said. "Can I just say that his legal grounds are not going to be the problem, as I'll share with you, because the Supreme Court precedents uphold the United States Constitution and confirm his Tenth Amendment constitutional challenge.

"However, that's not the problem with this Federal Government. Because they hate to lose, they won't play fair or according to the rules, so be prepared for a fight, especially when they know they're legally wrong and outside of their jurisdiction. They'll try to coerce Cliven to plea, scare him, threaten him; and if they can't get him to plea, they'll rig the trial, or the jury.

"So, prepare him for the fight of his life ... 'cuz the Feds do this every time, to every accused. It's the standard plea-deal justice system. Every detainee is charged as the worst criminal ever in history. Each is given the most amount of time possible, and the Feds never tell the truth. They don't have to. But he does. They'll try to play his family against him, and pit each of them against one another. That's what they do best.

"Let me share with you some legal precedents you can rely on to make the AUSA (Assistant U.S. Attorney) sh#! (well, you know) his pants. Cliven's case precedents include:

"Dave Mattis, Sheriff of Big Horn County, Wyoming, who in September 1997 forbid the Feds from entering his County, using U.S. Wyoming District Court case ruling that Wyoming is a sovereign state [as are all 50 states], and that the Sheriff is the highest law enforcement agent in the County. Dave Mattis said, 'If a sheriff doesn't want the Feds in the county, he has the Constitutional power and right to keep them out or ask them to leave ... I hope a lot more Sheriffs all over America join me in protecting their citizens.

"Two other brave Sheriffs, Richard Mack from Graham County, Arizona, and Jay Printz from Ravalli County, Montana, took on the U.S. Government in challenging the constitutionality of the Brady Bill, which mandated Sheriffs to enforce federal law. The Supreme Court of the United States held that the Sheriff did NOT have to uphold the Federal laws, and so the Sheriffs won their cases, [Case no. 95-1503 and 95-1478] on June 27, 1997, while the Government lost.

"You see, the 'lawful' Federal Government is one of limited powers, specifically delegated to it by the people through the Constitution of the United States. Where in the Constitution did the people delegate to the Feds the power to create its myriad of agencies; such as the FDA, the FCC, the EPA, the BLM, or even OSHA? And where was the power granted to the Government to regulate our vitamins, or radio airways, or the type of birds that may live on our property?

"The list of what might be considered a Federal Government usurpation of powers seems almost endless. In truth, those federal agencies are **not** Constitutionally-approved entities; but, were created to regulate the Feds' own employees, the inhabitants of D.C., and its territories, including enclaves under the U.S. Sovereignty. These are municipal corporate agencies, that have actually <u>no relationship</u> with the average private American citizen domiciled in one of the 50 states, because the Feds can **only** take criminal action against citizens of the U.S. 50 states for espionage, sabotage, destruction of the Feds' own property, interference with the U.S. mail, or fraud on the Feds, and that's it. Everything else is off limits to the Feds.

"For instance, take the FDA back in June 1994. It had spun so completely out of control that they became like a band of armed terrorist, perpetrating armed raids all over the country on alternative health care practitioners, health food stores, distributors, and nobody knew where they'd strike next. The FDA decided to make an example out of Rodger Sless, so, their agents moved in against Rodger Sless with deadly force, without determining if Mr. Sless was engaged in any criminal activity. This is a violation of his individual rights as a U.S. Citizen.

"Fortunately, the jury found in favor of Mr. Sless; otherwise, the FDA would have let loose a swarm of armed government agents to trample on people's rights in every health food store, vitamin distributor, and alternative medicine clinic in the country! That court case was decided in the U.S. District Court in Albuquerque, New Mexico, on June 6, 1994. Their reasoning was that the Constitution guaranteed the rights of its citizens to be free from the terrorism of the Feds, which had gotten out of control.

"The county commissioner of Nye County, Nevada, Dick Carver, states that the Feds do not own the land of Nevada; but rather, the land was passed on to the state of Nevada when the state was admitted into the Union. There are *no* Federal lands here; only state public lands. Mr. Carver has a significant following and support from the people to restore the State of Nevada its Sovereign rights to their rightful land. Nye County, Esmeralda County, and Lincoln County in Nevada have all adopted Carver's plan to boot the Feds out of these counties, and also have established their own public land commission to manage their own lands and get rid of the Feds' BLM. Nevada's revised statute NRS 321.5973 states, 'Subject to existing rights, all public lands in Nevada and all minerals not previously appropriated are the property of the State of Nevada and subject to its jurisdiction and control.'[4]

"Idaho and Oregon have introduced even broader laws to regain control of their lands. Colorado has enacted a bill, House Joint Resolution-941035, which declares 'Colorado's complete State Sovereignty.' Arizona, New Mexico, Mississippi, and Utah are considering similar measures.

"Wyoming's U.S. Congressman, Craig Thomas (R-WY, 1995-2007), introduced a bill to turn all the BLM land back over to the state as the proper and legally rightful owner.

"In 1992, U.S. Supreme Court Justice, Sandra Day O'Conner stated, regarding the Supreme Court's decision on New York v. United States, 'Congress exercises its confirmed powers subject to the limitations contained in the Constitution. If a state ratifies or gives consent to any authority, which is not specifically granted by the Constitution of the United States, it is null and void. State officials cannot consent to the enlargement powers of Congress beyond those enumerated in the constitution.' This means that neither the State of Nevada (or any other state) nor the people of any state have the authority to grant land jurisdiction to the Feds!

"Jurisdiction is an extremely important issue. It is by definition the authority of a court to hear and to decide an action and the authority

---

4 Author's note:

NRS 321.5973   Public lands and minerals are property of State; rights and privileges under federal laws to be preserved; administration of land to conform with treaties and compacts.

1. Subject to existing rights, all public lands in Nevada and all minerals not previously appropriated are the property of the State of Nevada and subject to its jurisdiction and control.

2. Until equivalent measures are enacted by the State of Nevada, the rights and privileges of the people of the State of Nevada under the National Forest Reserve Transfer Act (16 U.S.C. §§ 471 et seq.), the General Mining Laws (30 U.S.C. §§ 21 et seq.), the Homestead Act (43 U.S.C. §§ 161 et seq.), the Taylor Grazing Act (43 U.S.C. §§ 315 et seq.), the Desert Land Act (43 U.S.C. §§ 321 et seq.), the Carey Act (43 U.S.C. §§ 641 et seq.) and the Public Rangelands Improvement Act (43 U.S.C. §§ 1901 et seq.) and all rights-of-way and easements for public utilities must be preserved under administration by the State.

3. Public lands in Nevada which have been administered by the United States under international treaties or interstate compacts must continue to be administered by the State in conformance with those treaties or compacts.

(Added to NRS by 1979, 1365)

to prosecute. Before a court can act, it must first have jurisdiction over both the person and the subject matter. If either of these two are wanting (missing or absent), the court is without jurisdiction and the case must be dismissed."

As Mervin was giving me this incredible telephonic constitutional law lesson I recalled here Cliven's points that perhaps:

> Were the court to sever from the Nevada State Enabling Act of 1864 the condition in the Act regarding declaiming the public land ownership to the Federal Government as a condition of Statehood and declare it null and void, as the Congress' making or enforcing such a condition exceeds its power,

or −

> Were the court to agree that the public land underlying the exclusive-use rights of the Bundy Ranch did not bear any such declaiming condition when such land was attached to the State of Nevada from the Territory of Arizona in 1866 without any such condition,

... the Federal Government would not have any jurisdiction over this subject as it may relate to Cliven Bundy or the Bundy Ranch.

− or −

> Were the court to find that Cliven Bundy has not signed any contract with the BLM and is therefore not a party with the BLM in this matter involving the United States,

... the Federal Government would not have any jurisdiction over Cliven Bundy as a person.

− and −

... the court would have to dismiss the case against all of the accused, perhaps with prejudice so it could not be re-filed in any Federal Court. Mervin continued, oblivious to my mental rambling...

"No sanction can be imposed absent proof of Jurisdiction (Stanard v. Olesen, 74 S. Ct. 768).

"There are two types of jurisdiction, personal jurisdiction and subject matter jurisdiction. Personal is referring to the geographical local, while subject matter refers to the type of case in particular, because courts can only adjudicate specific types of cases and matters of law, like a traffic court cannot decide murder cases. This has broad court precedent:

> 'Once challenged, jurisdiction cannot be 'assumed,' it must be proven to exist' (Stuck v. Medical Examiners, 94 Ca2d 751 211, P2s 389.
>
> 'Jurisdiction once challenged, cannot be assumed, and must be decided' (Maine v. Thiboutot, 100 S. Ct. 2505).
>
> 'Federal Jurisdiction cannot be assumed, and must be clearly shown' (Brooks v. Yawkey, 200 F.2d 633).

"One of the main reasons citizens in all 50 states have been punished (accused and incarcerated) for laws not even applicable to them is because they did not challenge jurisdiction, and were therefore wrongly accused, and wrongfully assumed to be under the court's jurisdiction.

"Always seek to challenge the validity of the statute over the sovereign citizen, under the Constitution and law, rather than challenging the validity of the statute itself.

"The bottom line for Cliven is this – the states legally own the land within their boundaries, therefore ask yourself the question, 'Why then is the BLM telling ranchers how much they must pay for the grazing rights to their own lands? Why is OSHA in the state checking safety goggles? And for that matter, what right does the IRS have to seize property within a sovereign state?

"According to the United States Constitution, which is the highest law of the land, these Federal agencies are over-reaching their authority, which they have no right to do.

"That is the reason Sheriffs, like Lionel Koon of Madison County, Idaho, kicked the IRS out of his county, and Sheriff Dave Mattis kicked the BLM out of his county, and so on. I believe we must continue to fight legally for what is rightfully ours, or we risk losing it forever." He took a breath.

"Mervin, we're with you, remember, you're preachin' to the choir, here. But if it's so true, then why is Cliven sitting in jail?" I said, with a laugh, half chuckling and half irate.

"That's a whole other issue, Mike. It's the reason our forefathers set up the First Amendment to the Constitution; because they knew governments were hell-bent on oppression and usurping control and power where they had none. It is the nature of governments, and therefore Americans have their right to bear arms in order to ensure that no government rises up in tyranny against the citizens of the United States. So, tell Cliven to keep fighting. The people of America need him there ... and God willing, he will prevail."[5]

"Thanks, Merv," and that informative call ended with the arrival of count-time.

Due Process

I woke up late but managed to arrive just in time for a little breakfast: Oatmeal with an orange and a rock-hard cinnamon roll. I enjoyed the few things I could, while missing out on all the big stuff! That's prison life for you: a big trade-off. So, I made a coffee and headed over to see Cliven and the boys, ready to start another day.

As I walked up to Cliven's end-wall bunk, I noticed the boys weren't there.

"What's up Cliven?" I asked, while sipping on my coffee.

"Mornin', Mike – the boys are at the phones getting the latest news from home. I've already spoke with Carol this morning. I'm getting' up with the birds these days! Can't sleep much anyways with all the goin's on. Carol's doin' fine — despite all the many challenges she's takin' on fer me. She's a trooper. God's been good to me, and what about you, Mike?"

---

5 Author's note:
Congress shall make no law respecting an establishment of religion, or prohibiting the free exercise thereof; or abridging the freedom of speech, or of the press; or **the right of the people peaceably to assemble, and to petition the government for a redress of grievances.**
      – Constitution of the United States, Amendment 1 (Emphasis added.)
A well regulated Militia, being necessary to the security of a free State, the right of the people to keep and bear Arms, shall not be infringed.
      – Constitution of the United States, Amendment 2 (Emphasis added.)

"Oh, ... just got up ... and thought a lot about your issues last evening; but, to answer your question, yeah, I'm very blessed too. My Kim is such a wonderful soul mate to me all these years of my life. I'd have to agree, God's been good to me, too."

"So, what did you mean about thinkin' over my case?" Cliven said with a half-grin of curiosity.

"Oh, well, there's so much to ponder on, so many layers in your case to marvel at."

"Yep, I'm sure most Americans would never believe how the Feds trample on all our civil liberties, especially those guaranteed by our own Constitution. Like the simplest 'due process' protections that are practically, and for intents and purposes, lost to the plea-deal justice system that's replaced our rights to a speedy trial and to a jury trial by our own peers.

"Did you know the significance of a jury trial of one's own peers? Patrick Henry said 'peers are those who reside near him (the accused), his neighbors, and those well acquainted with his character and situation in life.' But this Government could select a Federal judge who might be from any of the fifty odd states, and with any background, whether familiar or adversarial, rather than from my own district who knows me, and jurors who also don't know me, and will be from at least 80 miles away and from a totally different community, life style, and culture than the community I live in.

"Mr. Wilson, an original signer of the Declaration of Independence, who later became one of the first Supreme Court Justices, was the one who stressed the importance of jurors personally knowing both the defendant and the witnesses; stating where a juror can be acquainted with the character of the parties and the witnesses; where the whole cause can be brought within their knowledge and their view; I know of no mode of investigation equal to that by trial by jury."

As Cliven finished, I couldn't help but consider a few points. It's reasonable to assume that if these key elements - intended as the safeguards and principles that we Americans have so long depended upon - were still in full effect, then Cliven Bundy and the rest of The Bundy 19 would have experienced an entirely different outcome than what they were going through, being in prison. Folks like the 19 were trapped in a legal hole being held in the Pahrump Detention Center, without due process rights. Similarly, there are thousands of American citizens in the same plight, with their families and children equally affected. Not to mention there were all those protesters who gathered from across the country, who had their rights trampled on for simply standing with Cliven and telling the Feds, "We've had enough!"

Obviously, our justice system is broken, and has been for a long time. For that we're all suffering the consequences, and reaping our worst nightmare...

... America has gone off course.

Chapter 6

– STORM CLOUDS BREW OVER GOLD BUTTE –
Fighting For a Way of Life

There is a common misconception thrown about in the media and among Bundy supporters that the standoff in April 2014 was about protecting the Bundy's land from the government stealing it. Cliven and his whole family – to a person – reject that notion. Outside of the 160 acres that his family homesteaded over a century ago is the some six hundred thousand (600,000) acres of open range known as the Gold Butte range.

The dispute lies in these 600,000 acres and Cliven's <u>property rights</u> over that land.

This is important, not because the Bundy clan has never deviated from the '15 Second Defense;' but because of what the government is trying to steal: His rights…his water <u>rights</u>, his grazing <u>rights</u>, his property <u>rights</u> in the way of range improvements and its use, and his inalienable <u>rights</u> to live the way that makes his life full and complete. These rights have been established over five generations and are his to enjoy, sell or pass down to his family in his will, they are counted in his assets, are assessed as his property, and they can – and he will be – taxed on them[1]. The easiest way to understand these rights is to look at easement rights of which most of us are familiar.

Here is a hypothetical illustration:

One land owner, Fred, has an easement for access across neighboring land owner's (Tom's) land. Without that easement, Fred would not be able to legally access his own land, in essence, making it worthless. So, an easement right is recorded to Fred to use part of Tom's land to access his (Fred's) land. It becomes Fred's *right* of access, not a permit and not a lease. Ultimately, it becomes an asset of Fred's, making his land more valuable.

Now, imagine the reaction of Fred, who holds this easement right, if Tom now wants to charge Fred rent for the use of that easement and only allow Fred to use his (Fred's) easement a couple of times a year –

---

1 http://www.landandwaterusa.com/Property-Protection/2014-Property-Protection/12-8Property-rights-on-western-ranches-amcintosh.pdf

or, better yet, Tom wants to lease to Fred the right to cross his land (a right Fred already owns with his recorded easement) … and this lease would allow Tom full access to the all of Fred's other lands and even encumbered them!

You can see that Fred would certainly resist this new proposal of Tom's - to rent or lease from Tom less access than Fred already owns and additionally, give away the access rights to this and all of Fred's other lands to Tom?

But essentially, that is just what the BLM (Tom in the scenario, above – sorry to all of my readers named 'Tom') has proposed – even *insisted* should be the new relationship between the BLM and the ranchers. The BLM is really big and blustery and believe that they can bully everyone.

In this debate, the ignorant often refer back to the Taylor Grazing Act of 1934 to repudiate this easement claim held by the ranchers. Selectively quoting from the act:

> …the creation of a grazing district or the issuance of a permit... shall, not create any right, title, interest, or estate in or to the lands.

But noticeably absent from that out-of-context, selectively-quoted provision, is the term 'easement over the federal land' which the Act *specifically* recognizes – both with grazing rights and rights of way / easement rights by stating:

> Whenever any grazing district is established pursuant to this Act, the Secretary (of the Interior) *shall grant* to owners of land adjacent to such district, upon application of any such owner, such *rights-of-way over the lands* included in such district *for stock-driving purposes* as may be necessary *for the convenient access* by any such owner *to marketing facilities* or *to lands not within such district owned by such person or upon which such person has stock-grazing rights, …"*
>
> (Emphasis added.)

Also, while the Secretary of the Interior was assigned authority to issue permits and enter cooperative agreements under Section 4, the Secretary is bound by Section 6 of the Act, which states:

Nothing herein shall restrict the acquisition, granting or use of permits or rights of way *within grazing districts under existing law; or ingress or egress over the public lands in such districts for all proper and lawful purposes.*

(Emphasis added.)

Cliven believes that these rights bring intrinsic value to his family and to his way of life as a rancher. In fact, without them, his way of life ceases. It's no wonder he is fighting so hard to maintain them. It's hard for most of us modern Americans to understand what the big deal is, because all you need to do is open a newspaper and you will find yet-another family business shuttering its doors. But farming and ranching are different. Farming and ranching are more than a good idea that has had its time in the sun and now is no longer needed.

Families like the Bundy's, have generation upon generation of family who settled this land. Every nail in every fence to every shingle of every building has a history and tells a unique story. The animals themselves have generational history and a man like Cliven can see the great, great grandsire of a cow in the very step of that mamma's baby calf.

But it is even more than all the history and connection to the land, it is a pride that says, as these farmers and ranchers would put it, "I am making a difference; I am feeding people."

After all, we all need to eat!

"Others think I'm a joke," Cliven said. "But I don't care what anyone says. This is the life I want to lead. I'm a cowboy and always will be." [2]

Without men and women like Cliven – who did not and have not given up for easier lives – the rest of us would suffer real and tangible consequences.

Cliven's story is not one of failure due to risky investments, fly-night-trends, or family in-fighting. Those are the stories that come from the business failures of "the cool kids" in our culture. Cliven's family suffered from the result of an act of theft by fraud: Someone tried to

2 https://lasvegassun.com/news/2013/sep/23/lone-rancher-prepared-fight-feds-land/

take something from the Bundy's that is not theirs to take, and making the victim think that it was theirs to take.

No wonder he is fighting mad.

The real difference between Cliven Bundy and the 50 or so neighbors put out of business by the BLM, is that Cliven knows his rights, knows the history of that land, and most importantly, is willing to fight for it. He told me once, "Mike, the State of Nevada is who should be fighting this out with the Feds, not me."

But I guess when a bully comes into your yard looking for your brother, then faces off with you because your brother is not there, you are the one who gets the scuffle.

Another misconception you'll read is that Cliven has been looking to go to war with the government all along. After all, it was he who said, "I have a gun." This statement is often *mis*-associated with "I will do whatever it takes" which he also said in a different context. Those two statements, which are often part of the media and Government narrative, are actually *dis*-associated from one another.

Yes, he has guns in his home, as most all ranchers in the west do. Firearms are part of a way of life in the rural west.

Will he "do whatever it takes"? Sure. In the same article, he goes on to say, "I'll gather my friends and kids and we'll try to stop it." And that is just what he eventually did.

But first, he tried to plead his case in federal court. It is fair to say both sides were frustrated, and the rhetoric and hyperbole surrounding the entire matter left many onlookers from around the world confused as to what actually happened.

But the Bundy family demonstrated time and time again that they wanted to see this battle end peacefully. Neither Cliven Bundy nor his family ever lifted a weapon against anyone, not in April of 2014, not before then, and not since.

Who is the trespasser here?

In an interview with Dana Loesch during her radio show April 10, 2014, Cliven said, "I believe this is a sovereign State of Nevada ... I abide by all of Nevada state laws. But I don't recognize the United States Government as even existing."

> **Dana:** "So essentially you have a deal already with Nevada and the Bureau of Land Management is essentially trying to revoke or renege that deal?"
>
> **Cliven:** "Yeah, it gets back to the ownership of this land. Who owns this land? Does the sovereign State of Nevada own this land within their borders? Or does the United States own this land with *their* borders? If United States owns this land, then I guess I'm wrong. **But what if this is a Sovereign State of Nevada and Clark County, Nevada owns this land?** The People of Clark County, Nevada owns this land." (Emphasis added.)

Cliven sincerely believes that the Federal Government has no right under the United States Constitution to dictate to the people of a sovereign state what they can and cannot do with their own property.

But the Federal U.S. District Court in Nevada has disagreed. Twice.

Cliven Bundy's family has enjoyed the right to graze their animals on the Gold Butte Range since before the founding of the BLM in 1948 and before the Taylor Grazing Act of 1934. Their grazing rights are rights, not 'leases' or the 'rental of grass' as they have so often been portrayed in the media. Why are they rights?

Two reasons:

First, they were established for the Bundy family as original settlers of the area while the land was still within the borders of Mexico, which gives the Bundy family preemptive rights under the Treaty of Guadalupe Hidalgo of 1848.

Second, under the Taylor Grazing Act of 1934, which does not encumber the land in itself as in real estate ownership or deeding the land to the Bundys would; but does give **this family** (as it would any other family or person, situated similarly to the Bundys) the *right* to graze their cattle on the open range – over **anyone else** - including the government.

Under the Taylor Grazing Act; however, the ranchers agreed to pay a small fee to the grazing board, and eventually the government, to maintain the records and adjudicate disputes. Ultimately, under the BLM, the BLM would also maintain the range improvements, as well. The Bundy's had installed over one hundred wells and hundreds of miles of pipe, corrals, and roads to maintain the ranch. In essence, the ranchers saw the fees they would pay for services that would be provided to them and that the fee was reasonable. So, it made sense. Cliven's father, his neighbors, and Cliven subscribed to this arrangement.

Over time, however, the requirement to maintain the improvements were migrated back to the ranchers – to the degree that the sadly-deflated 'service' that the BLM was to provide became "worthless," as Cliven puts it. "The only time you would see the BLM, was when they wanted to collect fees and I was more and more required to maintain the grazing improvements." From the perspective of the ranchers, it seemed that along the way from its creation in 1948 to 1993, the BLM had lost its way. In those years, the BLM became a bloated behemoth of a governmental regulatory body … and less and less a service provider.

Cliven explained it like this:

"You know, this is somethin'. Do you realize that, you know, we get into the grazin' fee thing and we'll talk 'bout how much the grazin' fee was 'n all that. Do you realize that when I had a contract, that contract was that I actually pay like 12.5% – an' I'm not sure exactly on that figure – but 12.5% of my grazin' fees would go to BLM wages and expenses. That's what that fee was about. Yeah, 12.5% of my grazin' fees was to pay for her service."

"Oh my," I responded, "and they were providing such good service."

Cliven continued, "That's what these fees are all about.

"Now, another point I want to make to you is remember the contract said that my grazin' fees would only be $1.87, I believe for AUM (AUM = "Animal Unit Month" is the fee for one cow, for a month of grazing). That was very cheap, that on private land it would at least be…" He paused to think. "10 times more."

"Okay," I said as I made notes.

"So … my grazin' fees on private property would be at least $18.70.

"Here's the point I want to make: Why is the government sellin' me grass, water, access to land, an' range improvements for only $1.87 per AUM? Well," he waited for a moment to emphasize his argument, "the point is, I'm not buyin' grass, I'm not buyin' water, I'm not buyin' access, I'm not buyin' range improvements n' maintenance. I'm not buyin' grass, and I'm not buyin' water because I own that grass, and I own that water. Them are rights that I have."

"Right! You own it – the grass and water – not the BLM," I responded, encouraging him.

"It's not theirs. If it was theirs, I would be payin' $18. But it's not theirs. All I'm paying of the $1.87 for is the management … out of that $1.87, I'm only paying her 12.5% of that, which only, what, 23 cents or something?" Cliven said.

"Right." I was beginning to understand.

"This gets back down to what is reality here. We _never_ have paid for our grass, or our water, or the land. We've only been payin' for management. The other part of the money goes for range improvements; it's supposed to come back to the land. So that makes their part in this whole thing very little, you know? It's only 12.5% of the whole business, the whole deal."

"Now Cliven, that is an excellent argument!"

"Okay, now here's another, just a statement, I'm goin' to make. The only tie I had with the Federal Government was the 12.5% of the grazin' fee that was for services.

"Okay? That contract I canceled in 1993 and, when I did that, when I canceled that contract, because I fired the BLM.

"Okay. Now, let me make one more statement here. This 12.5% of the grazing fee was paid for wages and expenses for Southern Nevada District (BLM)."

"I had no idea," I said.

"The other 87.5% was to come back for range improvements. Now when I canceled the contract, I said, 'I'm not goin' to pay.' This is what I said, 'I'm not goin' to pay for your services to manage me out of business and I will do my own range improvements.' So that's what I've done for the last 20 years.

"I quit payin' for their services, which their services was basically manage me out of business, and I have taken care of my own range improvements."

Just to clarify it in my own head I asked, "But Cliven, in the new contract they had presented to you was for grazing only for three months per year and those three months were in the summer, which anybody who knows anything about a cow/calf operation is the worst time in the year to turn your  animals out in the ... especially in southern Nevada… there is no water, no feed and 117 degrees! And they reduced your animal usage, too? Really what they presented to you was a contract that had no value, meaning even if you completely complied with the way they saw things, they still were giving you a contract that you couldn't do anything with."

I was understanding his disputes more and more.

"Yeah, it would have broke me in one year," he said. "That's why all my other neighbors all give up. They could see they couldn't live by that contract. See, it's already been through several years of just BLM harassment, and their numbers brought down, and their times – and everythin' – seasons went down and everythin'. Now they come out with this full-force and effect wordin'. They want me to sign a contract for 10 years with all the full-force and effect, or regulations in that contract.

"What I said now is, 'I'm not goin' to pay you to manage me out of business, and I'm goin' to take care of my own range improvements.' In other words, I canceled out the contract that they want me to sign."

By the time Cliven "fired them," as he put it, it was clear that the BLM was attracting other interests – with new revenue sources to fill their coffers, resourced through grants and political funding. These interests included special-interest environmental groups, especially the Center for Biological Diversity. And with this specific group's newfound political influence and a sympathetic federal administration under Clinton, came a gust of wind for their sails as the environmental special interests began to flex their 'muscle.'

Here is a relevant example:

In 1990, the desert tortoise became listed under the Endangered Species Act. By 1993, there was a massive political lobby pushing for a habitat designation and those same environmental groups began to file numerous lawsuits against the BLM and several other Department of the Interior bureaus for failing to protect the tortoise properly.

So, by 1994, nearly all of rural Clark County, Nevada, had been designated desert tortoise habitat. This designation area included the Gold Butte range where the Bundys had been grazing their cattle for years. In 1993, the BLM announced that they had new grazing restrictions (due to the pressure coming from the environmental groups). They communicated to Cliven that he would be restricted to a maximum of 150 head of cattle grazing on the ranch (down from the 1,000 head he had been successfully grazing there) and could only graze these few cattle when the grass had gone dormant (dried up). This meant that Cliven would need to remove his cattle from the range and during the peak of the grass season – just at the time when his cattle would be gaining weight and his cows would be giving birth to their baby calves – the most important time of the year in ranching! But he could return them to the range when the grass had the least nutritional value and water was scarcest. Inevitably, the under-grazed, fallow grass would become a powder keg of fuel for wildfires.

Where would he take his cattle? In reality Cliven would have only one option – the auction yard, to sell them off. Putting the cattle in a feedlot was really not an option. (Remember, this is the practice where a rancher would bring all the cattle into a small enclosure and feed them hay while waiting to use the range, allowing it to recover.) As we noted earlier, all of Cliven's cattle are bred to be on the harsh, open range in Southern Nevada. They are acclimated to that range and no other. Because they are 'range cows,' they likely won't stay in

the corrals anyway, "jumping out" as Cliven had told me, leaving their babies behind and exposed in those corrals.

Taking this plan further, if Cliven sold them and subsequently bought another herd each year, the new herds would not be accustomed to Cliven's unique range conditions and wouldn't likely survive the harshest time of the year, specifically the summer with its frequent periods of 117-degree heat.

In Cliven's eyes, this new plan was unsustainable and just another attempt to push one more rancher off the western state's lands, and in this case, the last rancher in Clark County.

The BLM offered Cliven a lease that no longer represented the traditional terms of their service-for-fees deal to which they long ago agreed. There it was in writing.

In the proposed lease, the Feds now officially claimed that they were the benevolent 'owners' of the land and Cliven's landlord. And now they would 'lord over,' a new authority they intended to take seriously. In this new document, the new claim was that the parties agree that the Federal Government had *ultimate power* over the lessee, as Cliven characterized it to me in the detention center in Pahrump. Cliven is adamant to this day about this being a pressure move benefiting the environmental groups at the cost of all ranchers. Apparently, the Center Of Biological Diversity agrees with his conclusion, stating:

> Challenging the Bureau of Land Management's grazing practices on arid public lands, we've helped protect millions of acres of fragile tortoise habitat.[3]

How do they practice this 'challenging' technique of theirs? They have a carrot-and-stick method.

Government agencies are to do what environmental lobbyists demand of them and in return for playing 'nice,' the environmental agencies will give them (in this case, the BLM) financial grants and for their (again, in this case, the BLM) support of the environmental agencies' political causes, these agencies will give them the support of their supporting politicians. If the government agency doesn't bow down, the environmental lobby sues the agency into oblivion and rallies all of their rabid supporters against that agency. You think I am exaggerating?

They even brag about their stick methods on their website:

> In 2000, we made significant gains for the desert tortoise when, as a result of our **legal efforts**, the Bureau permanently canceled all livestock grazing on 276,125 acres of the Granite Mountains Grazing Allotment. In 2002, we and our **allies won another landmark settlement** in which 1.9 million acres of the California Desert Conservation Area were protected against livestock grazing and 18,000 acres of tortoise habitat were closed to off-road vehicle access.[4] (Emphasis added.)

I wonder how many ranchers lost their livelihood, ranches, homes, maybe even families; certainly their way of life through this carrot-

3 http://www.biologicaldiversity.org/species/reptiles/desert_tortoise/index.html
4 http://www.biologicaldiversity.org/species/reptiles/desert_tortoise/index.html

and-stick method of the environmental lobby.

Under these terms, Cliven refused to sign the new lease and, in his words, he "fired the BLM." Which makes sense, since, from Cliven's long view of the services the BLM was failing to provide and that the new terms where totally unreasonable, even unconstitutional, how could he agree to them?

In our discussions of these practices, he told me: "That's how all these other ranchers have become victims to these federal agencies. Once they have you under contract, they can do whatever they want to – including put you out of business, like they did all my neighbors. But I refused to sign such a document!"

Thus, began a two-decade long battle that culminated by imprisoning (or 'detaining,' as they were only charged with crimes, not found guilty of them) 19 men without bail, each facing a lifetime of incarceration.

The most unfortunate side effect of this unprecedented power play by the government is that it goes 'misunderstood' or maybe even 'willfully ignored' by most Americans. The headline-grabbing commentaries, editorials, and articles – plus – the viral video content seem all too often void of the position that Cliven was trying to bring to our attention. It should serve as a strong case study for a 21st century review of the massive federal land grab and its asserted 'ownership' of so-called 'public lands' even as these lands are within the borders of the sovereign Western States.

With a federal budget out of control, increasing enforcement costs, and constant overreach by various federal agencies, the real story is being missed by the titillating and sensationalized media stories about 'militia' and 'armed conflicts.' If it were not for a small band of Bundy followers who have been forced into the limelight, I am afraid this story of abuse under color of asserted authority would have been lost to history.

Cliven has his day in court - *twice*
Cliven's battle, with only one side of it playing out in national and international news media, began in 1994 after Cliven refused to sign

the lease presented to him by the BLM. Eventually, Cliven's grazing rights were canceled for 'nonpayment of renewal' in 1994, according to court records.

The Feds claimed that the Bundy family continued to graze livestock on their ranch without permit and, in 1998, the BLM asked the federal court in Las Vegas for an injunction to correct the 'trespass.' The court ordered the Bundy family remove all non-permitted livestock by November 30, 1998 or face fines of $200 per head, per day. The family appealed to the 9th Circuit Court – only to be denied, the 9th dismissing his argument by the waive of the judicial hand in May of 1999.

Cliven managed all of these actions in pro per, meaning he represented himself in court. In other words, he took his constitutional argument regarding jurisdiction and property rights – on his own and argued them by himself – into Federal District Court. Along the way, a couple of family members and friends helped out. Why? Cliven told me as a matter of fact: "Because I don't have that kind of money, not like 'em reporters claim" (referring to erroneous media reports he's a multi-millionaire).

In 1998, Cliven's matters were in civil court. In the civil court, you are not given a Public Defender as you are in the criminal court. If you don't have money for a federal civil lawyer, you do have the right to represent yourself; but that is difficult at best. You need to teach yourself the law and rules of the court along the way, a Herculean task even for the highly educated, let alone for a man who "didn't much like school." He was quickly – and soundly – 'out lawyered,' with the Government winning by summary judgment, suggested to the court by the Government's highly trained and highly experienced federal attorneys who opposed him. He appealed to the 9th Circuit in San Francisco by mail and this appellate court dismissed his appeal.

"So, what did you do after you lost?" I asked.

"What could I do? I waited," he responded. "And waited…and waited."

Not until 2011 did the government make another public move.

While Cliven waited – through both the Clinton and Bush administrations – the BLM presumably performed a series of counts to determine just how many alleged "trespass cattle" were on the ranch.

According to later court records, federal agents noted increasing herd sizes on the land formerly 'allotted' to the Bundys and on tracts adjacent to it that had never been permitted to private parties. BLM investigators noted that "more than half" of the cattle did not bear any brand; but even though unbranded, were confirmed (somehow) to be the Bundys' property according to later government filings. Herd increase, of course, seems natural. Feral cattle, left unmanaged, will, in fact, reproduce and their herd will increase in size.

Federal bureaucrats claimed to take great interest in the increased grazing on a tract known as the 'New Trespass Lands,' adjacent to the old 'lease once held by Bundy' (the Feds' words).

Furthermore, Bundy brands were allegedly spotted in the neighboring Lake Mead recreational area. Of course, this is where the justification of the imaginary $1 million in grazing fees is later derived, from the combination of fines and fees for not just Cliven's cattle; but any and all feral cattle seen on the ranch. Neither any accounting of this demand nor accounting of these fees has ever been served upon Cliven or his family. This $1 million figure appears to be a number traceable back to a commentator on MSNBC, who threw the figure out once the story broke. Somehow it became the narrative - a narrative repeated over and over and over again, ultimately becoming the 'truth' presented by the government and the media for public consumption.

Finally, in June 2011 the BLM sent a cease-and-desist order with another threat to impound and seize stray cattle beginning July 2011, one month later. That November, the National Park Service (NPS) sent a separate letter regarding alleged trespass on the two new tracts, with a 45-day seize-and-impound threat.

Cliven responded with another order himself; but his was to the Clark County Sheriff demanding that he, the Sheriff, protect his property from the threatened 'illegal seizure.'

According to court records, in January 2012, the Bundy family told NPS they would work to round up stray cattle ahead of the deadline. But Cliven told me he was referring to rounding up the feral cattle, because they were becoming a nuisance and the range couldn't maintain their added presence. Logically, if he could get those

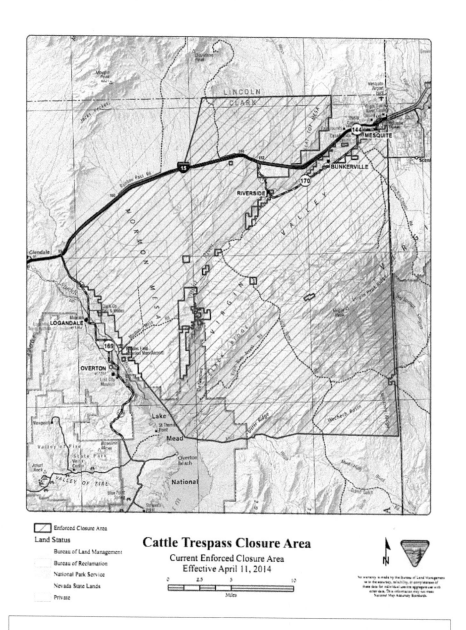

Cattle Trespass Closure Area

Current Enforced Closure Area
Effective April 11, 2014

Enforced Closure Area

Land Status

Bureau of Land Management

Bureau of Reclamation

National Park Service

Nevada State Lands

Private

0   2.5   5   10

Miles

The Bundy family can in fact claim to have enjoyed generations of grazing rights on federal land—with an arrangement originating in the 1870s. Adjacent to their personal property, the family was allowed to utilize what was known as the Bunkerville ranch.

competing cattle off the range, his cattle would be the better off.

Again, according to court records, in 2012 the BLM claimed to have surveyed 600 head of cattle on the New Trespass Lands – or *Nature Preserve* as the Government spun it – telegraphing their true intent. A month later, the figure was officially revised upward to 790, accounting for 'recently-born' calves. They also admitted they could only account for 120 head bearing Bundy's brand or 'markings.'

In April 2012, court records indicate that a final administrative effort was made on the part of the BLM to resolve (on their specious terms) the alleged trespass on the range traditionally used by the Bundy family and additional federal lands the Bundy family allegedly began using without permission on or around 2000. The offending cattle were clearly not Cliven's, but rather, the feral cattle that had been there for years and years.

"It's like all of a sudden they realized there are a bunch of cattle out there they never knew about – like it's a surprise or som'pin!" Cliven exclaimed at lunch one afternoon.

According to testimony, federal agents attempted to broker a deal involving the Clark County Sheriff that would allow cattle to be wrangled and transported to a sales market of the Bundy family's choosing and allow the family to keep all proceeds.

"But I didn't want the money for the feral cattle, they weren't mine! But if they tried to take my cows, I'd hold 'em accountable," Cliven told me. Court filings referenced Cliven Bundy's assertion that any such action to round up (his) cattle could lead to a 'range war.'

"Just not true," Cliven corrected.

Claiming to have exhausted all options, the U.S. Government filed a new civil lawsuit against the family that alleged specific trespass on the New Trespass Lands and the Lake Mead recreational area in May 2012. Court records reference Bundy's confirmation in deposition that the cattle – branded or not – were indeed his on the tracts. But Cliven denies any such claim to the unbranded cattle.

"I couldn't do anything with them if I wanted to. The Brand Inspector would never let me sell 'em."

A review of the deposition in which the government's claim that Bundy's confirmation that the cattle – branded or not – were indeed his, shows it to be dubious, at best. In the deposition, Cliven simply described how he can identify his cattle from the others. He didn't claim that they were his.[5]

Furthermore, the federal lawyers detailed the family's ranching improvements to the off-limits New Trespass Lands to include corrals, water troughs, hay and grazing supplements. Such improvements were explicitly prohibited for any party, according to their filings in court records. Cliven pointed out the silliness of this claim, noting that many of those range improvements had been there for "over 100 years, some were installed by my neighbors, some by my family (in past generations) and some by me."

The government repeatedly reminded the court that no grazing permits in the disputed area were ever offered in these areas. "It's an open range! If they didn't want my cattle to wander off to Lake Mead, it's incumbent on them to build a fence," Cliven retorted, referring to the BLM's responsibility to maintain range improvements.

When asked in deposition what reaction the Bundy family would have been, should an impoundment occur, Cliven supposedly said that he'd do whatever it takes, to include physical force (which, of course, is the Government's assumption), to stop such action. But that was not Cliven's testimony.

Referring to the removal of his cattle from his ranch, his exact testimony was the following:

> Q. Are you going to undertake any effort to physically stop that?
> A. Yes.

> Q. What efforts would that be?
> A. Whatever it takes.

5 Bundy Civil Deposition: Case 2:12-cv-00804-LDG-GWF Document 19-5 Filed 12/21/12

Q. Okay. Would that include – when you say "whatever it takes" – would that include the soliciting the assistance of neighbors, friends, family, supporters of yours to do whatever it takes in the scenario I just described?

A. Yes.[6]

It seems the government is again putting words in Cliven's mouth.

Throughout the civil litigation, Cliven Bundy defended his actions using similar defense theories from prior litigation – despite the federal court's rejection of them. He argued that the United States did not, in fact, maintain jurisdiction or ownership of the federal lands in Nevada, citing a specific Nevada law, NRS 321.596 Legislative Findings, which reads in part:

Section One:

The State of Nevada has a strong moral claim upon the public land retained by the Federal Government within Nevada's borders because:

Section Two:

(a) In the case of the State of Alabama, a renunciation of any claim to unappropriated lands similar to that contained in the ordinance adopted by the Nevada constitutional convention was held by the Supreme Court of the United States to be "void and inoperative" because it denied to Alabama "an equal footing with the original states" in Pollard v. Hagan, 44 U.S. (3 How.) 212 (1845);

(b) The State of Texas, when admitted to the Union in 1845, retained ownership of all unappropriated land within its borders, setting a further precedent which inured to the benefit of all states admitted later "on an equal footing, and

(c) The Northwest Ordinance of 1787, adopted into the Constitution of the United States by the reference of Article VI to prior engagements of the Confederation, first proclaimed the "equal footing" doctrine, and the Treaty of Guadalupe Hidalgo, by which the territory including Nevada was acquired from Mexico and which is "the supreme law of the land" by virtue of Article VI, affirms it expressly as to the new states to be organized therein.

---

6 Bundy Civil Deposition: Case 2:12-cv-00804-LDG-GWF Document 19-5 Filed 12/21/12

In July 2013, the federal court granted the Government's motion for summary judgment in favor of the BLM. The court reiterated its position that "the public lands of Nevada are the property of the United States because the United States has held title to those public lands since 1848, when Mexico ceded the land to the United States."

The Federal District Court in Nevada offered this curt summary of its ruling:

> In sum, this most recent effort to oppose the United States' legal process, Bundy has produced no valid law or specific facts raising a genuine issue of fact regarding federal ownership or management of the public lands of Nevada, or that his cattle have not trespassed on the New Trespass Lands.

In February 2014, Cliven withdrew his appeal to the 9th U.S. Circuit Court of Appeals, realizing that he could end up making a precedent – one the Government could use to "steal other ranchers' property with" if he lost. The 9th is the Appellate Court for Federal cases arising from the States of Arizona, California, Hawaii, Alaska, Washington, Oregon, Montana, Idaho, and Nevada; *i.e.* essentially, *half* of the US land mass west of the Mississippi River.

He needed the help of a real constitutional attorney, one whom he believed God would somehow provide. So, again, Cliven went about his normal daily business and waited.

This time it would only take a couple of months.

Given the fact that the cattle impound of April 2014 took 20 years, two federal lawsuits with appeals, and a number of administrative threats before actually occurring – what ended up getting the government to take action this time?

Since 2012, there was a motivating political force pushing it along.

Chapter 7

– "THEY'RE ALL A BUNCH OF DOMESTIC TERRORISTS" –

United States Senator Harry Reid

Then-Senator Harry Reid, long-time Democrat, the senior senator from Nevada, and U.S. Senate Majority Leader (now retired), came out of the shadows with vehement animosity towards the Bundys immediately following the Bundy's Protest of April 2014 (or, as the Government and media terms it, 'The Standoff').

Reid claimed the Bundy Ranch protesters were a group of "Domestic Terrorists and wannabes."[1]

Earlier he publicly threatened, "This is NOT over. We can't let people break the law and it go unpunished!" His U.S. Senate Republican counterpart from Nevada, Dean Heller, who, during their rare joint appearance on KSNV-TV, offered a more moderate approach when he said, "What Senator Reid may call domestic terrorists, I call patriots! … "We have a very different view on this."[2]

There was an even more moderate response by U.S. Senator Rand Paul (R-Kentucky), "There is a legitimate constitutional question here about whether the state should be in charge of endangered species or whether the federal government should be." Referring to Reid's remarks, Paul said, "But I don't think name-calling is going to calm this down."

Even Texas Attorney General Greg Abbott sat up and paid attention to the Protest, firing off a letter on April 22, 2014 to BLM Director Neil Kornze suggesting the agency "appears to be threatening" the private property rights of "hard-working Texans" – referring to the various, similar land grab actions by the BLM then occurring in his state. "Decisions of this magnitude must not be made inside a bureaucratic black box," wrote Abbott, who at the time was the Republican gubernatorial candidate who won his bid to become the Governor of Texas in 2015 and continues to hold that job.

So, why does Harry Reid find so much consternation in the Bundy Ranch Protest of 2014? He seemed to have taken an unreasonable,

1 MSNBC, Interview with Chris Hayes April 18, 2014
2 KSNTV, Interview April 14, 2014

even angry, stance in regard to this rural Nevadan from an area of the state where he had little rural political support and was often hated for his political policies.

Jon Ralston, respected political journalist in Las Vegas, Nevada, tweeted the following on April 6, 2016 @12:32 pm, two years later:

> Quoting Senator Reid, "I'm looking at something in Nevada, I hope the President (Obama) will start looking at it. It's called Gold Butte. It is a stunningly – not as large, and that's an understatement, as basin and Range – but stunningly unique. And the reason the President hasn't had an opportunity to look at that very closely is that is where the Bundy family raised the hell they did. Now most of them are in jail so maybe we can move forward on that."
>
> "Now that most of (the Bundys) are in jail," @SenatorReid says, "he might want another 'POTUS monument' call. Classic."

Followed two minutes later:[3]

Jon Ralston @RalstonReports · 6 Apr 2016
Reid legacy watch:
1. Bundy in jail. Check.
2. Once Bundy in jail, rub salt in by designating land near him as federal monument. Coming.
8
98
145

What does Ralston know that the rest of us have failed to see?

At the end of 2016:[4]

Jon Ralston @RalstonReports · 28 Dec 2016
I'm told POTUS will give his parting gift today to @SenatorReid: Designating Gold Butte, near the Land of Bundy, as a national monument.
7
127
349

3 Twitter.com/RalstonReports April 6, 2016
4 Twitter.com/RalstonReports December 28, 2016

Later in January 2017, Ralston writes:

> "I wondered, along with others, could Reid also coax the President to confer the same status on the Gold Butte area not far from where Cliven Bundy was protesting his right not to pay grazing fees other ranchers paid? That would be a fitting gift to Reid and a stick in the eye to Bundy and his backers ..."[5]

> "Last week, Obama said goodbye to Reid with another use of The Antiquities Act, creating another national monument out of 300,000 acres near Bundy's compound ...
> ... and the man they really should thank, besides Obama, for ensuring it finally occurred was one Cliven Bundy."

Now that seems like an odd statement. Why would Cliven Bundy, the man who does not believe that the federal government should own most of the State of Nevada, help see his ranch turned into a National Monument?

In Pahrump, I remembered when Cliven was working on helping his community in Bunkerville come up with a Land Use document regarding the National Monument Designation of Gold Butte. He was, in fact, preparing it for the pending visit and review of the new Interior Secretary Ryan Zinke. He had told me he thought it was a 'fine idea;' but not as much land as they set aside, some 300,000 acres. He went on to say, "There's some real pretty canyons back there, some petroglyphs and ancient native lands. Besides it's too harsh a country for running cattle."

However, that was May of 2017, many months after Ralston's article. Ralston's article laid out a nearly two-year timeline of trying to designate a National Monument in Gold Butte. Is that what this is all about; they just wanted Cliven and his cattle off the range so they could make it a National Monument? The timing didn't seem work.

Or did it?

---

5 https://www.ralstonreports.com/blog/how-harry-reid-brian-sandoval-determined-coalition-and-yes-cliven-bundy-helped-make-gold-butte

According to Ralston, Reid-ite Megan Jones had been in the forefront as the driving force behind the Gold Butte National Monument. She gave Ralston many details, as well as other sources.

"While Reid was always a champion of protecting Gold Butte, the Bundy standoff triggered unwavering support and he made it his mission to get it done," said one insider. "Ironically, it also put Gold Butte on the map – both nationally and locally – as a rallying cry to beat back extremism."

So, who was the 'unwavering support?'

"The strategy was simple, as Gold Butte backer Jones told me," notes Ralston:

> Through extensive research and polling, other political advocacy groups determined that amping-up hits on Bundy and tying the Bundy doctrine of land management around every elected official's neck was the only way to beat them (the Republicans) at their own game. Every move they made to hit Bundy was an attempt to ensure there was the political will for Obama and Jewell (Interior Secretary, under Obama) to do their job when the timing was right. Based on the election results in Nevada, I would say that we were successful in making sure that support for Bundy was toxic.

It was time to pay back the environmental lobby, the lobby that had so faithfully supported President Obama and Senator Reid. They used Cliven Bundy as their political whipping boy to make their case and push back the 'red tide,' referring to the recent Republican victories in the midterm elections. It even went as far as using Cliven's mug shot on election mailers to make the case that if you vote for a Republican, you're voting for an extremist.

The Democrat Party went further, tying Cliven to a cop killing in Las Vegas by a "Bundy Follower," carefully spinning the news coverage like this:

> Two months after the standoff, Jerad and Amanda Miller shot and killed two Metro police officers, Alyn Beck, 41, and Igor Soldo, 31, in east Las Vegas. The couple died in a shootout

with police. The Millers had visited the Bundy Ranch at one point to join the protesters; but, didn't fit in and left the group.

Cliven says the Millers went to the ranch, but he never met or spoke with them before they were forced to leave. Of course, this politically-motivated narrative omitted the fact that the cop-killers had only stopped by the Bundy Ranch for a short time, days after the Protest was over, and that the militia members themselves had sent them away, determining that there was something 'unhinged' about the pair. The Millers continued on to Las Vegas where they did commit the ambush of those two officers (and a civilian in the ensuing shootout) two months later. During the investigation of the shooting, Las Vegas Metro investigators found some literature and Facebook posts referring the Bundy Ranch Standoff in the killers' hotel room.

Without this last bit of information, no one could have – or would have – tied these two actually <u>disconnected</u> incidents together.

Yet clearly the details didn't matter to the Nevada Democrat party. They had funded the attack for Democrat Ruben Kihuen's candidacy for Congress against Republican incumbent, Crescent Hardy, who had surprisingly defeated incumbent Steven Horsford, a Democrat, in the previous election. And they added it to their overall "amped-up" voter campaign and continuing political messaging. Their underlying motives becoming crystal clear: to secure that land for Harry Reid's fitting gift.

Jon Ralston, in his coverage of Megan Jones' comments on the Gold Butte story, notes:

> This didn't happen in a vacuum, either. In the months before this happened, nonprofit backers of the designation repeatedly brought up Bundy as a *bete noire*. And his name also was constantly raised by Ruben Kihuen in his ultimately successful race to defeat Horsford-slayer Cresent Hardy. And when Bundy was thrown in jail, it only armed Reid with more rhetoric throughout the year.
>
> 'There was a conscious decision to separate Gold Butte advocacy groups from the efforts of those working on holding politicians accountable,' said Jones who led the coalition

efforts and advised third-party groups on strategy. 'On the coalition side, we continued to push out our business support and economic voices but also began to more forcefully highlight the injustice felt by tribal voices who hold this land sacred for ancestral reasons. We also documented extreme cases of irreparable damage to the area to call on a sense of urgency for permanent protection.'

So, according to Jones (as Ralston quoted her), this was all in an effort to hold Bundy-supporting Republicans 'accountable.' Using lies about Cliven Bundy, and falsely portraying cop killers as Bundy associates was ethically okay in their eyes as long as you appease your political supporters.

But, was this all about benevolent Harry Reid wanting to preserve the land, or is there more to that, too? If this had been all about cattle, tortoises, and environmental benevolence then why was there been such a laissez-faire attitude by the government in reclaiming the land for two decades – all of which was under Reid's watch? Cliven can't be that big of an obstacle to the all-powerful Federal Government.

Maybe the answer lies with the BLM? Their June 2016 news release assures us,

> Due to safety and security concerns, BLM employees have not conducted field work in the Gold Butte area in northeastern Clark County since early 2014. With the support of the local community, BLM officials have determined that the conditions are now right to resume work.

But, at the time of the release of this book in 2018, Cliven's cattle and the trespass feral cattle were still grazing happily, according to Cliven, but 'harassing' those darn tortoises according to the environmentalists – twenty months after the Bundy19 were arrested and 16 months after the all clear given.

And no more safety concerns.

The Tortoise two-step
U.S. Senator Reid recognized fourteen years ago that connections

between his official duties and the lobbying activities of his relatives could lead to ethical questions about his deal making. In 2003, he publicly banned relatives from lobbying him or his staff after newspaper reports showed that Nevada industries and institutions routinely turned to Reid's sons or son-in-law for representation. He knew this would lead to ethical questions. Most observers at the time thought it was a response to the public criticism.

But old habits die hard.

Reid had been one of the most prominent advocates in an effort by a Chinese energy giant, ENN Energy Group, to build a $5 billion-dollar solar farm and panel manufacturing plant in the southern Nevada desert. During a trip to China in 2011, Reid helped recruit the company, applying his political muscle on behalf of the project's coming to Nevada.

His son, a lawyer with a prominent Las Vegas firm that represents ENN, helped them locate a 9,000-acre desert site, near Laughlin, Nevada, approximately 150 miles southwest from the Bundy Ranch, and to buy that site well below its appraised value from Clark County.

The two Reids deny ever discussing the ENN project.

In an article headlined, **U.S. Senator Reid, son combine for China firm's desert plant**, Reuters reports:

> "I have never discussed the project with my father or his staff," said Rory Reid.
>
> ... *and* ...
>
> Kristen Orthman, a spokeswoman for the senator, said he had not discussed the project with his son. [6]

Well, that's embarrassing. I mean, this is a big deal by anyone's standard; $5 billion is a big deal for any state, let alone a smaller populated one like Nevada. And they both want the public to believe that they never spoke about it to one another, not even at the family barbecue? They should have, this project could have considerable

---

6 http://www.reuters.com/article/us-usa-china-reid-solar/u-s-senator-reid-son-combine-for-china-firms-desert-plant-idUSBRE87U06D20120831

meaning to the people of Nevada. We would hope that in making such a deal there would have been some significant coordination.

I guess Rory forgot that he was with his dad back in 2011 when then-Senator Reid was recruiting ENN. And Harry, I suppose, just thought that one of his entourage was a guy that looked a lot like his oldest son and just happened to have the same last name as his. So, the most powerful senator in the country recruits a Chinese firm to bring to Nevada a $5 billion project and the deal just happens to fall into the lap of a Nevada lawyer, ex-county commission chairman, with the same last name as the senator, who also looks a lot like his oldest son, who wasn't on the same recruitment trip to win over this very lucrative deal. Sure … the public buys that.

Sarcasm aside, let's take a look at the solar energy efforts here in Nevada and see how it has everything to do with Cliven Bundy.

Developing Natural Resources
Under the Obama administration, there was a clear and intentional effort to make renewable energy a priority. On the surface, it would seem that Nevada, Southern Nevada specifically, would be a natural location for such development. Nevada has large swaths of virgin land and, of course, the sun, especially in Southern Nevada's Mojave Desert. Let's not forget that the Federal government thinks that all of that land 'belongs' to them. So, it should seem easy to attract and develop solar projects to Southern Nevada.

The natural point-man in such an effort for his State would seem to be Reid, the Senate Majority Leader and the most-powerful and most-connected Senator in the Federal Government.

On a trip to China to recruit ENN (headed by Chinese energy tycoon Wang Yusuo, who made a fortune estimated by Forbes at $2.2 billion distributing natural gas in China), Wang had escorted Reid and a delegation of nine other U.S. Senators and their entourages on a tour of the company's clean energy operations in Langfang.

Reid featured Wang as a speaker at his 4th annual National Clean Energy Summit in Las Vegas in 2011.

Rory Reid (remember, he's a lawyer with a prominent Las Vegas firm that represents ENN), helped them locate a 9,000-acre desert site and a deal to buy it well below its appraised value from Clark County, where Rory Reid formerly chaired the County Commission.

Strangely, the deal spurred local controversy, and lots of it.

How far below its appraised value? Separate appraisals valued the land at $29.6 million and $38.6 million. Yet the County Commission agreed to sell it to ENN for $4.5 million. ENN also would assure the county that it had a power company willing to commit to buying energy from the solar farm.

Reid again pushed his political influence around, stating, "The project would start tomorrow if NV Energy would purchase the power... 95 percent of all of the electricity that is produced in Nevada and they should go along with this."

ENN, however, never could make a deal with NV Energy, which led to the deal's demise and the end of the Chinese firm bringing the project to Southern Nevada just months before the Bundy Ranch government round-up. Harry was left with egg on his face and Rory failed to make some nice, billable hours.

The Western Solar Energy Plan
Friday morning of March 22, 2014, and the onset of the Bundy Round-Up by the BLM, several dignitary-laden buses headed out into the remote desert. They traveled approximately 30 miles by road south of the Bundy Ranch Headquarters, but adjacent to the ranch's southernmost boundary, this time on the Moapa Band of Paiutes Reservation. Everyone was in a celebratory mood, as this hard-won project was to be built by First Solar, Inc., and it was a big one, installing large arrays of photovoltaic panels on a 2,000-acre portion of tribal land. This project was free of the pesky restrictions of selling the power to Nevadans that the Chinese had. The proposed plant had a Power Purchase Agreement with the Los Angeles Department of Water and Power (LADWP) to deliver renewable energy to Los Angeles residents for the next 25 years. The plant was anticipated to be fully operational by the end of 2015, but it only became operational

in March of 2017. It was sold 10 days after beginning operations on March 17, 2017, to Capital Dynamics, an international private asset management company.

Senator Reid joined with leaders and members of the Moapa Band of Paiutes that day, to celebrate the start of construction on a 250-megawatt solar generating power plant, the first of its kind to be built in "Indian Country."

"This is a day for celebration and for reflection," said Reid. "The celebration is evident. This is the first utility-scale project on tribal land and it will deliver much needed economic benefits to the Tribe and to Nevada."

Just eight days before this formal ground breaking for the First Solar project, the BLM announced its plan to develop much of the western states lands for solar energy in a March 14, 2014 press release:

> The BLM's current action builds on the Western Solar Energy Plan, a two-year planning effort conducted on behalf of the Secretary of the Interior and the Secretary of Energy to expand domestic energy production and spur development of solar energy on public lands in six western states. The Western Solar Energy Plan provides a blueprint for utility-scale solar energy permitting in Arizona, California, Colorado, Nevada, New Mexico and Utah by establishing Solar Energy Zones with access to existing or planned transmission, incentives for development within those Solar Energy Zones, and a process through which to consider additional Solar Energy Zones and solar projects. …
>
> The Regional **Mitigation Strategy** for the Dry Lake Solar Energy Zone is the **first** of several pilot plans to be developed by the BLM.[7] (Emphasis added.)

The Dry Lake Solar Zone (SEZ)
Just 26 miles from the Bundy Ranch headquarters and across US 95 from its southern border is the SEZ, having a total area of 15,649

7 BLM Press release: http://www.blm.gov/wo/st/en/info/newsroom/2014/March/BLM_Seeks_ Public_Interest_for_Solar_Energy_Development_in_the_Dry_Lake_Solar_Energy_Zone. html (has been moved or withdrawn at printing)

acres, potentially becoming Bundy's largest adjacent neighbor. The acreage was reduced through mitigation and the remaining developable area within the SEZ was 5,717 acres. In the most recent supplement to the plan, it was reconfigured to include only the southernmost area, northwest of I-15, in order to mitigate impacts on various resources, including impacts on desert tortoise and potential impacts on military training operations. In addition, 469 acres of floodplain and wetland non-development areas within the remaining SEZ boundaries were identified. In June 2014, the Bureau of Land Management (BLM) held a competitive leasing auction for six parcels in the Dry Lake SEZ, selecting three potential developers, according to the BLM's website.[8]

In researching all of this, it might be difficult to understand how all of the real projects and false narratives come into play with Cliven Bundy and his cattle.

As an example, it is also widely reported in the media that Reid secretly owns 80 acres adjacent to Cliven Bundy's ranch all in an effort to profit from the ultimate sale to the solar power concerns. I remember Cliven telling me that he knows that family, the "Reid family, they have owned that property for many years." In just a short research of county records, he appears to be right. If you look

at the records of transfers of the Bunkerville Trust, it appears that property has been in the Reid's family for 40 years or more. Mrs. Reid, its octogenarian owner, held the deeded property rights all those years, only recently transferring them into a Trust, managed by a Las Vegas CPA firm, a pretty common practice for aging property owners preparing for the ultimate resolution of their estate upon death. In all of the speculation and news, it becomes the narrative that Harry secretly owns that land. I asked Cliven if his neighbor Reid is related to our famous senator.

He said; "I don't know for sure, but you need to remember that the Reids are a Mormon family, who, like most Mormons, have big

8 http://blmsolar.anl.gov/sez/nv/dry-lake/

families. Just 'cuz they're named 'Reid' doesn't mean that they're closely related to Harry."

Another misreport in the media was ENN wanted Cliven's land for their project and Reid was trying to kick him off to give it to them. But, that was never truly a consideration. The proposed ENN project was better than 150 miles away from the Bundy Ranch and, unless you're a Nevadan, you might miss that small but important piece to the puzzle.

The bigger question in my mind was how they are all related – The ENN project, the Moapa Project, the potentially massive Dry Lake project, and the Gold Butte range (conveniently placed into National Monument status in the final hours of President Obama's administration by Executive Order). One thing is clear, just by looking at a map, Cliven Bundy's ranch sits in the middle of it all.

The next question is, why was one of the most powerful senators so angry, so focused on Cliven Bundy? He is just one small rancher in the middle of Clark County, who can't possibly be a real threat to the Reid's legacy…

Right?

"What is with Harry's animosity?"

Cliven Bundy seemed to understand all of it clearly. "Mike, it's all about a land swap."

"What do you mean?" I asked. "They want to trade you for another piece of land?"

"Nah, in order to make 'em Center for Biological Diversity happy, they set aside some land for the turtles, I mean tortoises," he said with a knowing grin on his face. "You see the law says, as I understand it, in order to keep the environmental lobby happy and keep from suing 'em they must set aside, fer-ever, some land for the tortoises, if they are going to take away tortoise habitat for commercial use."

"So, with all that solar development going on around you and throughout Clark County, they needed the land to set aside for protection of the tortoises?" I kept pressing.

"Yep, they got a bunch of promises they need to keep with all their lobbyists and political donors. And they have all this Government money they gotta spend on solar development in Laughlin, Dry Lake, and the Indian Reservations...

... and I am in the way."

"Do you think Harry Reid is getting rich on making all these back room deals?" I asked.

"I don't know, to say for sure. But I do know he's trying awful hard at makin' my life miserable. He seems to be real mad at me, so much so, to put me in here."

"Oh, I see. With all the deals going on, they need to set aside some land for the tortoises and to keep it for the tortoises forever in order to make the environmentalists happy and abide by the Endangered Species Act. Why don't they just make a preserve or something?" I still was not able to put all the pieces together in my head.

"They did," he stated so matter-of-factly. He was referring to the Gold Butte National Monument.

With that, he looked down, back to a note he had been writing to himself.

When you read the statements of the environmental lobby and the BLM, the word **'mitigation'** is in constant use – and a constant concern. It's a term that the general public seems to seldom use; but it's always at the forefront of the Government's policy-wonk vocabulary.

'Mitigation,' according to Miriam Webster Dictionary, means:

> *to cause to become less harsh or hostile: mollify.*

Then I remembered the BLM's hastily removed webpage that directly links Cliven's theory to the Solar Projects and environmentalist:

> Non-Governmental Organizations have expressed concern that the **regional mitigation strategy** for the Dry Lake Solar Energy Zone utilizes Gold Butte as the location for offsite

mitigation for impacts from solar development, and that those restoration activities are not durable with the presence of trespass cattle…

…The Center for Biological Diversity has demanded action to resolve trespass in designated critical desert tortoise habitat in several letters.[9] (Emphasis added.)

There it is in black and white; the environmental lobby had written a letter, threatening to sue the Department of the Interior over the Dry Lakes Energy Zone and Tortoise Habitat. They demanded that the Gold Butte area was to be an offsite 'mitigation' area. Eventually they would reduce the Dry Lakes project from over 15 thousand acres to fifty-seven hundred acres, in part; because, of those 'pesky' tortoises needed a place to roam and Cliven Bundy's ranch was just step one.

You can see it now, as pressures mounted from the solar industry, the environmental lobbyists, and with an administration that wanted to complete a legacy before handing the reins to the next President. Harry Reid was under big pressure.

The ultimate goal was to establish a monument that would settle, once and for all, the tortoise habitat, which was being endlessly encroached upon by first, the sprawling Las Vegas and then, the new solar energy projects. But, as journalist John Ralston revealed two years later, even President Obama didn't have the political stomach to force the issue in the more traditional, constitutional way for monument designation with a bill through Congress.

That being said, Harry was left to go to Plan B – and remove Cliven Bundy. He's the last rancher standing in Clark County, he hasn't paid his "grazing fees" in twenty years, and he's a small, insignificant, poor farmer who does not have any money to mount much of a fight. If they could get Bundy off his ranch quickly, then Harry could point to Cliven's 600,000 acres as designated tortoise habitat. Then, as President Obama's administration wound down, they could use the Antiquities Act to secure the monument, which designated over 900,000 acres for the tortoise and, if needed, the portion of Cliven's ranch that does not fall within the monument could be used for solar development if the opportunity presents itself.

---

9 http://archive.is/nvlzr#selection-213.0-213.313

And that is the **tortoise two-step**.

Step one: Steal that backward, ignorant farmer's property rights from him and drive him off his range.

Then,

Step two: Cash in some final favors with the President and get the monument designation for the solar projects to go forward in earnest.

It had to be done quickly; the plan couldn't wait for the more traditional approach of just placing a lien on the Bundy's for the fees allegedly owed. They needed to force a confrontation to move the timing along and get Bundy off the land. They didn't mind spending millions of taxpayer dollars to do it.

Only one problem,

    … Harry underestimated Cliven Bundy and the American people.

Chapter 8

– USEFUL IDIOTS –
'a dupe of the Government' [1]

There was a knock on the door of the Redd home, which sits on a knoll with its neighboring homes above Blanding, Utah.

As the door opened, Ted Gardiner greeted Jeanne Redd. "How you been, sweetheart?"

Ted is an antiquities dealer, specializing in native artifacts – a tall, weathered, middle-aged man; he certainly looks the part of a 'rock hound.' But, that was not his real job on this day. Instead, Ted Gardiner was a confidential informant (CI) for the federal government, the Bureau of Land Management, and the Federal Bureau of Investigation, and his handlers tasked him with infiltrating an alleged antiquities ring trafficking in rare Anasazi artifacts.

The Anasazi people had lived in the caves and mesas of the Colorado Plateau from before the time of Christ. By the end of the 1200s, though, they had disappeared, leaving behind elegant ceramic pots, effigy dolls, turkey-feather blankets, spears, and arrows. Settlers in the Blanding area discovered the Anasazi ruins in the 19th century and began collecting and selling the artifacts. By the 1950s and 1960s, 'pot hunting' was a deep tradition highly favored among Blanding's 1,800, or so, residents. In the 1970s, commercial pot hunters were digging with trenchers and backhoes looking for the artifacts - and the profits they brought.

Archaeologists and Native American leaders, however, protested the wholesale destruction of the Anasazi and other artifact sites. So, Congress made it a felony to remove ancient items worth more than $1,000 from Indian land, effectively ending the blatant commercial enterprise. However, this didn't end its tradition within the community of Blanding.

---

1 Author's Note: Concepts and wordings as used by Vladimir Lenin to refer to those whom his country had successfully manipulated the citizenry. Holder, R. W. (2008), 'useful fool,' Oxford Dictionary of Euphemisms, <u>Oxford University Press</u>, p. 394, <u>ISBN 978-0199235179</u>, useful fool – a dupe of the Communists. Lenin's phrase for the shallow thinkers in the West whom the Communists manipulated. Also, translated as 'useful idiot.'

In 1986, the government conducted a raid in Blanding that swept up two county commissioners, causing, as one would imagine, tension between the Federal Government and local officials. Even though Utah's U.S. Attorney decided not to file criminal charges, the hostility remained.

From that time forward, things remained quiet between the BLM's enforcement efforts and the locals. Sure, there was an occasional arrest of individuals, but the arrests didn't lead to felony convictions or prison time. Pot Hunting remained a community tradition that was a fun weekend hobby enjoyed by many of the local area citizens. Besides, there remained thousands upon thousands of uncollected items on the desert floor for the hobbyist to find.

Jeanne and Jim Redd were just such the hobbyist couple. Jeanne was actually the collector; Jim was the local doctor who liked to spend time with his wife, often accompanying her on her walks in the desert.

Dr. Jim Redd was a longtime, well-loved, and respected doctor in Blanding. He was the kind of community doctor who presided over your birth and remained such a constant figure in the community that you would naturally return to him for the birth of your own children. He raised a beautiful family, with wonderful grandchildren in his beloved Blanding.

In 2006, the BLM approached Ted Gardiner to become a confidential informant, and the timing was perfect … for Ted. He had just been separated from his second wife and child, unemployed, and recently released from rehab, again. He was flat broke and not sure where to turn. He had sold his family's grocery store chain and somehow piddled away all the proceeds. Eventually, he moved into a cabin in the mountains near Salt Lake City and became a hermit, burning furniture to keep warm. Desperate for money, he decided to cash in on his 'expertise.' He opened an online business, trading in Anasazi items and bought private collections. When he couldn't make ends meet, he started dumping his artifacts on eBay.

Then came the government with an offer - an amazing offer! Two agents from an FBI Art Crimes Task Force approached him with a request for information on collectors and dealers of prehistoric artifacts. Gardiner divulged information about a highly organized black market in prehistoric Southwestern artifacts. He listed off the names of well-known collectors and dealers from Phoenix to Austin to Santa Fe.

The government paid him $10,000 for his initial information.

Joe Mozingo, a reporter for the *Los Angeles Times*, uncovered this information and more. He conducted more than 200 interviews with the federal task force, defendants and their families, archaeologists, artifact collectors, appraisers, and Native American Leaders; reviewed FBI investigative files, court records, and interviews by others with Ted Gardiner and many others.

With this in hand, Mozingo documented the Redd case in detail in the September 21, 2014 issue of the *LA Times*:[2]

> Special Agent Gibson Wilson, in asking superiors in Washington for authority to put Gardiner undercover, said Gardiner "admittedly traded in the past in objects which were of 'questionable' origin and … appears to be legitimately motivated to make amends."

Wilson promised an investigation that would go after not only the excavators; but, the collectors and dealers he described as "the root cause of the problem."

Wilson brought in a BLM special agent, Dan Love, and a Utah state insurance-fraud agent, Ryan Cleverly. Neither of them had any special knowledge of Southwestern antiquities; but in Gardiner, they had a whip-smart informant with an encyclopedic grasp of the antiquities market.[3]

The agents returned with another offer for Gardiner – $7,500 a month, plus expenses, a leased Jeep Cherokee, and cash – lots of cash – to buy illegal goods. The task force was intent on going after the 'complex and well-organized criminal underground' whom they were convinced were making millions and decimating the heritage of the Native American peoples. It was a righteous cause and now they had a 'useful idiot' to make their case.

2 http://graphics.latimes.com/utah-sting/
3 *Ibid.*

Again, according to the *LA Times*:

> The task force wanted to send a message: The decades of impunity were over. Agents called the operation 'Cerberus Action' – after the three-headed dog in Greek mythology that guarded the gates to the underworld.

The Blanding husband and wife had previously experienced a run-in with the law over their hobby some ten years earlier. They had been collecting in an area that was improperly mapped as private land. While there, a local sheriff's deputy happened across them and cited Jim and charged him with misdemeanor trespassing and felony desecration of a grave, because there were human bones at the site. The local judge, who knew Jim as the local doctor who delivered his son, threw the case out. His ruling was that the law with which Dr. Redd was charged was intended to keep people from digging up graves. The law was not intended to be applied to those who collected on lands that had thousands of shells, arrowheads, and other artifacts on it - and just happened to have shards of human bones on it, too. The judge saw that Dr. Redd was being overcharged and knew that the man he had before his court was not a criminal mastermind.

The prosecutors wouldn't have their office challenged in such a clear way, so they appealed, dragging the case on for years.

The charges deeply distressed Jim. He was tormented by the thought that he could be seen as a felon. "You know, it's so bizarre. I don't even like this stuff," he told his assistant, Debbie Christiansen.

Eventually, the charges against Jim were dropped, because, according to the prosecutors, his wife "was the prime mover and the one most interested in these sorts of relics." Jeanne pleaded no contest to a misdemeanor and was sentenced to six months' probation.

The *LA Times* reported:

> The outcome infuriated archaeologists, Native American leaders, federal investigators, and rangers, who believed it sent the wrong signal to pot hunters across the region.

It was August 29, 2007, when Ted Gardiner made that first knock at the door of Jeanne Redd's home. It was a warm summer desert evening around 9 PM. Ted was wearing a buttonhole camera, secretly recording the conversation for his Government handlers. They had spoken once or twice on the phone but had never done business or met in person. The agents listened to the conversation from a truck nearby.

Ted had brought some items with him – most of which he had purchased from other collectors with the cash his Government handlers had provided him – with the intent to sell or trade them with Jeanne. The two went back and forth, discussing different items and describing where they had acquired the various pieces. The conversation is exactly as you would expect to go between two people passionate about their hobby: laughs were exchanged, wonder expressed, and admiration shared for what they both had collected. For Jeanne, it seemed innocent. Nothing dirty or criminal about it. Except, in viewing the undercover video, you just want to scream a warning to Jeanne: "Stop! You are being SET-UP! Manipulated!"

Gardiner had recorded plenty of conversation that day, none of which incriminated Jeanne. Jeanne was forthcoming about where she'd gotten her collection, some from friends, some from other collectors in the Blanding area. All artifacts were collected from 1940-1979. Much of the artifacts were collected well before Jeanne was even born. Frustrated the way the conversation went, Ted's government handlers wanted conclusive evidence of the antiquities ring they were sure existed, so they set out to catch collectors in the act of looting. In Cedar Mesa Canyon, west of Blanding, Gardiner and Special Agent Dan Love set in place motion-detecting cameras to record the looting by the "antiquities ring."

Gardiner now lured Brad Sather, an Austin, Texas collector, to the Utah desert for an undercover sting. Gardiner showed him a juniper bark ring that had been used to hold ceramic vessels vertical. It was a rare find.

"Why don't you take it?" said Gardiner. Sather refused. Then, Gardiner offered to carry the item for him back to the truck.

Sather insisted he didn't want it. They left with no evidence of wrongdoing.

Again, the *LA Times* reported on the operation:

> Agents tried again with Vern Crites, a retired businessman from Durango, Colorado. Gardiner accompanied the 73-year-old collector and a friend to dig on a mesa in Hovenweep National Monument in San Juan County, as agents hid behind rocks and bushes, having erased their tracks with leaf blowers.
>
> Crites and his friend broke ground and quickly found human bones and a skull. Crites suspected looters had hit the spot long ago, taking anything that was valuable. "We're in the right area, just 50 years too late," Crites said.
>
> They put the remains back in the hole.

Jeanne Redd never went with Gardiner on any of his outings in search of artifacts. In fact, she did not appear all that interested in what Gardiner had to offer. Not without Gardiner's persistence. Gardiner had made three attempts to buy or sell artifacts to Jeanne to no avail.

Early on she made a small trade with him; some broken pendants she traded him for a turquoise piece. This was just not the evidence Dan Love and the task force expected. Because these were trades, the Feds revalued the items to meet the criminal dollar threshold of $1,000.

Jeanne just seemed to be happy with her personal collection and the items *she* collected. As for Jim, he had no interest at all in the collection, Gardiner's visits, or the cash that could be made. In fact, Jeanne once lamented to Gardiner on tape that Jim was "not interested in this stuff."

The problem for operation Cerberus Action is that they didn't seem to be uncovering much of an organized ring trading in millions of dollars in rare antiquities. So, the task force decided to redouble their efforts on the Redds. They had priors, after all.

Confidential informant Ted Gardiner once again knocked on the door of the Redd home on March 2008. This happened just a few weeks after Jim had recently found a 'White Bird' on one of his outings with his wife. A 'White Bird' is a small, bird-shaped shell half the size of a dime located on Black Mesa in Arizona.

Jim drew attention of this item to show it to Gardiner, but he was not interested. Though it was probably 800 years old, traded between tribes from its source in the Sea of Cortez, the shell was worth only about $75 and again, wouldn't achieve the $1,000 felony threshold that he was instructed to achieve.

Four months later, in July 2008, Gardiner again showed up at the Redd's door.

"Jeanne, beware of Greeks bringing gifts," Jim joked. "Oh hi, Ted."

"Got any perishable stuff I can talk you out of?" Gardiner asked Jeanne.

At first, she declined. Then, after a bit of talking, she reconsidered. Her daughter Jamaica was planning a wedding and some extra cash would be helpful.

"If you need money for your daughter's wedding, I got cash," Gardiner said.

Jeanne had some crude sandals of braided yucca she could part with. Gardiner offered her $2,900 for four of the sandals, though all four were only valued at $400. Jeanne was hesitant to sell, but Gardiner offered $3,000 and she agreed. He pulled out his envelope of cash the government agents had given him and started counting.

The investigation of nearly two years, and numerous attempts to close down the underground antiquities ring trafficking in rare Anasazi artifacts, had come to its important conclusion.

On the morning of June 10, 2009, the task force raided twenty-six innocent Americans' homes in **full tactical military gear and weapons – swat team style** – known as 'Full Kit' in military jargon[4], to bring the alleged trafficking ring to justice. Families of retired, or near retirement, hobbyists who had enjoyed collecting rocks and artifacts they had found occupied most of these homes. The Redd's were determined to be the ringleaders in the conspiracy.

That morning, Jericca Redd, Jeanne and Jim's daughter, was making breakfast with her mother when, through the kitchen window, she witnessed military-looking personal racing up to the front of her mom's house.

"Holy cow," she said. "What is this?"

Men in full kit moved up the steps, weapons drawn.

"Federal agents!" they yelled.

She unlatched the door, and the officers pushed in.

"Where's the white bird?" one shouted.

Agents, all hand selected by Special Agent Dan Love, handcuffed Jeanne and hauled her out of the house to the front yard. Then began their interrogation about the white bird. Fifteen minutes later, armed agents – who were hiding in the juniper shrubbery along the driveway – ambushed Jim at gunpoint, who was returning from patient visits. He was yanked from his vehicle, forcibly handcuffed, ultimately isolating him in the garage.

Needless to say, the Redds had no idea what was going on.

Average, law-abiding citizens were stunned to see arrests handled this way. They were confused and disoriented by the aggressive law enforcement actions. Most people in America have been taught to believe that all law enforcement is the good guy and that military-style raids are reserved for the most hardened and dangerous criminals in our society. It's just assumed to be necessary to protect the officers

4 http://www.military.com/equipment/personal-equipment

and community in the execution of their duties.

It was natural for the Redds to think that this is all just a big mistake and cooperation would be the fastest way to bring to light the agents' error.

Jim was harshly interrogated in his garage for four hours as he cooperated. According to the family, the BLM Special Agent Dan Barnes interrogated Redd during those four hours. The agent taunted him, pointed to garden tools and asked, "Which shovel do you like to dig bodies with?"

Jim was threatened that he would lose his medical license for illegally removing an ancient artifact from the Navajo reservation.

Interestingly, it's unclear how Dr. Redd was even targeted in the raid. In reviewing the FBI investigation, FBI Agent Gibson Wilson, who launched the investigation, did not even consider Jim a target. The undercover camera footage by CI Gardiner did not capture Redd violating the law, nor did it capture the conversation about the White Bird he had found.

According to the *LA Times*:

> FBI reports on the undercover operation had not mentioned the white bird. One report written shortly after Jim Redd showed Gardiner the piece said the task force had evidence to indict 26 subjects. Jeanne Redd was among them. Jim was not.

What the government needed was a prominent figure and Doctor Jim Redd was deemed to be the one. Prosecutors, Special Agent Love, and another newly assigned FBI agent reviewed Gardiner's tapes and decided they could charge the doctor for possessing the shell. He became the prominent figure they needed to make it '**newsworthy**.'

U.S. Interior Secretary Ken Salazar, adorned in a cowboy hat, and Deputy U.S. Attorney General David Ogden flew to Salt Lake City to announce the raids, in which the Justice and Interior Departments (in a news release) called the "nation's largest investigation of archaeological and cultural artifact thefts."

Forest Kuch, executive director of Utah's Division of Indian Affairs, said that the raids broke up "a big ring that's been operating for many years."

"It also includes Dr. Redd and his wife, who were basically slapped on the wrist a couple years ago," Kuch said. "A lot of us were not happy with that case, but we think it's being redeemed now."

FBI Special Agent in Charge Timothy Fuhrman told reporters the illegal trade was a multi-million dollar industry. "They are people who know what they are doing," he said. "There's a network."

The Redds were later taken to the BLM office a half-hour north in Monticello. Humiliated, they were chained to the other defendants in the allegedly 'criminal enterprise' from Moab, Utah for a 'perp walk' in front of the media.

Jeanne was eventually charged with seven felony counts: two for selling the sandals, one for trading for the turquoise pendant and three for possessing other items that Gardiner couldn't get her to trade or sell.

Jim shared the seventh count with Jeanne for taking the white bird. But in order for Jim to be charged with a felony, the white bird would need to be valued at over $1,000. The feds simply reassessed its worth at $1,250!

The Federal Judge told them they were facing 35 years in prison.

In one afternoon, the Redd's lives were destroyed by the full weight of the Federal Government and, as it turns out, the over-zealous and power-intoxicated BLM Agent Daniel P. Love. He had a 'useful idiot' in his employment of Confidential Informant Ted Gardiner – who spent $335,685 in government-provided funds to buy 256 artifacts – some illegal and some legal. Presumably, Gardiner had collected $224,000 (plus expenses) for himself and a nice Jeep Cherokee to use. Gardiner was the only person connecting all 28 defendants; none of whom knew each other. No charges were filed against the biggest collectors.

Special Agent in Charge Dan Love, and his team of Federal Agents, searched the Redd's home for nearly 12 hours. Jericca said Love told her that 140 agents were in and out of the house. A neighbor said ***snipers*** were perched on the roof; a tactic we will see used again in 2014 at the Bundy Ranch.

They seized computers and the artifacts listed in the search warrant, all except the white bird. When they departed, it was left sitting unnoticed on the bottom shelf of Jeanne's display case.

Jim Redd was mortified by the shame and the stress of the pending trial that was in his family's future. He told his family they would "never get out of this," remembering the years of court proceedings they had faced before.

Jim went about his rounds the day after being released from the courthouse. He came home late that night and went out on the patio in the rain and began to make a series of recordings to his staff in regard to his patients' future care. His last message said, "Debbie, I am sorry that I didn't finish all my dictation on my patients." He told his five children how he admired them and loved each of them. Of course, he had a message for the love of his life, Jeanne. The last recording to his family he said, "With me gone, there will be one less charge to contend with." Later that night he went down to the pond near their house, leaving a note inside, "I am down by the South Pond. Love Jim." Jericca found him there at daybreak, knees muddied from praying all night. Though he appeared fine, she could see the deep hurt in his eyes, "I love you, Daddy," was all she could muster. He said, "I love you, too. You are a wonderful daughter and a great mother to Sebastian." He also said he'd be up to the house soon to get to work.

Later that morning Jim parked his silver Jeep Rubicon behind the pond bank where the Jeep wouldn't be seen from the house. He put a garden hose in the exhaust pipe and placed it through an open crack in the driver's-side window. Overcome by the shame that was thrust upon him by the country he loved, Jim committed suicide sometime before 1:00PM that day, just days after the BLM raided his house. His family believes Jim gave his life to protect his family.

Blanding erupted. Jim Redd's family was devastated. The townspeople of Blanding gathered at the end of the Redd's driveway, most weeping, some cursing the agents who were so power hungry to act in such an unjustified way.

More than 900 people attended Redd's funeral. The line for the viewing went out to the street and around the block.

At the church, Jay Redd, Jim and Jeanne's son, could barely get through his eulogy. "The situation that occurred, my dad, I know. I know he gave his life for his family. I know that … I love you, Dad. And I'm going to see you."

But that was not the end of the tragic outcomes from operation Cerberus Action. A week after Dr. Redd died, another defendant, Steven Shrader, 56, a salesman from Albuquerque and an artifact collector, went to a local elementary school late one night and fatally shot himself in the chest.

Shrader had simply accompanied two other collectors when they had sold a pair of sandals and a basket to Gardiner. Of course, he was charged with two felonies for being involved in the transaction.

In the wake of two deaths, the agencies involved in operation Cerberus Action would callously make an oversized medallion with the three-headed Greek dog Cerberus on it, to commemorate their operation. Special Agent Daniel P. Love would receive an accommodation for the operation and subsequently be named BLM 'Agent Of The Year,' leading to his promotion to the Head Of Law Enforcement in the BLM district that includes Utah and Nevada.

And the tragedy would continue.

The town of Blanding was angry with Ted Gardiner, Dan Love, and their Government. There was outright rage in the township when the subject of Cerberus Action would be discussed at the local coffee shop. So much so that a local ex-con with mental health problems was arrested after telling Love he would tie Gardiner to a tree and beat him with a baseball bat.

Ted Gardiner eventually went into hiding. Again, he piddled away the government's money he had received for his CI work, consequently losing his cabin to foreclosure. He started drinking again, was fired from the restaurant job he had taken after his undercover work (and money) ran out, and then hospitalized for pancreatitis brought on by the excessive alcohol. He stopped paying child support and fell behind on his rent.

Gardiner would soon have to face the people he had snared, as the first trial was approaching in March. There, in the courtroom, he would come face-to-face the people he entrapped.

The *LA Times* chronicles Ted Gardiner's days leading up to the trial:

> On Feb. 27, 2010, he called Tina Early, his racquetball buddy. "I'm done with this," he cried. "I can't take it anymore."
>
> She rushed to his house to find him holed up in his bedroom, drunk and waving a .38-caliber revolver, crying uncontrollably.
>
> "These people thought I was their friend," he yelled. "I'm such a liar. I pretended to be their friend."
>
> She tried to tell him he had done a good thing fighting the artifact trade, but he bellowed over her.
>
> "I caused two deaths," he said. "I killed two people. They thought I was their friend."
>
> She called 911. Police took him to the hospital on a psychiatric hold. Two days later, on March 1, Gardiner's roommates heard a gunshot in his room. When a patrolman arrived, Gardiner pointed the .38 at him.
>
> "You're going to have to do what you're going to do," Gardiner yelled from his bed.
>
> The officer fired. His bullet missed. Gardiner slumped out of sight. From behind the bed a single shot cracked, then silence.
>
> Gardiner was dead from a gunshot above his right ear.
>
> In his pocket was an operation Cerberus Action coin.

Government prosecutors kept up the pressure on the Redd family, now piling felony charges upon Jericca Redd. Jericca had become an extremely vocal critic of the government operation that killed her father. In searching the family computers, investigators found a picture of Jericca allegedly taking three artifacts from Hoskininni Mesa in the Navajo Nation. These additional charges would bring seven years if she was convicted and she would lose custody of her child.

That was it. The Government got what they wanted.

The attorneys for Jeanne and Jericca worked out a plea agreement with prosecutors for the two. Jericca and her mom accepted a plea agreement: Jericca would serve no prison time and keep custody of her child. Prosecutors would recommend a prison sentence of 18 months for Jeanne.

U.S. District Judge Clark Waddoups, however, gave the two of them much lighter sentences. Neither would serve prison time. Jeanne was given 36 months' probation and a $2,000 fine, Jericca was given 24-months' probation and a $300 fine.

Then, he expressed sympathy to the two defendants, saying, "I know this has been a terrible experience for all of you."

In the end, the family told me they believe Jim's death may have saved his wife and daughter from going to prison and the loss of Jericca's custody of her child. He was not willing to comply with the double-edge sword the government had put to his throat. First, if he fought the charge, the Feds would pile more and more charges on them all, with a potential of facing years and years in prison for the three. The other edge of the sword was, if he plead guilty to a crime he didn't commit, he would face losing his medical license, enduring ridicule and his good reputation would be shattered, not to mention face prison time. He refused to play their evil game. Instead he chose to protect his family and by his death hopefully to bring light the horrible treatment they'd endured and the lies the government had conjured up.

For the remaining 25 defendants, court records reveal 11 received felony and eight misdemeanor convictions; all arranged by plea-bargain. For the remaining six defendants, the charges were dismissed.

No one was sentenced to prison.

The BLM and the Department of Justice maintain that operation Cerberus Action was a praiseworthy law enforcement action, moreover, worthy of the ***millions of taxpayer dollars*** it took to close down a so-called, nefarious criminal enterprise.

The artifacts were locked up in an evidence locker at the BLM headquarters, for safekeeping.

Or so one would think.

A Foundation is Laid

The importance of operation Cerberus Action would appear to be an incident separate and unrelated to Cliven Bundy. It had, after all, taken place hundreds of miles away and years earlier. The Redds and the Bundys had never met prior to the attempted impoundment of the Bundy's cattle in April 2014 and there is no reason to think they had ever even heard of one another.

Still, there are two important and connective pieces of the Bundy puzzle to be found in the Redd's story.

Puzzle piece one is Special Agent Daniel P. Love.

Puzzle piece two is the BLM's curious and seemingly institutionalized (for Utah and Nevada, at least) appetite for inappropriate, over-the-top, enforcement actions, i.e.:

> The use of 'Full-Kit' military attack-style arrests and treatment of unarmed and apparently compliant suspects,
> The use of Confidential Informants (CI), those manipulated 'useful idiots,' used to entrap suspects (targets, as BLM would term them) where no crime would otherwise have been committed, and finally (one would hope),
> The over-enthusiastic demand for victory at any cost (to the taxpayer, of course).

It also includes the so-called 'nefarious ring' taken down ($335,685 for entrapment by the CI, alone) in Utah and the attempt to get the Bundy's cattle off of Gold Butte land in Nevada (at the cost of, perhaps, $200 million … so far).

Confidential Informants in the Federal Justice System

The average American thinks CIs (as opposed to undercover, sworn peace officers) are "sleazy stool pigeons ratting out their mob boss to save their own skin", as quoted from and portrayed on <u>The Sopranos</u> or other TV shows. CIs are neither police nor law enforcement officers. Frankly, they are usually criminals paid as contractors to entice or even participate in criminal acts – *with immunity* – for the purpose of documenting the criminal acts of others. But, in today's modern Federal Justice System, CIs are the go-to method to prove the existence of a criminal action.

In other words, if investigators and prosecutors have a target that they want to pursue, they contract with CIs to establish case facts.

The use of CIs has a long history according to The Attorney General's Guidelines Regarding the Use of Confidential Informants:

> Since the inception of the FBI in 1908, informants have played major roles in the investigation and prosecution of a wide variety of federal crimes. The FBI's Top Echelon Criminal Informant Program was established in 1961 when FBI Director J. Edgar Hoover instructed all Special Agents in Charge (SACs) to "develop particularly qualified, live sources within the upper echelon of the organized hoodlum element who will be capable of furnishing the quality information" needed to attack organized crime. In 1978, the FBI replaced that program with the Criminal Informant Program. Its mission is to develop a cadre of informants who can assist the FBI's investigation of federal crimes and criminal enterprises. Informants have become integral to the success of many FBI investigations of organized crime, public corruption, the drug trade, counterterrorism, and other initiatives.

Directors of the FBI frequently make reference to the value of informants while acknowledging that they present difficult challenges. In a June 1978 article, Director William Webster stated:

> Not many people know very much about informants: and to

many people, it's a queasy area. People are not comfortable with informants. There is a tradition against snitching in this country.

However, the informant is THE – with a capital "T," capital "H," and capital "E" – THE most effective tool in law enforcement today - state, local, or federal. We must accept that and deal with it.

But today, the paid confidential informant is used in virtually every federal case. Not only against the "hoodlum element," as J. Edgar Hoover envisioned; but also, against average American citizens as clearly documented in the operation Cerberus Action.

The problem with this is, that once investigators determine there *may* be a crime, they target a high-profile 'suspect' and hire a CI to *make the crime happen – and document it as it unfolds*. And, if the CIs don't make it happen to the extent they hoped for, their job is to gather enough information so the investigators can file some type of charge to justify all the expense and effort expended in the investigation. Then, the Government hyper-exaggerates the importance of the investigation in the sensation-hungry media with press releases and press conferences pumped-up to make the case that they – the investigative body and the prosecutors – have somehow made the American people safe again – from a threat we didn't even know existed (but, was supposedly worth all of that taxpayer money spent in the pursuit of its case) regardless of whether there ever was any threat to begin with.

Clearly, this is neither how we picture federal law enforcement would operate, nor what is described in developing "a cadre of informants who can assist the FBI's investigation of federal crimes and criminal enterprises" (the FBI's Guidelines description). It may be more accurately described as an effort to 'develop a cadre of informants who can *develop crime where its suspicion arises, for the sole intent of getting a conviction'* for … something … ok, *for anything!*

In operation Cerberus Action, even a layman can see that never, not once, did it ever enter into the minds of the BLM or FBI investigators that these collectors, the 'targets' as they are commonly called, where not an evil criminal organization existing for the sole purpose of raping our heritage for the ethereal 'millions of dollars' they certainly must be making. These investigators and prosecutors seem to be blinded to the possibility that those they focus upon are just average people, making a living in genuine and honest ways, while enjoying a hobby, a hobby that might be technically illegal.

They also seem to have lost the very fact that they decided to pay stacks of money to a desperate and clearly broken human being (Gardiner) to *instigate* the crimes and make the weakest of connections between all of the defendants to create the case of an "illegal trade (that) was a multi-million dollar industry." Never mind the obvious difficulty of Gardiner having a clear conflict of interest in keeping the operation going as long as possible – to make as much as much money as possible – with the pressure to produce results any way possible *whether they were actually there or not* – in order to make Government handlers happy.

Now, here's the tie between the Redds' story and the Bundys' story.

At the time of the writing of this book, three trials have been concluded in the Cliven Bundy, *et al.* v. United States of America criminal case:

> One trial in Oregon and two trials in Las Vegas, held in the Nevada Federal Courts.

The budget for the Bundy-related cases is estimated to be over $200 million dollars. In those totals are: Investigative costs, evidence discovery, private investigators, court fees, incarceration costs, attorney fees, expenses – and (you guessed it) payments to confidential informants.

It is unclear how many CIs were involved in the Bundy case. The defense team has estimated somewhere around 15. There is no definitive answer. That's because the prosecutors refuse to release this information in order to keep their CIs, well, confidential. Their stated reason is for the CIs' safety, because these CIs might be used in other investigations and their value would evaporate were their status publicly divulged.

But the fact is: a productive CI's job can become a long-term – *and lucrative* – gig.

With some careful study of the open trial transcripts one can begin to
see some names in common among the witness lists and attendees of:

> The protest at the Malheur Refuge in Oregon (a protest
> and subsequent trial, in which two of Cliven's sons
> were exonerated in 2016) and
> The protest at the Bunkerville overpass in April 2014
> and after.

Of those 15 potential CIs, 12 of them were carrying weapons, mostly
'long guns' (the term the BLM uses for a rifle of any type).

Ironically, the prosecution's own court records demonstrate that
there were approximately 18-20 guns held by those in the Protest in
Bunkerville – among the estimated 240 protesters. That would mean
the majority of those possessing weapons were CIs, the rest of those
armed (6-8 protesters) were presumably locked up in Pahrump. This
leaves a majority of The Bundy 19 (11-13 men) who ***didn't have a
firearm with them*** at all – including Cliven.

Embarrassingly, it turns out that one of those defendants happens to be
a CI – a fact that was not disclosed to the defense team before any trial.
And surprisingly, this status was revealed by the CI's own lawyer in
the open courtroom!

Who slipped up? Was this *failure to disclose* a prosecution slip up – or
a tactic to emplace a spy in the midst of the defendants? Was the CI's
lawyer's revelation a slip-up – or was it a ploy to get the prosecution
off the procedural disclosure-failure hook?

Imagine how betrayed you would feel if, in the trial of your life, you
find out that the man you had been preparing with and reviewing
discovery with *for months*, the man sitting next to you at the defense
table in the very trial – was actually a confidential informant for the
Federal Government. And the only way you find this out is because
his attorney happens to reveal it in open court! Had he been leaking
your legal defense plans and strategies to the prosecutors and you
only find this out in the midst of your trial? For the defendant, and for

the public as well, this glaring failure of the discovery process – so casually revealed – gives you little confidence of the fairness of the justice system.

More importantly, there were identified CIs that first appeared in Bunkerville, and then later in Oregon, but now have simply faded away (but, not without having inflicted their damage). In Oregon it is clear the CIs were the ones who brought the large masses of ammunition to the protests, the very action that the prosecutors used to charge the defendants. As was demonstrated in court; however, the preparation for armed defense of the refuge in Oregon was actually a 'target practice to blow off a little steam,' orchestrated by a CI to gather video evidence – under instruction of his Government handler to do so. Federal prosecutors later characterized the events at the refuge as "defense drills" against other nearby federal agents. Fortunately, the Feds' ruse was seen for what it was by all three juries so far and consequently, resulted in acquittals of nearly all the charges.

We may never know for sure the actions that all of the paid Confidential Informants played in the Bunkerville Protest, but if there use remains true to the practice of investigative technique of Special Agent Dan Love, this technique was questionable at best. Never forget, as with Ted Gardiner, it takes a toll on the soul of the people who willfully practice such deceit against those who once put their trust in them. It allows me an understanding of the mistrust the Bundys had for me when we first met.

Handler of the 'Idiots'
The BLM and other Federal agencies have long been under the scrutiny of the public for their expressed need for their own law enforcement agencies. After all, in the rural west where the BLM primarily operates, the county sheriffs could provide what little enforcement that may be required. But, under the Obama administration, there was a concerted effort to amass additional law enforcement and prosecutors in every agency of the Federal Government and put them into local communities. [5]

After service with the Air Marshals, where he received much of

5 https://cops.usdoj.gov/pdf/taskforce/taskforce_finalreport.pdf

his terrorism training, Special Agent in Charge Daniel P. Love was transferred to the BLM. As mentioned, Love had a meteoric rise in the ranks of the BLM for his aggressiveness and attention-getting operations. But, as the supervisory agent of Utah and Nevada, he also came to raise the ire of the local sheriffs, representatives, and citizens. One sheriff in Garfield County Utah actually arrested a BLM agent in Dan Love's charge:

> Sheriff James "Danny" Perkins says, "Wasn't me that pulled the trigger on that deal. Do I think he needed to come to jail? I do, the guy's a fruitcake." The BLM agent was allegedly illegally issuing citations to campers. [6]

It's up to Sheriff Perkins and half a dozen deputies to patrol Garfield County, a county about the size of Connecticut. "The country's big and it's vast," Perkins said. "I mean it's like this for miles and miles and miles." Federal land makes up 94 percent of this county, so you'd think that Perkins would welcome the help of federal authorities.

Think again.

He, like Cliven Bundy, doesn't think the government has a constitutional right to own large swaths of land. In his eyes, the government agencies have overreached their authority. And he isn't the only sheriff who thinks this.

There are dozens of sheriffs in Utah and Nevada who are of the same position. They call themselves Constitutional Sheriffs. They're not organized, but they share the same problems that come with coexisting with a federal government that is always pushing at the locals whom they represent.

This overreach is the impetus behind former U.S. Congressman Jason Chaffetz's (R-Utah) proposed bill to get rid of BLM and Forest Service law enforcement all together on federal land. Then-Utah's Representative Mike Noel, (R-Kanab), proposed State legislation to rein-in the feds and require the BLM to defer more to local law enforcement.

---

6 http://www.npr.org/2016/05/31/480100279/utah-sheriff-threatens-to-arrest-rangers-if-they-try-to-close-public-lands

"I don't believe they have the right to be out there except as a proprietary officer for protecting their own resources, Noel told the Salt Lake Tribune. "I definitely don't believe they have the right to arrest you or me for traffic citations or violations on county roads."

In 2010, sheriffs from around the west gathered in Las Vegas, Nevada, to discuss the ongoing problems with the overreach they experienced.

The Denver Post reported on some of the sheriffs' comments:

> Elkhart County, Ind., Sheriff Brad Rogers told of chasing federal regulators out of his county after they repeatedly did inspections at an Amish dairy farm that was selling raw milk. He threatened to arrest the regulators if they tried to come back.
>
> Sheriff Tony DeMeo of Nye County, Nev., recounted how he had to threaten to bring out his SWAT team to go up against a federal government SWAT team when federal agents were seizing cattle from a local rancher.
>
> Sheriff Dave Mattis of Big Horn County, Wyo., told the conference about the edict he has issued in his county. Federal agents are forbidden to enter his territory without his approval.
>
> El Paso County Commissioner Peggy Littleton, who attended with El Paso County Sheriff Terry Maketa, gave a presentation that took another tack. She told how her county recently passed a resolution to nullify the National Defense Authorization Act. She urged other counties to do the same.[7]

Clearly, it is these acts of overreach – that set the precedents regarding federal government power to arrest and detain citizens without filing charges or seeking convictions – that garners most of the attention associated with the Constitutional Sheriffs group. But, these are our sheriffs' concerns, too – not just Cliven Bundy's. And at the center of much of the unease was Special Agent Dan Love, responsible for the BLM's Federal Law Enforcement of Utah and Nevada, a man who has proven he has a big ego and access to the use of military-like force to back it up.

7 http://www.denverpost.com/2012/02/11/emerging-movement-encourages-sherif-fs-to-act-as-shield-against-federal-tyranny/

Before I tell you about his central role in the Bundy's case, let me leap ahead to what appears to be the end of the Dan Love saga.

After a decade of overreach as the supervisory agent in charge of BLM's Law Enforcement in Utah and Nevada, those who had been victims of his ego saw Love served his 'just desserts.'

On February 14, 2017, U.S. Congressman Jason Chaffetz (R-Utah), wrote a letter to Ms. Mary Kendall, Director of the Office of the Inspector General (OIG) of the Department of the Interior.[8] In the letter, Congressman Chaffetz, the well-respected Chairman of The Committee on Oversight and Government Reform, *publicly calls out* an investigation of Daniel Paul Love that the OIG's office had initiated on Love over two years earlier.

Just two weeks before his letter, the OIG's office had released its findings in a severely redacted report, which resulted in keeping Agent Love out of the limelight.

Chaffetz would have none of that. In his letter to Ms. Kendall, he called out Love by name and listed his alleged offenses:

> By first accusing Director Neil Kornze (the former Director of the BLM, appointed by President Obama under the nomination of U.S. Senator Harry Reid (D-Nevada) – having been Senator Reid's Chief of Staff from which he was ushered in to his new position just weeks before the attempted impoundment of Cliven Bundy's cattle) of tipping off Agent Love of the pending request the by Congress for the records the day before, the very day the records were purged, Love is then accused of:
>
>> Intentionally withholding documents for a Congressional Committee,
>>
>> Instructing subordinates to destroy documents and "scrub emails," and
>>
>> "Coaching witnesses" in his (Love's) own investigation during which Love allegedly gave subordinates "talking points and rationalizations" to give the OIG investigators after the investigation had begun.

---

8 https://oversight.house.gov/wp-content/uploads/2017/02/2017-02-14-JEC-Farenthold-to-Kendall-DOI-OIG-Dan-Love-Investigation.pdf

Chaffetz ends his letter instructing the OIG's office to investigate...

> As a federal law enforcement officer, Love's actions have the potential to not only taint your investigation, but to seriously undermine the trust in BLM's law enforcement office and thwart congressional oversight of the Bureau. As such, I request that you investigate the specific allegations raised in your interviews of destruction of federal records, witness tampering, and obstruction of a congressional investigation.

The initial investigation into Love's alleged misbehavior began in 2015. Investigators found the supervisory agent broke federal ethics rules when he bought three tickets and special passes to Burning Man in 2015 after it was sold out. Burning Man is a huge counter-culture festival in the desert of Northern Nevada that costs $390 per person and many other access fees. The average person pays well over $500 just to attend. Love was in charge of BLM Law Enforcement at the event. On Jan. 10, 2014, Love participated in the initial negotiations of the 2015 event. During a BLM meeting with top Burning Man officials at the festival's San Francisco headquarters he wore mirrored sunglasses and a Glock pistol on his hip, according to multiple sources.

"Talk about a passive, peace-loving place," said Mike Ford, a former BLM official who was at the meeting and was consulting for Burning Man organizers at the time. "That heavy, macho, armed attitude, that doesn't serve the agency well."

A year later, a *Reno Gazette-Journal* investigation revealed BLM – Love in particular – had demanded the festival provide enhanced accommodations for agency officials, including flush toilets and access to Choco Tacos, M&Ms, licorice, and Chobani Greek yogurt, in exchange for receiving a permit to operate.

Love paid with his own money; yet he also brought along his girlfriend, allowing her to stay in BLM housing, which he had made sure was very comfortable, and toured her and other friends around the event in government vehicles. When gently questioned about it by other BLM employees at the event they were commanded by Love to forget what they saw.

The investigators also found evidence Love had manipulated the hiring process of a friend in order for him to obtain a job with the BLM.

This letter from Chaffetz was a strident call for the OIG's Deputy Director to deepen the investigation into Daniel Love. The OIG Investigators went to work.

Additional investigation reports that in spring 2016, Love told an employee to take seized stones, known as Moqui marbles, out of an evidence room so he could give them to a contractor who had done work on the facility in Salt Lake City. Moqui stones are unique geological formations of iron oxide that form in sedimentary rock. They were stored in dozens of 5-gallon buckets, and Love told an employee to get him four of the best rocks for gifts. The agency had thousands of Moqui stones seized as evidence during an investigation into whether they had been collected illegally from a national park, having an estimated their retail value of up to $520,000.

The employee told investigators he had a 'bad feeling' about taking the stones from the evidence room; but he followed instructions because Love was a law enforcement officer and "scary" at that.

Several other employees also had the stones, and one told investigators that Love was "giving them out like candy." They were later returned.

During the investigations, Love refused to turn over his government-issued laptops, saying they'd been lost – something he previously told colleagues that he planned to do if he ever got in trouble. He declined to be interviewed by investigators.

These actions, of course, lead to the obvious question: Was this evidence that was seized from the Redds?

June of 2017, the *Free Range Report* filed a Freedom From Information Act, inquiring as to the evidence in the alleged theft of Love's being that of the Redds: [9]

---

9 http://freerangereport.com/index.php/2017/06/28/probe-into-dan-loves-criminal-conduct-by-oig-bolstered-by-additional-evidence/

Free Range Report (FRR) issued a Freedom of Information
Act (FOIA) request to the OIG earlier this month, however,
because the investigation is active, we are unable to obtain
detailed information about the scope and implications of
Love's apparent criminal conduct.

The OIG's office in Washington denied the request as there was an
"ongoing investigation."

The *Free Range Report* goes on to report:

> Love ordered a subordinate to drive a government issued
> vehicle to run personal errands for him. There have been
> some outside reports claiming the subordinate found ancient
> Indian artifacts in Love's vehicle during this process, but the
> most egregious allegation was still to come.
>
> After a raid on the Redd Family of Blanding, Utah, that also
> involved several other collectors of ancient Indian artifacts in
> the surrounding area, Love demanded the Utah Department
> of The Interior Evidence Custodian to retrieve several of the
> artifacts from the evidence room so he could display them on
> his desk. The internal investigation also states that Love gave
> at least several BLM Agents, other "Federal Agents," and one
> private contractor "Moqui Marbles" to keep as a trophy after
> the 2009 raid he and FBI Special Agent Greg Bretzing called
> Operation Cerberus.

Information in the wrongful death lawsuit brought by the Estate of Dr.
James Redd against Dan Love and the Federal Government furthers
the contention that Love makes this sort of behavior a practice. This
wrongful death lawsuit alleges that Love even kept some crude
artifacts Ted Gardiner acquired from Jeanne Redd – and took them
before they had been entered into the evidence locker following the
raid, but they were not. Instead, the FBI found that Love had kept
them for his own personal use.

The artifacts should have been entered into the evidence locker
following the raid on the Redd home, but they seemed to find another
home. The FBI conducted a search for the evidence of the Redd's
home and found it in Dan Love's car.

According to the *Free Range Report*:

> An FBI document contained in the wrongful death lawsuit (exhibit 11) reveals that Dan Love was reprimanded and written up for keeping Jeanne Redd's artifacts for his personal use, and failing to enter them property into evidence. When the Redd Family filed this, the federal government quickly had this document (exhibit 11) sealed so no one could see or read it but it is mentioned in the lawsuit itself:

> 94) Defendant Love's lack of the respect for the Constitution and proper law enforcement procedures was illustrated when, in April of 2008, 48 artifacts alleged to have been traded in August 2007 by informant Ted Gardiner with Jeanne Redd failed to appear in the case evidence file, and were instead discovered by FBI agent Gibson M. Wilson in Defendant Love's vehicle. These 48 items of evidence had been kept over nine months by Defendant Love, and were not recorded as evidence until Defendant Love was written up by Defendant Gibson.

It's also important to note that in the first two trials of the defendants in the Bundy Case in Las Vegas, early in 2017, the Government prosecutors were adamant in keeping Agent Love from testifying on behalf of the defense. The defense teams desired to call him as a witness, as the investigations of Agent Love came to the public attention and, although Dan Love was the primary witness in the Grand Jury hearing that led to the indictment of each of The Bundy 19, the Government objected and Judge Gloria Navarro agreed (!).

Odd isn't it that the prosecutions key law enforcement witness, and the key witness for the Government's actual indictment, is called by the <u>defense</u> and the Federal prosecutors then fight diligently to keep him out of the very trial for which he was the Government's key witness.

Odder still, that Judge Navarro agreed with the prosecution on their refusal to produce him!

August 24, 2017, the OIG's office issued its final report on the investigation into the misconduct of Dan Love. They had "substantiated all but one of the allegations."

Not long after, Daniel P. Love was fired.[10] This is not the kind of publicity that extends a career with a government agency – no matter how protective (or even supportive) the agency may be or may have been.

September 2017, in a memo circulated by Deputy Secretary of the Interior David Bernhardt, BLM employees were finally told that:

> Daniel Love had been fired.
> Misuses by Department of The Interiors' employees will not be tolerated and
> The Deputy Secretary renews a commitment by the new leadership of the Department of the Interior, now under Secretary Ryan Zinke, to deal quickly with any further abuse (how convenient), and
> The Deputy Secretary also encourages employees to report any abuse that they may witness.

All of this was of little consolation to the Redds, or to Cliven and the rest of The Bundy 19 as they sat in the Pahrump Federal Lock-up, or to their families.

Nor should it be to us.

---

10 https://www.doioig.gov/sites/doioig.gov/files/MishandlingofEvidencebyBLMLEManager_ Public.pdf

Chapter 9

– THE PROTEST –
Operation Gold Butte

Government Field Preparations …

Field preparations began March 27, 2014 for the BLM's "Gold Butte Operation" – the long-threatened round-up of Cliven's cattle – which would commence ten days later. Anticipating a much larger than normal round-up, (several smaller-scale round ups they routinely conducted each year across the West – involving, perhaps, a dozen or fewer cattle per operation) the BLM built a massive compound in the middle of the high desert of Clark County, about 15 miles northwest of the Bundy Ranch headquarters.

It consisted of several corrals, outbuildings, a command center, a communications facility to handle both the Operation's internal communications among its several participating agencies and operatives and its external communications with both the public and with the participating agencies' regional and national headquarters. It also included office accommodations from which both the contract cowboys and the BLM and Park Service agents involved in round up activities would work and from which the BLM's law enforcement contingent would work. The FBI contingent also had a van within the facility and provided both live surveillance presentation and an agent / equipment operator as liaison to the Operation's command team. The Operation's agents had also set up a checkpoint near the State Route 170 and an observation point high on a bluff overlooking the Bundy Ranch headquarters, and the overall operation.

In addition, BLM officials had established two orange, plastic-fence-enclosed plots of land as official "First Amendment" areas to allow for (confine) public protest. One area was just over the bridge from Mesquite on the way to Bunkerville on Riverside Road. The second was at the Riverside exit off Interstate 15. These two areas were to be only occupied by 25 people at a time (in shifts), including the media, according to Gayle Marrs-Smith, BLM field manager.

There were over 200 BLM, NPS, FBI agents, contract cowboys, helicopter and fixed-wing aircraft pilots involved in the Operation and its security, most of whom were staying in local hotels in Mesquite, just 7 miles up the road from the operation.

As the Operation began, the BLM closed the surrounding 300,000 acres to all public access – a closure area that could grow to a targeted total of 600,000 acres total area, if necessary. The Federal Aviation Administration closed the airspace above entire area to all air traffic not related to the Operation.

To conclude that this was a major BLM operation is the largest of understatements.

Preparations at the Bundy Ranch

Seeing the Operation's field preparations come together - but, little if any law enforcement presence or preparation from the Clark County Sheriff's office - Cliven Bundy began to gather his family and friends to protest to Sheriff Gillespie about his and his office's failure to protect Cliven's life, liberty, and property from the Operation's Federal Agents' now-expected usurpation of Cliven's constitutional rights (as he saw it).

He had made several demands on the Sheriff to intervene in the BLM's activities on his behalf. Cliven believes that the duly elected County Sheriff and his deputies are the highest legitimate law enforcement authority in a sovereign state. He and the entire Bundy family remain consistent in their respect for the Sheriff's authority remained steadfast in that respect during the Protest and in the days and months that followed.

The Lead-up: Sheriff Gillespie tries to talk some sense into Dan Love

In the weeks preceding the round up the Clark County Sheriff attempted to divert the imminent confrontation that BLM's preparation actions would precipitate.

On July 2, 2014, just six weeks after the Protest, Sheriff Douglas C. (Doug) Gillespie met with the editorial board of the Las Vegas Sun Newspaper to discuss his efforts and the BLM's actions against Cliven and his family.

Gillespie's knowledge of Bundy began two years ago. That's when the BLM first wanted to move in and take his cattle. After doing research, Gillespie said he pointed out to BLM officials that the court orders against Bundy said nothing about seizing the rancher's cattle.

So the government went back to court to refresh and update the order against Bundy.

Gillespie said he initially agreed to a request from Bureau of Land Management officials to assist in the roundup of Bundy's cattle from public lands after Bundy's refusal to pay federal grazing fees. But when he learned the feds weren't being truthful with him and he saw they weren't going to listen to his advice, he told them he wouldn't send his officers to Bundy's ranch near Bunkerville.

"'This is what normally happens,'" Gillespie said, paraphrasing the BLM's conversation with him before the roundup began in April. "'The local sheriff backs out. We know what we're doing.'"

At first, Gillespie was amenable to helping; then he said he found the BLM wouldn't take his advice and didn't tell him the truth.

For instance, Gillespie said, he urged putting off any roundup until the fall. The BLM held firm to a spring roundup.

Gillespie said the BLM told him Bundy's sons weren't at the ranch, which meant there would be less of a chance for confrontation. The BLM's people also said the feds had secured a place to take the seized cattle.

Gillespie found out otherwise.

"I go up there to talk to Cliven (before the roundup), see if I can talk some understanding to him, and the boys are there," Gillespie said. Further, he learned the BLM had no place to take the cattle.

"That's when I call the BLM and say my folks are not participating in this," Gillespie said. "You're telling me things that I'm finding out not to be true. I don't like the way this is going, and I think you need to put this off and look at the fall."

"I said all along to the BLM and to anyone who would listen, no drop of human blood is worth any cow," Gillespie said.[1]

BLM's Special Agent in Charge Dan Love failed to heed the Sheriff's direction, which ultimately led to Sheriff Gillespie's refusal to take the lead in the roundup operations.

The Sheriff had Cliven's respect. Cliven respected his authority; Cliven believed that ONLY the county sheriff has policing authority in Clark County or any other county. He and his sons have continually held to this belief. Sheriff Gillespie's statements also explain why the BLM needed to return to court. The first court order didn't allow the seizure.

If …

      Dan Love's ego had not gotten in the way,

      The punitive militarization of the BLM and Park Service had
          not escalated the situation; and

      Dan Love had backed off the operation and obeyed the orders
          of his superiors,

… the events of the round up operation would have resulted in a far different outcome.

But then what really happened?
The following is the exhaustive account of the activities of the Protest of the Clark County Sheriff by the Bundy Family and their supporters. It's better known as the 'Standoff,' as the National and International Media portrayed it. This chapter was compiled through hundreds of hours of video taken by protesters, bystanders, and uniform and dash cameras of the law enforcement at the site that day. Along with these videos, there are both personal interviews and media interviews of the participants. What I have tried diligently not to do is use private or public commentary as evidence as to the activities of those events.

I want you the reader to decide where - if at all - the fault lies.

1 https://lasvegassun.com/news/2014/jul/02/sheriff-breaks-silence-says-blm-bundy-share-blame-/

The July and October 2013 Federal Court Orders Authorizing Operation Gold Butte

Under a Federal Court Order, which had been embattled among the parties in court since 1998 and finally refreshed by the Federal Court in July 2013, the BLM finally began "Operation Gold Butte." The mission was to seize and remove the "trespass cattle" in late March, 2014 by sending Cliven a mid-month letter announcing their intent to impound the "trespass cattle" from the public lands that comprised his ranch.

Case 2:12-cv-00804-LDG-GWF Document 35 Filed **07/09/13** Page 5 of 5)

...

IT IS FURTHER ORDERED that Bundy shall remove his livestock from the New Trespass Lands within 45 days of the date hereof, and that **the United States is entitled to seize and remove to impound any of Bundy's cattle that remain in trespass after 45 days of the date hereof.**

IT IS FURTHER ORDERED that **the United States is entitled to seize and remove to impound any of Bundy's cattle for any future trespasses, provided the United States has provided notice to Bundy** under the governing regulations of the United States Department of the Interior. --Extract pertaining to Operation Gold Butte (Emphasis added)

Case 2:98-cv-00531-LRH-VCF Document 56 Filed **10/09/13** Page 5 of 6

...

IT IS FURTHER ORDERED that the United States is entitled to protect the former Bunkerville Allotment against this trespass, and all future trespasses by Bundy.

IT IS FURTHER ORDERED that Bundy shall remove his livestock from the former Bunkerville Allotment within 45 days of the date hereof, and that the United States is entitled to seize and remove to impound any of Bundy's cattle that remain in trespass after 45 days of the date hereof.

IT IS FURTHER ORDERED that the United States is entitled to seize and remove to impound any of Bundy's cattle for any future trespasses, provided the United

States has complied with the notice provisions under the governing regulations of the United States Department of the Interior.

> IT IS FURTHER ORDERED that Bundy shall not physically interfere with any seizure or impoundment operation authorized by this Court's Order. --Extract pertaining to Operation Gold Butte (Emphasis added)

The scope of these court orders strictly limited BLM action to rounding up and impounding the Bundy's cattle. This newly defined 'New Trespass Lands' area completely enveloped the Bundy Ranch and extended considerably beyond its boundaries.

The demand letter sent to Cliven by the BLM and NPS provided the required notice and declared that his cattle would be impounded and held for 45 days to allow Cliven to claim his cattle from among those rounded up by the BLM. It is important to note that any action other than rounding up and impounding the Bundy's cattle would be beyond the order's scope and would require separate court authorization.

As Scottish poet, Robert Burns observed 270 years before:

> The best laid schemes o' mice an' men
> Gang aft a-gley." (/ Go often awry.)

And "gang a-gley" they did, here in *"County Clark."*

The Events Of April 2nd 2014 near north of Austin, Sevier County, Utah

When a government *request for bid* goes to the public, the "cat is out of the bag." When that request reveals that the government wishes to sell a very large herd of impounded cattle very quickly – and the soon-to-be-owner's name is Bundy, the cat gets to other ranchers, county government, state government and Federal Government very quickly.

Ryan Bundy, Cliven's son, organized a protest for Wednesday, April 2, three days before the BLM's gathering of his father's cattle was to begin back on the ranch. The protest was in the form of a line of family members and like-minded ranchers and sympathizers carrying signs expressing their protest of the impending auction in front of R Livestock Connections, LLC, near Austin, Utah, the auction house selected by the BLM. Ryan had contacted Sevier County Sheriff Nathan Curtis before the protest to ensure that the Sheriff knew of their peaceful intent and hoping that this Sheriff would affirm his responsibilities to protect life, property, and peace as his Dad had requested of Clark County Sheriff Gillespie. The Richfield (Utah) Reaper covered the story and reported:

> As of Reaper press time (for its Tuesday, April 8 issue), no cattle had been transported from Clark County to R Livestock, but the BLM had tallied that 234 total trespass cattle had been rounded up by the end of the day Monday.
>
> …
>
> Some Utah counties, like Iron County, quickly drafted letters issuing ultimatums to the BLM to abide by their own policies with wild horse herds in their area before spending money to take Bundy's livestock away.
>
> "The decision of the BLM in Clark County, Nev., to force trespass on private citizens has triggered our interest … and has spillover ramifications," said Iron County Commissioner David Miller in a letter sent to BLM officials. "Why do you have money to deal with noncompliance as in the case with Mr. Cliven Bundy, but no funds to keep yourself in compliance?
>
> "We charge you to fulfill your responsibility to address the concerns found herein and being brought once again to your attention, as in previous communication."
>
> The letter issued an ultimatum to the BLM, stating that unless the agency created a plan with county officials to remove excess horses from the land to achieve "appropriate management levels," by Friday, county officials would take action by "necessary means to reduce the numbers of feral horses … on the western range within the county."
>
> "This is not a threat," Miller said. "This is a plan of action.
>
> "While state BLM officials are working with Iron County

commissioners to hammer out a plan to reduce herd numbers
on the range, officials and ranchers in Piute County are taking
a stand with the Bundy family.

A handful of ranchers from the Kingston area turned out
to support Ryan Bundy's Protest in Sevier County April 2,
while others, including Piute County Commissioner Darin
Bushman, have taken to social media to show their support
for Bundy's cause."

"A lot happening with this and seems Sevier County may not
be able to avoid the controversy," said Piute County recorder
Shane Millett. "Piute County is standing with Cliven Bundy."

Cause for concern

Sevier County commissioners did call an emergency meeting
to address concerns raised over the issue Friday morning, and
drafted a resolution urging the BLM to hold off on shipping
the cattle to Sevier County until conflicting information
regarding the situation could be cleared up, also urging them
to reconsider shipping the cattle to Utah altogether.

And with such warning, Utah officials would not allow the cattle
entry into the state for auction: Utah Gov. Gary Herbert (R) said state
veterinarians were concerned that the animals may not have received
regular health maintenance and could carry livestock diseases.
"Serious illnesses, such as Trichomoniasis, external parasites, Bovine
tuberculosis and Brucellosis, could be present in the herd," Herbert
wrote in an April 2, 2014, letter to BLM Director Neil Kornze.

Utah's two Republican senators and Republican Representatives
Chris Stewart, Rob Bishop and Jason Chaffetz concurred in a letter
to Kornze one week later, warning that BLM's auction plan "may
endanger the health of Utah herds and place Utah state employees and
other Utah residents in danger."

According to a letter written by Nevada State Assemblywoman Fiore,
it appears that none of the cattle were sold at auction. The Nevada
Brand Inspectors office wouldn't permit the cattle across state lines
into Utah.

In other words, the BLM's disregard for the court orders' limits (gather and impound) and their ill-thought plan to illegally sell 'trespass cattle' (Bundy's and the feral cattle) at an auction yard they had already paid was stopped before it even started.

The Round Up. Events Of April 5th – 12th 2014 near Bunkerville, Nevada

Even over the Clark County Sheriff's objection and urgings to delay until fall, the BLM begin "Operation Gold Butte" to seize and remove (under a Federal Court Order) what were being called "trespass cattle" in part belonging to rancher Cliven Bundy. The situation quickly escalated from a small local news story onto grabbing the attention of a national and international media. The matter finally came to a head on Saturday, April 12, 2014, when Federal Agents vacated the area, leaving the cattle and compound behind. The Clark County Sheriff's Department released the cattle back to the Bundy family. Again, as in 2012, but this time too late to prevent an embarrassing back off, the order to withdraw came down from Dan Love's Washington D.C. superiors two full days earlier (April 10, 2014). That was days before the Standoff.

The cattle remain on the Bundy Ranch at the release of this book in winter of 2017.

Saturday, April 5, 2014

The federal round up of Bundy's cattle begins. The BLM chose to use contract cowboys, hired through federal contractor Shayne Sampson, who would be paid $966,000 to "seize" … "the Bundy cattle" (according to court records). They began the roundup using horseback, motorized, and helicopter methods.

It's spring and the middle of calving season. The cows are either heavily pregnant or have just dropped (gave birth) their calves. This is the worst time of year to attempt such an operation and, in fact, would never be attempted by an experienced rancher. Cliven explained it would have taken a month or more to gather that many cattle in the best of circumstances with just grown or no calves alongside their 'mommas.' "No self-respecting cowboy would try somp'n like what they did. It was a bad idee," Cliven huffed. "The Gold Butte Range was the only home these wild cattle had ever known and would be very protective of their babies, 'sticky,' meanin' they will not want to leave their babies. But, if forced to, they'll hide their babies in the brush and return to 'em later. This is the natural instinct of mother cows to protect their babies from predators and the gen'ral immobility of a young nursing calf. If they're forced to run, as they were by the helicopter and motorized vehicles, the babies will not be able to keep up, so they'll hide until the mother's return. Also, the pregnant cows could be run to exhaustion, even death."

The remoteness of Cliven's ranch and the complete lack of domestication of both Cliven's and the feral cattle of the range also made conditions for a massive roundup extremely difficult. It is why Cliven uses humane 'cattle traps' to gather his animals, though this practice was later criticized by the Federal Prosecutors, calling it "bizarre." Cliven's ingenious traps are large sturdy pens where he uses feed, water, or both, in which the cow (and babies) are lured. At this point the gate is quietly triggered and closed behind the animals. What Cliven could have done with just one or two cowboys, the federal government needed hundreds of men and machines. The time of year, spring, also explained the low numbers of cattle gathered each day.

Government Roundup Operations on the Ranch

Simultaneously, with the beginning of the round up, the BLM Law Enforcement contingent and the FBI personnel attached to the Operation, began a military siege of the Bundy ranch – with roving patrols, checkpoints, and both observation and sniper teams. When I first heard of "sniper teams" in lock-up I thought it was an embellishment on Cliven's part. His son, Ammon, had said in a jailhouse media interview that even the red laser dots of snipers' rifles targeting the Bundy children's "little bodies." In my subsequent research of the incidents explained in this book, the sniper teams are clearly seen in the video footage. Ultimately this was all confirmed in the courtroom testimony of Dan Love – under oath – on October 23, 2017. But, of course, this is an intimidation practice against U.S. citizens that Agent Love used in the past, at least on one occasion at the Redd's home in Blanding, Utah, some eight years earlier.

The BLM's contract cowboys rounded up 76 head of cattle that first day.

Sunday, April 6

BLM officers took David Bundy, Cliven's son, into custody while he was standing along State Route 170, between Bunkerville and Riverside, taking video footage of the roundup operation. I got to know 'Davey', as he is known to his family and friends, while in lock-up and asked him about his experiences during the Protest. As we were all talking together in lock-up, I asked, "So, how did this whole thing begin anyway?

To which Davey explained: On Sunday April 6th, 2014, he was heading to Las Vegas, to report for work as a new airline pilot for Sightseeing Tour Company, conducting tours into the Grand Canyon. It was a day of emotion, also being his mom's birthday. He'd picked up some flowers and planned on swinging by the ranch for a short visit and a 'hug.'

He had also gotten word from his sisters that the BLM had moved onto their ranch and had begun impounding 'dad's cattle.' All Davey wanted to just "hug" on his Dad and let him know how sorry he was for him.

It seemed to Davey that 160 or so years, literally generations of family ranching, had come to an end. And, like all his siblings, he had no financial interests in the ranch, each of them loved the life of ranching, like most would after growing up this way.

Now a grown man with a family of his own, Davey's passion was all focused around avionics, or flying. He had become an instructor and been gainfully employed as a commercial pilot. He was always reading aviation magazines or books about flying, or talking about it with anyone who would listen and reciprocate. Just by watching Davey while in lock-up it was easy to see this passion.

Crossing over the Virgin River Valley via Highway 15 that day, Davey could see the massive BLM compound to have seemingly sprung up out of the desert from nowhere. "Just the sight of it set me back,"

Davey recalled after he arrived at the ranch and exchanged greetings with his family, presenting his mom with flowers and wishing her a happy birthday. Subsequently, they began a long conversation, which turned quickly to the matter surrounding the BLM Federal Compound.

His sisters were quick to convey information about spotters and sniper teams in the hills around the ranch, performing what appeared to be military operations, just a short distance from the ranch itself. They described Federal Agents in full kit with military style rifles strapped to their chest and patrol teams.

Word comes from another family member about the government's contract cowboys who would soon bring down a gather (herd) of cows and calves through a canyon that would lead the animals directly to the road near the ranch. Also noted were dozens of vehicles in a convoy, including a couple of one-ton trucks pulling cattle trailers, traveling across the ranch.

With this information, Davey and his sisters decided they wanted to see the Feds and view how the cowboys were handling and treating their animals. Davey pointed out that he really never saw his dad that day. He expected his father was in his bedroom, on the phone or in prayer, as was his usual custom.

Fittingly, together they went down to the intersection of the state highway (SR 71) to observe the scene. Safely parked off the highway's shoulder only a few hundred yards from a smaller BLM compound, they observed a couple dozen heavily armed agents congregating. Davey got out of his car, leaned against the hood where he began videoing with his iPad the armed men, the cowboys and cattle drive including all the goings on.

Then others began to stop alongside them. Davey wasn't sure who these people were. He doesn't remember. He certainly didn't recognize many of them. About twenty minutes passed when Davey's brother Ryan, returning from church, came by with his wife and kids. Everyone was just plain curious. Stopping in the middle of the road, Ryan then stepped out of his vehicle to "holler" at his brother and sisters. With that, the BLM agents actually drew down on Ryan, with wife and the kids still in the vehicle.

At this point I asked Davey, "What do you mean by "drew down?"

"They took positions behind their vehicles and pointed their weapons (guns and rifles) at us."

They observed four agents climb in their SUV and drive out to the road, while the remaining agents marched down in formation from the compound to the highway. From the lead SUV, over its loudspeaker, the small crowd gathering was ordered to "Disperse" ... because they were allegedly unlawfully assembled. At that announcement, the bulk of the bystanders got in their cars and departed. Ryan and his sisters remained a while; eventually they decided it was best to remove the children while Davey continued to video the entire scene.

Coming upon Davey, the agents directed him once more to disperse. Davey retorted that he was exercising his constitutional right to be on a public highway and there was no legal reason to make him move. Their response was to advise him to "relocate to the First Amendment Area," approximately three to five miles away. All the while video was rolling, Davey asserted his constitutional rights.

"FIRST AMENDMENT AREA"

With that, abruptly and unexpectedly, about a half a dozen federal agents seized him and began to jump on him. Falling, he tried to brace himself, but he couldn't completely because federal agents firmly gripped his wrists. He fell headfirst onto the country road, smashing his face into the shoulder's gravel surface. With full weight, one agent landed on him with a thud, driving his knee into Davey's head, tearing more of the flesh from his bleeding face, and pushing him deeper into the gravel. All the while Davey had snarling police dogs within inches of his bloody head. After handcuffing him and yanking him to his feet, agents placed him in the back seat of the SUV where they drove him up to the major BLM compound.

Once at the compound, he sat in the back of that SUV windows rolled up in the heat of the day, while bruised and bleeding. At one point, they pulled him out of the vehicle and paraded him around the compound in a 'perp-walk', a trophy walk usually done in front of the media. This time, though, it was in front of other agents. Agents then returned him to the vehicle where he was left.

Davey reflected a moment. "It seems they didn't know what to do with me... Finally, they changed out my handcuffs for a waist chain with leg irons."

"Wait," ... I stopped him. "You mean like the leg irons and waist chains they use to transport us prisoners in here?"

"Yep," he responded.

I thought to myself how odd. That means that they were preparing – and planning on – arresting dozens (or more) of people. Although common for custody officers, like the Correctional Officers of the Pahrump Detention Center, its rare for law enforcement officers to have transport chains on hand. Why would BLM agents have transport chains, unless they were expecting and anticipating making mass arrests? But there were no masses, no crowds at this point. It was a full week before the "Standoff," as the national media would dub the events that were soon to take place. I speculated there was something going on; some piece of a puzzle to unravel sooner or later.

Eventually, Davey was transported to the Henderson Jail, located in the suburbs of Las Vegas, Nevada. For all his family knew, he just simply disappeared from the highway that day. The next morning the US Marshal's Service moved him to the Federal Court House. Pointing out his mistreatment by the federal agents, Davey cites, "I never saw a doctor and the two marshals handled me roughly, cuffing my hands failing to trip the locking mechanism." (This refers to the counter-locking mechanism that keeps handcuffs from tightening with every click of the ratchet. In other words, his handcuffs continued to tighten with every application of the transport vehicle's brakes or accelerator in order for his cuffs to cut into skin.) "It was excruciating pain for the entire 45 minute drive to the Federal Court House."

At the Courthouse he was interrogated for hours without the presence of legal counsel. Davey recounts, "One of the things they kept asking me was if I hit my wife." Unaware, agents behind the one-way mirror were, at the same moment in time, verifying by telephone each answer with his wife. "I was confused as to why federal BLM agents were asking me about marriage. What in the world does my personal life have to do with my videoing the BLM operation?" he exclaimed with incredulity.

"That *IS* odd," I responded. "Sounds to me like they were fishing for anything."

In the end, the federal gents left the room, handing Davey Bundy a mere citation for "failure to disperse" and for "resisting arrest." Once the citation was presented, the U.S. Marshals walked Davey to the courthouse front door, handing him a bag of his personal belongings while wishing him a "nice day." Arriving at the entry, Davey now had no phone or iPad, both of which agents refused to return, the iPad containing all his video data of the entire incident. (Davey never did see his phone or iPad again. The agents kept them and then, "lost them," according to court records.) He also had no cash either. Quickly walking to a gas station on Las Vegas Boulevard, he traded a credit card purchase of $10.00 of gasoline for the use of a cellphone. He was able to contact his family who, in turn, called his dad, Cliven, who was just leaving Sheriff Gillespie's office in Vegas. Cliven was able to pick Davey up on his way back to the ranch.

Davey said, "I was never so glad to see that old truck of my dad's coming down the road."

Cliven added: "Ya know, he didn't tell ya that was a lot more dramatic than what he told ya. He told it; but he just basically, don't ... he don't want to dramatize it any.

"They put him down on the ground, and they really hurt him. They put their feet on his head and grabbed his face and put it right into that gravel. They was hurtin' him. They wasn't just monkeyin' around, they was hurtin' him.

"Another thing, what happened to Stetsy.' Cliven continued; 'What happened to Stetsy happened (just) before Davey. The main thing that happened there is, I want to make two points.

"Stetsy challenged their, you know, all the jurisdiction authority. She'd already gott'n permission to be on the side of the road. She was on the road just like Davey was, only there's a turnoff that goes to a side road. Davey's probably about 150 feet before he got to that road where he was parked, then there's an exit road that goes off towards the mountain. That was the road that they was goin' to bring the convoy with the horse trailers, or the stock trailers down.

"Well, Stetsy was on the other side of that exit, probably maybe 200 feet, and maybe even a little further. She'd pulled off the road there, and highway patrol had come along and had talked to her. And she asked if she was off the road enough and it was okay for her to park there. She already had permission from the highway patrol to be there and that she was in a safe enough location, and all of that, was all taken care of the highway patrol."

Angry at the situation involving his daughter, Cliven continued, now more animated; "Then the BLM came and started to harass her. She said that she had permission, and they'd okayed that she was in a good place. Course, they wanted her to go to the First Amendment zone, said she didn't have no right to be there. They had First Amendment zones they'd created, designed, and set apart places for her to go protest. She made the statement, 'I can protest, use my First Amendment right and protest any place I am in this United States, you know, in America.' She made that statement.

"And then she made ... they was goin' to arrest her. In the process of them tryin' to arrest her, she was telling them they have no right. She had a right there. She wasn't breakin' no law. She had the right to protest. The only thing she was doing ... I don't think she even had a camera. She was just sort of watchin'.

"So now, they're goin' to arrest her, they're threatenin' to arrest her if she don't leave. She said she has the right to be there. So now, what happens is about the time they're gettin' really physical with her, somebody comes up, one of the BLM people come up, and they said, "We have been notified that we do not have arresting power."

With a knowing grin, he said, "So they recognized that they do not have arrestin' power, so they back off and leave her alone."

"There's two things happened there." With great expectation, we all waited for Cliven to continue.

"One is she makes a statement about the First Amendment thing. That brings that all to the surface about the First Amendment zones, or areas. I call them Human Corrals, 'em Pig Pens. That brings the fact that they recognize they do not have no arresting power. They'd been told by their authorities real clear … where that come from, I don't know, but they actually announced there that they have no arresting power.

"Then we go back to Davey, which I think this happens a few hours after Stetsy's ordeal. … let me pick up where I left off on Davey. They put Davey in a ... they handcuff him, put him in the car, and they take him from there over to where the cattle are, over at the compound.

"When they get him over there, they keep him handcuffed, and he says they treated him like a trophy. He's hurting. They've got him in there, and he's probably handcuffed in the back, you know how that all is, in the seat. He stuffed in sort of a tight quarter and he's hurting. Then they walk around him and took in and hassle him like he's a trophy, like he's a wild animal."

Cliven heatedly went on. "That goes on for several hours, maybe two and a half hours or something he sits in that car. Then they transfer him down to (the Henderson detention center – about an 80 mile ride) and put him in, book him Henderson jail. He spends the rest of that day and the night, and then they pick him up out of Henderson jail and take him to the Federal Courthouse in Las Vegas, the Federal Courthouse.

"Now, I don't know how much hassling they gave him in Henderson, but he indicated that they... somebody… mainly questioned him but hassled him while he was in Henderson. Then they take him to the Courthouse, and he said, 'By the time I got to the Courthouse,' he actually said, 'I thought my life was over.' He said that he felt that they was actually goin' to kill him. That's what he felt." With understandable sadness for his son, he paused for a moment.

"And then he said that they … and then he said everythin' just changed. He said they brought him in a lunch, gave him a lunch, un-handcuffed him, and sent him out the door, out on the Las Vegas Boulevard.

"Other words, it was over that fast. It was over. Now, I had been down talkin' to, I think it must've been the same time," he pondered out loud, "I had been down talkin' to the sheriff. That's the only time, so had to've been down talkin' to the sheriff that mornin'," nodding as he recalled the events from that day, "and I was on the way home, and I'd got that... I think I'd got up to about that Love's station on the way home, where the exit goes on 93?

"And I got a phone call and said that they'd turned Davey loose, and that he was in Las Vegas turned loose on the street, and he told me the address. I think it was Stewart and Las Vegas Boulevard, or not Las Vegas Boulevard. Yeah, Las Vegas Boulevard. Stewart and Las Vegas Boulevard. Said that he was there at the service station, so I just turned right around and headed back there.

"On the way back, I called Channel 8 newspaper, or TV, because they'd been wantin' contact with me. So I told them, 'He's there. I'll meet you there.' Course, when I got there, they was already there, and they had him, and there's interviews, and there's pictures. You don't have access to all this stuff, but there's pictures of what he looked like when I got there." Sadness enveloped his face as he reflected back on the sight of Davey.

"We had an interview right there in the service station parking lot there. We had an interview on TV, and then I picked him up and brought him home. He was in pretty bad shape, but he never tells you those things."

After another moment deep in thought, he went on.

"If you really want to get to the beginnin' of this whole ordeal that we're dealin' with, you got to realize that Stetsy and Davey basically laid the foundation of this thing. They basically resisted the First Amendment thing, they said they had the right to be there, and then they had the statement that they had no arrestin' power, and yet they went ahead and did all this abusin', and abusin', and it's still going on and on. That's what's happening ... It started there. It started with Stetsy."

With these events social media heats up – first-person news commentary – and first-hand video of the action.

National, local and social media began to actively follow all events happening on the Bundy ranch. Locally, of course, there had already been many stories written about Cliven's legal fight over jurisdiction and the BLM's use of public lands. But now, what the BLM was doing was what many observed as unprecedented.

Well, it seemed so in Nevada anyway.

Davey's arrest was the first of two incidents that became flash points, starting one of the most significant property rights movements in the history of our country. In rural states, and across America, citizens continue to get more and more fed up with the over-reaching and usurping of power by the federal government into their everyday lives. Not to mention the fact we can witness the acts of corruption, lack of responsiveness to the average citizen, and the persistent *laissez-faire* attitude by most bureaucrats, in regard to trampling the basic constitutional rights of the American people.

This unsettledness, anger and outrage manifested itself in the "Tea Party Movement," a grassroots, organic movement of American voters and citizens representing conservative American views. People of faith perceived they had lost their voice in any meaningful way with the government; a government leaning so far to the left in its definition of values that it was literally redefining America's constitutional values on the fly.

And the American citizens, especially rural freedom-loving people, were emotionally beginning to simmer — and what happened to

Davey Bundy that Sunday, April 6, 2014 turned up the stove.

But the pot was yet to boil.

Moving into the Pahrump facility's recreation area, I posed the question to Davey as I sat down with my back against the chain-link fence: "Do you think the protesters came out because of the injustice of how you were treated?"

"Nope," he answered surprisingly quickly. Ordinarily, Davey is a quiet man, deliberate in speech and thoughtful, quick to listen and slow to speak, as the Bible would suggest.

"What got them all stirred up then?" I asked.

"It was them signs," he says.

"What signs?" I pressed.

"Those first Amendment signs!" he heatedly blurted out.

The Federal Agents had set aside two First Amendment Areas miles away from the activities of the BLM round-up operations. They had also requested that the FAA close the airspace to all non-government aircraft to keep the media from a fly over and videoing the operation.

These two designated First Amendment areas were each roughly 100' x 100' square. It was into these two small areas where the BLM intended all press and protesters remain. Of course, this was an absurd idea and was widely ignored. The Feds even posted 'Tax Payer Funded' signs on those two areas appearing to be "human corrals – pig pens," as Cliven termed them.

Davey explained further, "That's what made everyone so mad. That's what set this pot to boil!" He continued, "But what made the pot boil over was what happened on Wednesday, April 9, 2014. Now THAT was the reason people got their cars and drove hundreds, even thousands, of miles to a little patch of green in the southern Nevada desert, here, to the Bundy ranch."

During the first Bundy trial, the federal prosecutors made unfounded accusations and assertions that somehow the Bundys sent out a "Call to Arms" to local militias and government haters across the country. The assertion was these folks were coming to protect the Bundy ranch from the Feds as they executed a lawful court order.

Davey clarified, "In fact, I didn't even know what a local militia group was, or that they even existed, until they started arriving on the 11th of April."

Cliven reminded me, "I'm a constitutionalist, and I don't think we are allowed to even form a private local militia," referring back to Article 1, Section 8 clauses 15 and 16 of the United States Constitution.

Cliven went on. "I think that describes the National Guard."

"So, why did private militias supposedly and reportedly come out to the ranch?" I asked.

"All kinds of people came out to protest, for all kinds of reason," Cliven answered. "Some groups wanted me to send 'em a letter invitin' them. Some of which were private militia groups. But I told them, NO and never signed anything...and I'm so glad I didn't!" he said with a smile of relief. "I wouldn't be surprised if they were actually a government set-up. You gotta remember, most people there were just regular folks – women, little kids, families, my neighbors – those who felt they had just enough."

"But, then, this media attention also attracted whack-a-doos, didn't it?" I asked Davey.

"Yeah, but remember it was just their words, not their deeds that the government says makes this a conspiracy. Words that were said weeks and even months later," Davey reminded me.

Davey was referring to some of the The Bundy 19 defendants who made boastful, vain, and alarming comments to an undercover CI working for the FBI.

Cliven explained, "I didn't even hardly know most of the April 12, 2014 protesters, though I may have shook their hands and said howdy."

Nodding his head in agreement, Davey said, "I never seen most of those people ever since. I didn't even get to know the men here in prison with us until we were all showed into this place together."

For both the first and second Bundy trials, the jury agreed with the Bundy's story; that there was no call to arms, no conspiracy, and therefore no conviction.

Then, if there was no "call to arms" by the Bundy's, what *DID* cause the pot to boil? Davey's arrest hit the news and word accelerated its way through social media of the BLM's actions there. All across the west, farmers, ranchers and rural-living people began to take an interest. It's not hard to find people in the Western States who have had terrible firsthand stories of the "tyranny" experienced at the hands of BLM, EPA, Forest and Park Service.

It's true; following the coverage of Davey's arrest, protesters began to arrive in small groups, the catalyst of which was his refusal to move into a "human corral," supposedly designated as a "First Amendment Area" or zone. The Stars and Stripes went up along the road where it had taken place, and people began to picket with protest signs, mostly for passersby and the occasional media coverage.

But, it was one video clip of one woman taken by a cellphone and posted on Facebook that became, not just a call to arms, but a "clarion call" all on its own. It made vividly clear that the U.S. Government was undeniably trampling on Americans most precious constitutionally protected civil right: the right to free speech, the right to speak up against our government. It was a right that was insisted upon by a small, frail senior citizen who dared to stand up to militarily-clad Federal Agents, carrying automatic weapons in order to subdue this "one-women threat."

The "one-woman threat"? Margaret, Cliven's sister. But that was to come a few days later.

The incident with Davey prompted Cliven to send out an announcement on Sunday evening declaring a protest against the Sheriff's failure to protect him from the government's action. A rally at the Bundy ranch was planned for the next morning and regional media was invited.

Another 60 head of cattle were gathered on Sunday, according to numbers released by the BLM.

Monday April 7, 2014
More than one hundred people gathered early Monday morning at the Bundy ranch to protest Davey's arrest, the federal roundup that was ongoing and Sheriff Gillespie's deafening silence.

The rally remained a peaceful protest. The participants eventually moved to a location on private land, just north of the Riverside Bridge. There they erected two flagpoles with a banner posted across them stating "Liberty, Freedom for God We Stand."

Despite the federally designated "free speech zones," this area became the focal point and the picket line for the Bundy cause.

BLM reported gathering 100 head of cattle during the day on Monday.

Tuesday, April 8
State Assemblyman, and U.S. Congressional candidate, Cresent Hardy

arranged for two local residents to meet with Nevada's Governor Brian Sandoval to relate the events unfolding at the Bundy ranch and across northeastern Clark County. The meeting was held in Las Vegas and included Hardy, Assemblyman James Oscarson, plus Logandale residents Lindsey Dalley and Dustin Nelson, both of whom are board members of the Partners in Conservation organization.

"We were able to take him (the Governor) from being 100 miles away from this issue, to bringing him up to date on just what was happening on the ground," said Dalley after the meeting.

That afternoon, Sandoval released a written statement decrying some of the methods of the BLM in the roundup.

> "Due to the roundup by the BLM, my office has received numerous complaints of BLM misconduct, road closures and other disturbances. I have recently met with state legislators, county officials and concerned citizens to listen to their concerns. I have expressed those concerns directly to the BLM."

> "Most disturbing to me is the BLM's establishment of a 'First Amendment Area' that tramples upon Nevadans' fundamental rights under the U.S. Constitution. To that end, I have advised the BLM that such conduct is offensive to me and countless others and that the 'First Amendment Area' should be dismantled immediately. No cow justifies the atmosphere of intimidation which currently exists nor the limitation of constitutional rights that are sacred to all Nevadans. The BLM needs to reconsider its approach to this matter and act accordingly."[2]

It's important to note that Brian Sandoval left his life-long appointment as a Federal District Court Judge to become Governor of Nevada. This was significant statement for a man who spent his life interpreting the rule of law under the United States Constitution.

BLM reported 41 cattle rounded up on Tuesday.

2 http://gov.nv.gov/News-and-Media/Press/2014/Sandoval-Statement-on-BLM-Roundup/

Wednesday, April 9, of 2014

On Wednesday, April 9, Margaret Houston, Cliven's 57-year-old sister, along with several others had gotten word that the BLM had cut a new road across the desert. (Ordinarily, creating a road like this would most likely be denied for environmental reasons.) But in just a few short hours the U.S. Government had built this road to accommodate their issues over Cliven's property. The BLM dispatched a dump truck with trailer, loaded with a backhoe, to drive over this newly built road. That action gave the entire Bundy family hours to speculate what the government could be doing with such equipment. Eventually, they concluded that the BLM's contracted cowboys, with the assistance of the helicopter, likely ran some of the cows to death or that they cavalierly shot some of the troublesome cattle and orphaned their calves. If true, it would be a violation of the court order, which stated they were only to seize and impound the cattle. The order did not allow the BLM to sell, destroy or kill the animals. It made sense that the government, if indeed they had killed some of the cattle, would want to get rid the evidence. Further, if the government wanted to get rid of the evidence, the carcasses of dead cattle, the perfect equipment would be a backhoe to load the animal carcasses into the dump truck, where no one would suspect or see them.

Then word came that the dump truck was returning along the new road. So, Margaret, Ammon and some protesters decided that they wanted to see what was actually inside of that dump truck before any evidence was lost forever.

"We figured they were up there shooting cows and burying them in the mountains," Margaret said. "So we decided we were going to check it out."[3]

Equipped with her cellphone and its camera, they went to the intersection of the new road. As the dump truck with trailer approached, the protesters, including Margaret, try to stop the driver and demand to see the contents of the dump truck. Now this seems to be a wildly courageous move, considering all the military activities, snipers and hostile acts that have occurred so far. But, we need to understand that these cows are almost part of the Bundy family, and have been for generations. Cliven and his family have raised these

3 http://mvprogress.com/2014/04/16/timeline-of-a-tense-week-in-northeast-clark-county/

animals since they were babies and acclimated them to their unique environment there at the ranch. Oftentimes they hand-raised a small percentage of the animals, and certainly doctored them when they were sick and cared for them like one of their own, which they were. So, if any of their cows were really dead, then this becomes a very personal matter to the Bundy family, if indeed, that was what was actually happening.

Margaret and the protesters attempted to stop the truck. What the protesters didn't know at the time was the truck didn't contain dead animals, merely the range improvement materials that the Operation's BLM agents had torn out, consisting of several lengths of pipe, watering troughs and the like. These were improvements that the Bundy's installed at their own expense over the years. This removal was NOT part of the court orders the BLM claimed to be using as their authority. The court orders were merely for the seizing and impounding of the cattle. Cliven's ancestors installed the improvements, consisting of hundreds of miles of pipe to furnish water, over the many, many years, and the water rights, for which Cliven holds the rights, are not only for grazing cattle, but also for wildlife.

As soon as the sniper teams were in place, more military-clad Federal agents were immediately dispatched to the location of the interaction. As they arrived, Margaret and Ammon stayed on the state highway, just as Davey had been, and not on federal land.

This time, the BLM federal agents ordered the few citizens there to disperse. But these citizens were protesters, not bystanders as in Davey's situation just a few days earlier. Refusing to leave, once more the crowd is told to "relocate to the designated First Amendment Areas" (those 'human corrals'). However, by Divine providence and clearly unbeknownst to the federal agents, all of what came to pass was captured on cellphone video, then posted to Facebook for the whole world to see first-hand and in near-real-time with their own eyes!

There stood Margaret, toe-to-toe with these intimidating and armed federal agents, looking up (as the agents are taller than she is) straight into their eyes. Squaring off with the agents, she replied, "My First

Amendment rights are wherever I am!" With that, she moves past them where one of the park rangers grabs, picks up, and throws this little grandmother hard to the ground.

"All of a sudden I got hit from behind by one of the rangers," she said. "It was a football tackle and he threw me onto the ground. I was shocked that somebody would actually do this!"[4]

Ammon, who was standing by, came to the aid of his auntie, racing up on his ATV. He blocked the dump truck, for which the Agents tased him with a Taser gun ... not just once to render him immobile – they tased him four times!

At a speaking event in which Ammon shared his experience of that day, one of the audience members asked why would the government confront the protesters in such a way?

Ammon explained: "Earlier, they had set up these perimeters, they call it the First Amendment Area. You only have the right to protest in those first amendment areas, according to them. And if you protested outside of those areas you are breaking the law."

"So, they got out to confront us because we were not in our First Amendment Area. They were saying, they were reading off this code ...

"And they actually would say this code to us. 'Code, code,' and then they'd have their Tasers, and we're confronting them, basically telling them to go away, this and that."

Describing what happened to his aunt Margret, he continued: "They come, snuck up from behind and took my Aunt Margaret and literally just slammed her right on the ground, right on the asphalt. So they did that, and of course the crowd just went crazy. The protesters were just like ... just to give you an idea, there are about 35 of them and there are probably about 40 to 50 of us.

"They've got their dogs, they got their Tasers. So, then what they did is, my sister Stetsy is pregnant, sicced their dog on her. And then as we began to protest loudly, we're protesting, they hit me with the

---

4 Margaret Houston video - https://www.youtube.com/watch?v=iT97SRyaJA8

Taser. And it hit me; the first one I think hit me in the neck and the chest. It's a 50,000-volt Taser, and it will put your whole body in convulsions.[5]

"My body is convulsing, I turned and kind of stepped away and I end up getting one of them out, and as soon as you get one of them ... 'cause they arc across each other. But as soon as you get one of them out it stops. And then we went back, began to protest, they sicced the dog on me. Couple of times I ended up kicking the dog, getting it to back away from me. Then they tased me again.

"By this time, everybody's kind of getting wise, and they start tearing them off. So then they tased me a third time. And the other protesters are tearing them off. They shot a fourth time, but fourth time, they didn't hit. So every time someone gets tased, they go to the ground. You get hit, and you go to the ground. And they asked, 'Well, why didn't you go to the ground?' And at first, I was kinda being real funny, I said, 'Well, I didn't know I was supposed to.'"

I have watched the video over and over. It's very detailed, so much so you can see the other protesters push forward and jerk out the live Taser wires hooked on to Ammon. It's a powerful and sobering video to watch. What you see is onlookers seeing a need, a need to stop what appears to them to be excessive physical abuse and save Ammon's life. Watch the video and see with your own eyes how the common American citizen's civil rights and physical safety could be at

5 Ammon Bundy Tased - https://www.youtube.com/watch?v=RO-d0HYJRZA

issue. The video may be shocking.

Like the incident with Davey a few days earlier, there were no charges filed on Ammon or Margaret that day by the Federal Government. Not even an arrest, like there was with Davey. Though later, Davey's charges were completely dropped, as you've already read. As Davey told me that day in the recreation yard, "I called the Court to verify every week for two months my citation number or ticket, because I actually wanted to go before the judge and tell him the truth about what happened."

"Were those charges added to this indictment?" I asked.

"Nope, they just seemed to disappear," said Davey.

Cliven thought someone told them they had no policing powers or state land jurisdiction where Davey was parked that day where the incident occurred. That also explained why Ammon and Margaret were both never arrested.

"They've just plain no business being there," says Cliven. "Besides the fact that they did nothin' wrong!"

Margaret Houston stated that the area felt like a war zone. "I was worried that I wasn't in the United States anymore."

For the third time, the Feds, BLM, and Park Service agents were ordered to retreat from their positions that day—without gaining any ground to speak of, other than that of the detention and incarceration of The Bundy 19, coming some two years later.

But even more telling than their retreat had been, the video of the entire incident with Margaret and Ammon and the BLM Federal agents, along with the protesters, couldn't be contained or retracted by the Feds. Yet, the Government had been able to control the media and subsequent outrage from the encounter with Davey, seizing his iPad containing the video he shot of the event when they were arresting him. They refused to return it, knowing that by keeping Davey's personal property the Feds could keep the actual events far away from the American people.

However, the video of Margaret standing toe-to-toe with the Federal Agents of the BLM went viral on Facebook almost immediately, and became "the Clarion Call" for protesters from around the country. These U.S. citizens chose to take time off work, pack their kids in the car and drive to the Bundy ranch to show their support against possibly illegal acts perpetrated on the American people by U.S. Government Agents.

And, more importantly, protesters came to stand up for the God-given civil rights of every American citizen as protected by the U.S. Constitution. Many of these patriots came knowing that if it could happen to the Bundys, then it could happen to them. Others had already experienced first-hand the Feds unjust abuse of power and authority over them.

Still, some just came to support their neighbor. Did some bring guns? Sure. Nevada has a long-standing tradition of being an 'open-carry' state, meaning, unless local ordinances prohibit it, guns are allowed on your person, as long as they are in "plain sight." But, by far, most of the 2,000 people (accumulating over time) who showed up to protest the government action and support the Bundy's rights were not armed. One thing is sure, never was this an armed assault, as was alleged through the narrative created by Federal Government and broadcast by the sensation-hungry (useful idiots?) media outlets.

"Never once was a gun pointed at Federal Agents.[6] Not one rock was thrown nor one drop of blood spilled by the protesters," stated Davey Bundy.

To contrast, the only evidence the Government could show at the first and second trials was their own Federal Agents raising and pointing their weapons at unarmed American families, including women and children.

Meanwhile, federal prosecutors, in a desperate attempt to re-write, re-spin, and re-characterize the true events of that Saturday, renamed the line of protesters, calling it a "skirmish line" and / or "combat

---

6 Authors Note: The first two trials of Bundy, et al. v. United States, the defense was able to prove that none of the protesters pointed a gun at agents. Even the famous picture of Eric Parker (one of The Bundy 19) laying prone on the freeway overpass was not actually pointing a guns at anyone, but instead posing for the camera's.

214

line," saying the horses were a "cavalry," while the spectators on the highway bridge above them were "spotters" for "snipers." This is exactly the kind of psycho-sensation-babble spin these Feds sought with which to capture the media narrative and thus, frame the events in order to advance their 'Lord of the State' (police state) agenda. No wonder the American people are protesting!

Even more telling, Special Agent in Charge Dan Love was forced to admit under oath (October 23, 2017) that the 'Communication Plan' was changed to make the BLM out to be the "victims" rather than law enforcement by his superiors in Washington after the "Standoff" concluded.

That same day, National Park Service announced it was expanding its closure area to include St. Thomas, Overton Beach, and Stewarts Point. Contract crews and BLM Ranger vehicles passed, at high speed, through the Moapa Valley community throughout the day bringing cattle out of the National Park area.

At around noon, Wednesday, Nevada Senator Dean Heller released a statement expressing "great disappointment with the way that this situation is being handled."

> *Law-abiding Nevadans must not be penalized by an over-reaching BLM.*
>
> *I remain extremely concerned about the size of this closure and disruptions with access to roads, water and electrical infrastructure. I will continue to closely monitor this situation, and urge the BLM to make the necessary changes in order to preserve Nevadans' constitutional rights.*

Later that evening, over 300 people attended a local Moapa Valley Town Advisory Board meeting where Cliven Bundy gave a presentation. Over two hours of public comment ensued during the meeting, mainly in support of Bundy. State legislators stated publicly that Governor Sandoval was fully engaged working behind the scenes to bring a solution to the impasse.

A total of 75 head of cattle were reported gathered on Wednesday.

Thursday, April 10 – Tensions Escalate

The BLM quietly took down its "First Amendment" areas. BLM officials said they had heard the Governor's concerns and "made some adjustments" in their practices.

"We are allowing people to congregate on public land as long as they don't inhibit the operation," said BLM state director Amy Lueders in a conference call with reporters on April 10th.

The crowds continued to grow at the Bundy's Ranch and protest site.

The issue became a national debate as State lawmakers across the western United States - mostly Tea Party Republicans or Libertarians and patriot groups - expressed public support for Bundy.

In addition, a call to arms went out over the internet within the Oath Keepers (a non-partisan association of current and formerly serving military, police, and first responders, who pledge to fulfill the oath all military and police take to 'defend the Constitution against all enemies, foreign and domestic'), and within other militia groups for armed militia members in places like Montana, Arizona, Utah and other western states, to gather at the Bundy Ranch to provide protection to the protesters against federal brutality.

Two brothers from St. George, Utah were detained and cited by federal authorities on Thursday afternoon for climbing under a gate and entering a closure area at Overton Beach in the Lake Mead National Recreation Area. The two men, identified as Tyler and Spencer Shillig, were held for about an hour and released. They received citations for interfering with a BLM agency function, disorderly conduct and violent behavior.

Pete Santilli, an independent journalist and radio host from Ohio, had been following the story (Santilli was eventually named in the 2016 indictment and was held along with Cliven as one of The Bundy 19). Although Pete claims a significant role in the Bundy reaction to the roundup, a very surprised Cliven Bundy told me, when we were reviewing the developing manuscript, "Pete is claiming that he's a liaison between me and BLM. Well, I never even knew this happened until I read it in your book, here! So, all this is totally new to me. I knew Pete was sticking his nose in things a little bit, but never knew that this thing ever happened here, so this was a whole new thing. The main thing is, I never gave him permission or told him to do anything, you know?"

Pete was able to secure an interview with Special Agent Dan Love in an attempt to deescalate the tensions. Here is a portion of transcript of the conversation (It has been edited for clarity).

Pete Santilli: I think that everybody's on to and I wanna relay the question and you just respond to it appropriately. Where are the cattle?

Dan Love: In town.

Pete Santilli: I know. Specifically, is it here?

Dan Love: No, we've got them. They're undisclosed. We've got it.

Pete Santilli: Okay, why is it undisclosed?

Dan Love: Because we don't want to create a flash point for conflict. You guys have shown that this isn't about lawful demonstration, this is about...

Pete Santilli: Hold on a second. Hold on a second. Come here for a second.

Dan Love: I got it.

Pete Santilli: I want to make sure I get this right, if you don't mind. You want to avoid conflict?

Dan Love: Absolutely.

Pete Santilli: Okay, okay.

Dan Love: Look, we're all about free speech. I mean that's the same constitution. The one, the very amendment you speak of, we defend. So, we understand free speech, we get it, but you know, people holding rocks above their head to throw at police officers…

Pete Santilli: All right. We have to talk our way through this. I have to be the liaison to talk our way through this. We want zero, and I mean zero, conflict. Confrontational, nose-to-nose, I mean the conversations we're have because ... You guys we're all freaking doing your jobs. You believe you're doing what's constitutional. We're defending and we're having a discussion. We're defending their rights as well. If we really believe that heavily in what we're doing, it's their rights as well. They have families. They've got jobs. They've got bosses that say, "You're going to follow orders."

If they're unconstitutional orders that's a different scenario. You debate it somewhere else. But we're going to have these face-to-face confrontations in the following fashion.

For instance, I'll give you just a scenario. I'm not saying operationally what we're going be doing. Let's say as a result of the media hell storm, you know what's going on with the media hell storm, right?

Dan Love: Right.

Pete Santilli: We've had 20 satellite trucks already, and it's going go ten fold. As a result of that, now we have thousands and thousands and thousands of people and I think I've mentioned that this was going to be coming about. So hopefully you understand that I've seen this escalate to this point. Now we know we're going to get thousands and thousands of people, they're all going to be coming. So, what are we going to do with those people?

Let's say, for instance, if the decision is made to line up in single file ten thousand people, and then they come right here. One by one, everybody addresses you guys and says, "Let the cattle go." Are we going here screaming at you? You're going to be tasing? Is there going be that type of confrontation? What we're trying to do with this to completely get de-escalated. 100 percent.

So I'm here to tell you this warning. Okay, what we want to do to make sure that there is zero conflict, we now have political support. And I mean big, big time.

We have sheriffs, constitutional sheriffs.

Dan Love: Sheriff Mack? I know who Sheriff Mack is.

Pete Santilli: Sheriff Mack is coming out to hear our problems, and Sheriff Mack…

Dan Love: I know exactly who he is.

Pete Santilli: Right. We have political representatives on the congressional level.

Dan Love: Very familiar.

Pete Santilli: Yes. If, and this is what we're going to ask for, to de-escalate and make sure that we're not in that confrontation with you. What you're doing, you're taking care of your family and you're doing your absolute right job and we've got energy at this level. When the media's here you're gonna be in trouble. You're gonna think of your uncomfortable position if we start being belligerent. You're gonna be doing your job, we believe we're doing our job. That's gonna force a bad situation. So want to let you know we're going to come here, and it's gonna be non-negotiable, okay?

Dan Love: Less constitutional.

Pete Santilli: What we believe in and what we believe are political authorities and law enforcement authorities believe it's the right thing to do. If that situation comes about, we want to make sure that…

Dan Love: Go ahead.

Pete Santilli: …any individual is given that opportunity to stand down. That they won't [inaudible 00:04:14] and as an individual, if you make the decision…

Dan Love: Yeah, that's not going to happen. So here's the deal. So…

Pete Santilli: No, wait, wait, wait.

Dan Love: No, I'm done here Santilli. So let me explain this

219

to you.

Pete Santilli: I have to…

Dan Love: I understand where you think you're doing what's right.

Pete Santilli: No, no, no, no.

Dan Love: The constitution you speak of, we actually have two federal court orders issued by two federal judges or interfere you will be arrested. You impede, you interfere with US attorney, I got off the phone with Main Justice out of D.C. today, you impede or interfere you will be taken into custody.

Pete Santilli: Okay, tell D.C. Justice this is non-negotiable.

Dan Love: And I'm telling you this…

Pete Santilli: Hold on a second, this is non-negotiable. This message is not communicating well. [inaudible 00:04:54] Come about. If it escalates after this point, after what I've just expressed to you. If you make the decision to not accept the fact that we will be trying to get people help. That if you stand down, you're believe that standing for the constitution is the right thing to do, you've got a very nice lady standing here and you're turning your back to the situation, but you're not going to lose your job, okay? But if you chose to go face to face and people get hurt we're going to hold you personally accountable.

Dan Love: And I will hold you legally accountable and I guarantee you that the constitution is on my side, not that side.

Pete Santilli: That's not a guarantee.

Dan Love: Oh, I guarantee you.

Pete Santilli: But see, that's where you…

Dan Love: I guarantee you.

Pete Santilli: I don't want to have…

Dan Love: I'm the one that has sworn an oath in office. From

220

the U.S. Government and I'm going to uphold that.

Pete Santilli: But, we are, that's why it's non-negotiable.

Dan Love: That piece that you're talking about, that's in a court of law. You don't decide that on a...

Pete Santilli: You don't...

Dan Love: The constitutions aren't decided on the dirt.

Pete Santilli: Tell D.C. it's a...

Dan Love: Yeah, but [inaudible 00:06:17] the law, you will be taken into custody.

Pete Santilli: You're impeding the U.S. Constitution.

Dan Love: Mr. Santilli, I appreciate that you're absolutely right. You can fight that argument from jail if you choose to take that action.

Pete Santilli: It's not going to be a fight; it's going to be a non-negotiable term peacefully...

Dan Love: Yeah, I'm not...

Pete Santilli: If you bring...

Dan Love: I'm very clear as to what the terms are. I want you to hear me. You interfere, you impede, you will be arrested. Are we clear? Again, you interfere or impede you will be arrested. I don't know how you plan on arresting me, but good luck with that.

Pete Santilli: Well, there's going to be some law enforcement officials that are going to be going to jail if they're unconstitutional.

Dan Love: Okay, yeah. Don't do that. That's not going to end well for you.

Pete Santilli: I'm not going to do that.

Dan Love: Yeah, that doesn't happen and I've seen your

numbers right now. You'd better hope the ten thousand show up. Because if you show up with those numbers, we got plenty of people here to take all those people to jail. So don't do that.

Pete Santilli: Sir, please this is not ... Okay, don't challenge us.

Dan Love: I'm telling you right now. I'm telling you not to interfere or impede. You're telling me you're going to show up and arrest officers? That's not going to happen.

Pete Santilli: I didn't say I was going to do that.

Dan Love: It's not going to happen.

Pete Santilli: If anyone is unconstitutional, is not following by the U.S. Constitution they are going to be arrested, including the sheriff of this town.

Dan Love: Okay, well you can start with him. Go arrest "Uncle Espie." Once you accomplish that, you come back.

Pete Santilli: He will still be incarcerated if he fails and refuses to uphold his oath to the U.S. Constitution.

Dan Love: You let me know when that occurs.

Pete Santilli: He will go to jail.

Dan Love: Okay, let me know when that occurs. Once that occurs, let's you and I have a discussion about what the next step looks like.

Pete Santilli: Right.

Dan Love: All right.

Pete Santilli: We don't want anyone to come here aggressive, okay; it's not under aggression. You can turn your back.

Dan Love: No one's turning their back.

Pete Santilli: You have the option.

Dan Love: No. You have the option not to create any conflict and I'm telling you right now. I'm putting you on a warning, okay, you on warning as the messenger: If you violate, you impede, you interfere with two lawful court orders you will be prosecuted, you will be arrested.

Pete Santilli: They're unlawful court orders.

Dan Love: Sir, again, I appreciate that. You are not a judge; you are not a lawyer.

Pete Santilli: But me personally, if I was going to be that person that you would be addressing. That you believe that I'm impeding, okay?

Dan Love: You will lawfully go into custody, under the constitution. You can go before a federal magistrate; you can argue your case about the lawfulness of court orders.

Pete Santilli: I did not come here to do anything, but to give you the opportunity to prevent a scenario where you're going to make a decision to cause harm to people.

Dan Love: Again, that decision will be made by your supporters in that camp.

Pete Santilli: Your presence has incited...

Dan Love: No our presence we're lawfully here. Look, you see all these signs? You're in a closed area; you're on federal land. You don't have to like it, it is the law.

Pete Santilli: It is not federal land.

Dan Love: It is federal land.

Pete Santilli: You think so?

Dan Love: I'm positive.

Pete Santilli: I'll bet you lunch.

Dan Love: Mr. Santilli, if you were right, I wouldn't have a job. So you know what? Be right, get everything changed, and then I'm happy not to wear this little blue shield that I have on my hip.

Pete Santilli: You're managing it. You're not the owner of the land.

Dan Love: Go get Gillespie. If that is your theory, do it the legal way. Go get the sheriff, come on down with the sheriff.

Pete Santilli: It's not a theory, that's what I'm saying. You've been misinformed.

Dan Love: Okay then make it happen. Where is he then?

Pete Santilli: Do you know how dangerous it is?

Dan Love: Where is he Santilli?

Pete Santilli: All I want to say is, you know how dangerous it is for you to run around with a gun and badge with what you just told me? That you think it's theoretical? That you actually believe that you have the constitution and the law behind you, and the entitlement? And you have a badge and a gun?

Dan Love: Yeah, we do have the constitution, sorry.

Pete Santilli: I'm very concerned at this point.

Dan Love: I'm very concerned, too.

Pete Santilli: I'm going to tell you. You're actually with confidence at this point, you're basing everything on the numbers, is that what you said?

Dan Love: Again, we are very confident we will continue to do what's lawful in this country. If you come here, impede, you interfere, you don't obey lawful orders, you will be taken into custody and prosecuted. Period.

Pete Santilli: Okay, you have the opportunity to avoid an unnecessary conflict.

Dan Love: Impede, interfere, or violate the law you will be taken into custody.

Pete Santilli: Respectfully, I'm just trying to give you the option.

Dan Love: We're not coming down there. You don't see us down at his house. See us on his private property? See us on anybodys private property? We're on federal land, which is managed by the United States Government. Something I think you can appreciate.

Pete Santilli: Managed by the United States Government.

Dan Love: Managed.

Pete Santilli: Managed.

Dan Love: Owned by the public. Managed by the United States Government, gives us our legal authority to be here. Again, if you come unlawfully, you impede, you interfere, you will be arrested. Non-negotiable.

Pete Santilli: Okay.

Dan Love: Seems fairly simplistic. Right?

Pete Santilli: Yes. Make the right decision.

Dan Love: You do as well.

It appeared that de-escalation was not in the cards for Dan Love. Pete Santilli was trying to get Love to understand that the Bundy Protest was beginning to escalate beyond family and friends of the Bundys. National and international media was taking an interest and social media was beginning to blow up, with over one million views from the videos that had been posted of Davey's arrest and the assaults on Margaret and Ammon. And, of course, the First Amendment areas were becoming explosive issues as well.

Additionally, Love's superiors were taking notice of the protest size and media attention being gained and decided to cease the operation. It seemed unpalatable that so many lawmakers were criticizing the BLM actions and as the BLM director of media relations stated, they never seemed to be able to get ahead of the narrative that the media was carrying by saying "it was frustrating." It's also clear that this order was received by Love, because as revealed in the October 25, 2017 (and following), testimony – under oath – of the BLM agents

who ran the Communications Center and the Operation's Agent
Dispatch desk therein, the agents in the Communication Center at
the BLM compound were ordered to start packing up and shredding
documents on April 10th. Note: this was two full days before the
events of the "Standoff" on the coming the Saturday.

The BLM reported rounding up 25 head of cattle on Thursday.

Friday, April 11
Momentum continued to build for the Protest near the Bundy Ranch.
People continued to arrive from all over the country and beyond to
join in the demonstration. This included heavily armed and equipped
militia members from all over the western U.S.

A group of five armed militia members from Prescott, Arizona, offered
to act as Cliven Bundy's personal security detail. They had arrived at
3:00 a.m. on Friday morning.

In Las Vegas, three southern Nevada Tea Party groups organized
another protest event outside Las Vegas sheriff's headquarters on
Friday morning. The group called upon Sheriff Gillespie to "do his
job" and protect the Bundy family.

Friday evening, National Park Service officials announced that the
closure on the west side of the Overton Arm at Lake Mead had been
lifted. "Lands near St. Thomas and Stewarts Point are now open in
time for the Clark County Fair and Rodeo," the statement read.

On that same Friday, BLM Director Kornze approved the final
decision to terminate the operation and ordered the agents to pull out.
The decision was made based on an intervention on Sheriff Gillespie's
part to end the roundup operations. He just didn't feel any cow was
worth any human injury. BLM Deputy Director Steve Ellis (retired
2016) stated, "The optics of this is going to be horrible ... We did not
anticipate those large numbers of people coming ... "Surrounded by
people with guns ... I was thinking of how serious this has become ...
It's not worth it to get anybody hurt ... So, I told them to pull out, to
pull out now ... They can gloat all they want, but everyone went home

safe, I also knew the wheels of justice would start turning, that was not the end of it."[7]

But that night, according to the testimony of Dan Love on October 25, 2017, Love had a conference call with the U.S. Attorney Dan Bogden in Las Vegas. Together, they planned how they would bring Cliven to justice. If they could get Cliven to be the one to release the cattle – or "Pull the Pin" (which meant to remove the pin on the gate holding the cattle) as it was referred to – then they felt they could charge him with impeding a federal officer in his duties and then tie Cliven and his boys into a conspiracy in relationship to all the other charges of weapons and assault of The Bundy 19.

The BLM reported rounding up 12 head of cattle on Friday.

7 PBS Documentary "American Patriot" May 16, 2017 http://www.pbs.org/wgbh/frontline/film/american-patriot-inside-the-armed-uprising-against-the-federal-government/

Chapter 10
– THE ~~PROTEST~~ "STANDOFF" –
Disaster averted

Saturday, April 12, 2014

It had been a long week and Cliven's 67-year-old body was feeling the effects. His mind and spirit were responding similarly. The night before he had watched a disconcerting video of a shooting of a civilian by the BLM Rangers near The Red Rock State Park entrance.[1] He was tired and feeling embattled from the previous weeks activities. It was about 5:30 AM as he rolled out of bed and his feet touched the cool floor. He began his day, as every day, with some time alone in prayer and scripture reading. But today before he began, he needed to wash his face and the 'sleep out of his eyes,' as his mom would say.

Heading into the kitchen, Carol was aware of the stirring family (sons and daughters) and friends inside the house and of those who were camped outside the house at the Bundy Ranch headquarters. Carol, always concerned for others' comfort, began breakfast for the myriad of sleeping bodies lying about the house. The house looked like someone had moved an office into the main area of the house, with whiteboards on the walls, makeshift tables, chairs, and stools crowded near each. To make room, the household items seemed tossed to the side in a hurried fashion. However, on careful observation, one could see each of these items had been carefully placed, not haphazardly thrown about. The household items were well cared for out of respect for their owners. The sleeping bodies were all those who had come in support, spending days coordinating massive volume of phone calls, text messages, emails, and social media. They, too, were exhausted.

Out on the front porch, several of the private militiamen taken up their positions, as they had around the house, as well. These men were deeply concerned for the Bundy family's safety, especially Cliven's. Hundreds of people had arrived throughout the night, most of whom the Bundy's had never met. The militiamen were not only concerned about the Federal agents' military operations around the house, but also with the mounting security concerns over those

---

1 https://www.reviewjournal.com/local/local-las-vegas/red-rock-henderson-police-fatal-shootings-ruled-justified-video/

arriving. They recognized immediately that some of those arriving had 'different motives' than to protest the Sheriff. As such, they organized themselves as bodyguards for the Bundy household. Cliven told me at Pahrump, that "I really respect 'em militia men ... they gave up their lives back at home, sometimes for weeks, well after the Protest, to protect me and my family. I didn't even know 'em; but they came to protect me! And they asked for noth'n in return. They didn't even want to come in the house, 'cuz they didn't want to be bother'n us. They just took shifts on my porch, camping there. And they did it for day after day after that day (referring to April 12th) ... they were just plain gentlemen."

The morning progressed. In order to focus and pray, Cliven took his breakfast in his room. He could feel that something was stirring; he wasn't quite sure what, but he was certain something was happening, certain something beyond his understanding was about to break.

About 7:45 am there came a knock at his door. It was Ammon.

"Dad, the Sheriff is on the phone and he wants to see you privately."

There was a pause; Cliven didn't know what to think.

"He says he wants to meet with you at the house."

Cliven paused. "Tell Sheriff Gillespie I'll meet him at the stage at 9:00 am and he can tell 'We the People' what he has to say."

Curious at his response, I asked, "Why did you do that?"

"Mike, when I get up each morning and I spend my time with my Heavenly Father, I don't have a plan on what I'll do. I just believe that I am following what He wants me to do as the day come along."

"Okay…" Puzzled, I asked, "Wait, what does that mean here?"

He paused a moment, then continued. "It means that I felt that The Father was saying he (the Sheriff) needed to tell *the People* what his plans were, not me. This had gone beyond just the two of us."
"What did you do next?" I asked, wanting to hear more.

"I went back to reading my scripture." He smiled.

"Well, then what?" I was getting anxious now.

Cliven continued with Ammon's reply:

"Dad, he wants you to know about some developments from last night."

"Just tell 'em to meet me at the stage at 9:00 am."

And with that, Ammon had left to tell the Sheriff.

"That was it?" I asked.

Cliven paused again, thinking back at that specific moment in his life. "You know, I just wasn't in the mood for more talk. My family had been trapped, under siege, in our family home. They'd sicced dogs on us, tased Ammon, thrown my sister on the ground, had us surrounded by snipers, and an army! After all that, it was time to stop talking and they needed to leave," he said sternly, clearly recalling the moment, "and I expected the *SHERIFF* to do it!"

I was taken aback. As a first in our time together, Cliven had revisited his emotions of the moment and it surprised me. Had I pushed him too hard or was he just projecting those emotions of that morning towards me? Then he paused again, turned his head and smiled that big cowboy grin, eyebrows raised and eyes mischievously looking up at me. He had allowed those feelings to surface. He was smiling because he realized he just let me see another side of him. Cliven is a man who is measured, thoughtful, and not given to quick emotional expression. But, in that moment, I could see there was also anger – a righteous anger – in his heart for what happened on April 12, 2014. He wasn't angry about his circumstances sitting there in Pahrump. He was angry the government of the country he loved would behave in such a way.

The events of day of the Standoff were in motion. Still at home, another 45 minutes or so passed and Cliven was ready to head to the Stage area. He had just nibbled on his breakfast, as he and Carol got ready. The militia pulled a Humvee around to the house gate to escort Cliven and Carol the short drive to the stage area. This is where the gathered protesters would hear from Cliven and begin the day's activities.

They bounced down the dusty ranch road and turned onto SR 170 on the way to the staging area. Cliven was stunned at the amount of people that had arrived. There were cars and trucks from numerous states all bumping along that same road, headed the same direction. There were also people walking along the road, families with little children and teenagers, all dressed patriotically. With flags in hand and smiles on their faces, you would have thought they were heading to an Independence Day fireworks display.

As he and Carol neared the staging area, he saw many horses with cowboys and cowgirls astride, some waiving massive flags in the wind. About 50 horsemen had come from all over the west to join in the Protest. Most had come from northern Utah and Nevada, many were ranchers who had had 'run ins' with the BLM over the mismanagement of the wild horse problem in the northern part of these two states. These ranchers felt that riding their horses was an appropriate statement to make to the government. In the early morning hours, they chose to load up their horses in their trailers and made the trip to the Bundy Ranch to make a stand alongside Cliven.

Cliven could also see that Sheriff Gillespie and a handful of officers had arrived, waiting for him and to share the news together with the gathering crowd.

The Stage
At 8:30 am, as the people and the media gathered in front of the stage, Ammon took the stage, wearing just a black T-Shirt, denim pants, and a straw cowboy hat. He fidgets, a little uncomfortable with public speaking. An opening prayer was offered, followed with the Pledge of Allegiance. Then Ammon began a testimony of the week's events.

The gathered friends and family quieted down, intent on what Ammon would say.

"I just wanted to thank everybody for being here, and just talk about the events of what's gone on the last week. It's been amazing what's gone on, as many of you and all of you are aware. What's been most amazing is the people of this country and their response to this, and how many of us were in kind of our own little world, thinking that we had these thoughts and these beliefs, but there wasn't very many people out there that had the same thoughts and the same beliefs. We had these problems and these challenges; but, we might be the only ones in our area, or our communities … might be the only ones that are having this problem, and through this, we know that it's not that. We know that the over-reaching Federal Government is in all the states, and that's why we're here. That's why we've united. We're certainly making a statement, right?"

Hoots and hollers erupted from the crowd in response.

"I also want to talk a little bit about our feelings. When we, a week ago, when I rolled in here, I rolled in right here, and my brothers had these flags all set up, and it was pretty amazing. We did it with a little rundown forklift, and those wires are barbless barbwire coming down here, and I came in here, and I was pretty proud of what they did. I love the sign, and I was ready to fight, and I looked up on those hills, and they were completely occupied, and we were under martial law by an unauthorized agency.

"That's the way it was. If we stepped off the road, they would pounce off on them and shove our faces in the dirt, and to have that feeling, I've never had it before in this country. To have the feeling of freedom taken away from you, my friends, it is not a good feeling. It is not a good feeling.

"My family and the community have run these hills and enjoyed these hills for generations. Never once, in this history of this nation, have those mountains ever been restricted from us. Never. And yet, this week, they were.

"So, a battle began. A battle on the roadside where my brother was taken down by about 20 Agents and taken to a Federal jail, and we had to battle for him, and then they didn't even prosecute him, just dumped him out on the street once they knew that everybody was going to make a big enough scene, right?

"We had another young man down here that pulled off on this little road right here. He's done it his whole life. He's 16 years old, and they surrounded him and began to do the same thing. Then, we had about 30 or 40 people over here, and we headed over there as fast as we could and we backed them down. We pushed them off. That's what we did."

Again, the crowed hooted and hollered, along with amens and hallelujahs.

"And then we had another incident, after they had cleared all the cattle up here, we had to deal with their helicopters, and their snipers, and their rifles, and their guards, and all of that garbage, we had to deal with that here, for almost a week, while they gathered <u>our</u> personal properties to sell. And then, to top it off, they had the gall to take a backhoe and a dump truck and go up there and destroy these waters that have been out here over 100 years.

"So, we decided to put an end to that; but, we were up against 13 armored vehicles … these men were highly armed, and they had dogs. We went down there, and we backed them off and we found out what was in the back of that truck, and then we sent them packing. And yeah, there were some fatalities … Not fatalities. There were some people hurt and some things happened; but, we did it peacefully in the sense that we were just pushing back … and just pushing back … and that we did what we had to do, and then, we sent them packing.

"We showed them at that time that the people have the power. When united, we have the power."

The crowd applauded and cried out "Yes!" in reply.

"Friends, this battle is not over, and it's not over here. Okay? And the war is just begun. But, I also want to say this … I know we have a huge variety of people here, and many of you have different faith. Or many of you consider that you have no faith. But, I'm here to tell you that the American People, the American People to God, whatever you may call him. He is a … We have a Creator, and that Creator is looming over us, and caring for us, and He is leading this fight, okay?

"I'd like to just explain something. That Creator wants us to choose Him. He does not want us, He does not force us, to choose Him. In order for us to choose Him, what do we have to have?

"Well, yeah, freedom. We have to have the agency to choose Him, right? So, agency is most important to our Creator, otherwise we cannot choose Him, and His hand has been all over this, this battle. His protection has been all over this, and I'm telling you that this battle is at the point, and you guys are going to find this out soon, this battle's at the point where we, the people in this area, have nothing to fear. Okay? We have nothing to fear."

At that, more shouts of "Amen!" and "Praise God!" erupted from the audience.

"We can carry our weapons if we like, right?" (The crowd yells in reply "Yes we can!") Because we have the Second Amendment Right. And those are God-given rights, thank you. Those are rights. Those Second Amendment Rights are just rights that are inevitably given to us, and we wrote them down on paper and said, "We're going to respect these rights." So, those are our rights, but ...

"I say; but because, we don't have to carry them right now because we're afraid, okay? I'm telling you that right now. There's been a lot of people that are afraid, and I know that feeling. Just a few days ago, just yesterday, even, just yesterday evening, I was really afraid.

"I was, and my family's had a lot of manipulation going on; but, you know what? Today, we have been confirmed from our Creator that we do not need to be afraid. Okay? This is His battle. This is His battle."

Applause and cheers erupted as Ammon ends his speech.

"I was wondering if my Uncle Steve would come up here 'en talk to us? And I know I'm putting him totally on the spot, and that's a big group; but, I also know where his convictions are and his dedication to freedom is, and I would like him to come up and talk to us."

Waiting on his uncle, Ammon continued.

"Just so you know what's going on is, we're waiting for our County Sheriff to join us. And my father is coming, and they're going to talk about something that we don't know, because the Sheriff called my dad. He said, 'I want to talk to you. Can we go in a back room and talk?'

"And my dad said, 'No. If we're going to have this dialogue, we're going to have a dialogue in front of the people.'

"So, my dad doesn't know what the Sheriff is coming to talk about. He does not know, and so it will be a true dialogue. The only thing I ask is that we be respectful. I know we have ... We realize he has not stood up to what his Constitutional duties are. We know that; but, let's just hear him out, and let's see what he has to say, and let them have that dialogue, and then we'll know where we're at when we're done, okay?

"I'm going to turn the time over to my uncle, Steve."

Cliven's brother-in-law, Steve Kelly, took the stage.

"I'm even less of a speaker than Ammon claims to be and he's done really well. So I'm in a bad situation, but ... I just want to tell you people how proud I am to see what's happened here from Monday morning, I come down here and there were three of us, and you could count 50 armed vehicles. We have snipers on these hills up here, and I had that feeling of desperation, that our freedoms are gone."

From the crowd, murmurs of surprise mixed with boos rumbled.

"I don't know how we'll ever see them back again. How do you ever get back what you let slip away like that?"

"We take it back!" someone in the crowd yelled.

Steve Kelly continued. "I don't want to see any violence; because as soon as I turn to violence, I abandon what I believe as the basis of our country, as a country of law."

"Live free or die!" another yelled. Others echoed the sentiment.

Steve continued. "The order of law provides us that freedom, and if we don't support that order of law, and if we don't manage it as a free people, we lose it. As I look at that, I have seven sons and I have a bunch of them, and one is on one side, and one's on another, and the bottom line is, is we have a common interest in our freedom, and I see our whole society being picked apart by forcing us into little groups that won't stand together.

"You got this group over here and they're worthless, and this group over here, and they're this, and they're that, and this is that, and everybody's divided. Everybody has some kind of conflict that they can't stand up for the other one, and this divides our society from being able to stand here, and I see people from every walk of life standing here, and this has changed my life from Monday until today."

"My feeling about my…, and about the hope we have for our country, and how great it could be again. These types of regulations are turning us into a third world country. And it's not just the man, it's education. It's our food supply. I work in the timeshare industry. They're regulating us out of business. There's paperwork for every little thing. 'Where's your trash going? Where's your documentation?'

"And we've taken care of it, forever, without them. Why do we now have to pay them to come tell me how to do what I'm doing? They come and ask you, "What are you doing here?" And then they come back and tell you how to do it and how to document it. Well, this kind of regulation divides us, Cliven was at odds because he hasn't paid range fees, and that's one of the most negative things in this thing is that range fees weren't paid; but, they wouldn't be accepted, and under regulation, right now, there's not a person standing here, a business in this country, that can't be destroyed through federal regulation harassment.

"It's the IRS, it's OSHA, it's your ... It's everywhere you live. And if we're going to make a difference in our country, we need to correct this. What started here started with the EPA. I was in the federal courts in Las Vegas when the ranchers scraped together enough money to try to appeal the ruling for them to remove their cattle off of this land. "They said, 'You're ruining us. We can't remove these cattle the only time of year there's any decent feed.' They appealed it to the Federal

Court. They hired one lawyer. Karen Budd-Falen was her name, from Colorado. She stood up there and made a case that documented that the ranchers had improved the range. There were more turtles than before, that the range is more productive, and not only that, they're producing a commodity that benefits all of society off of a desert. There's only a couple people I know that's tough enough to live out here and make something worthwhile out of it.

"But, this Federal judge was under the Clinton Administration, and he stood up and said, 'I'm finding in favor of the ranchers.' And during this whole case, the lawyers, the State of Nevada's lawyers, the Conservation Group ... We had all the 'greenies' there ... Every one of their lawyers got up to speak any time anything was said. And after they had lost the case, obviously, they stood up and the only thing they had to say was, 'You have no jurisdiction over EPA law, and there were no rights to oppose the EPA in any regulation. You have no federal recourse in the law.'

"And he had a situation where he's already paid for the grazing out here. This fee that they're charging him is just an arbitrary fee, they say, 'Well, you can put this many cows out there and it's going to cost you this much.' And next week, it's something else. And then next week, it was, 'Well, you could have put out 150 cows. Now, you can put out 50.' And you can either comply or go out of business as they've done to all the ranchers around, all the people on the mountain. They want to be able to completely be able to control what's in regulation.

"I don't know that that's their plan; but, that's what's happened to our country, and one at a time they can take out anyone in this country that opposes them, and you can bet your license plates and your faces are now on the Federal Registry."

A crowd member hollered, "Good!"

"Would you be surprised if you're audited?" Steven responded.

"No. I'm waiting for it," the crowd member hollered back.

Steve continued. "Anyway. I'm carrying on. I get ... I'm going in the wrong direction with you people. What I'm saying is, is that when people of a common interest stand together, whether it's in the Lord's name, 'Two or three gather in My name, I'll be there.' Whether it's in the name of freedom, we gather together and stand *because* of our differences, not in spite of them. They got us standing separately, all the time.

"If we can get that message out, we have a chance to turn the direction of this country around, to get back to the greatness that this country was. Look at the change that we've made in the world with this freedom that's being taken away.

"We have raised the living standard, we have raised the conditions. We have, as a country, I can't do anything. I didn't even serve. My dad was World War I. He chased tanks across Europe. I'd lotteried out at 200 ... No ... 364 in a 365 lottery, so I didn't go to Vietnam, but there are plenty of people here that have seen the ultimate price paid for our freedom.

"I mean, people are willing, with one leg, have to have a house built so they can brush their teeth because they stood up for us. When our nation was called to stand, they were there, and I see you guys as exactly the same type of patriots. You see the need in this country right now, and you're here instead of watching the cartoons, you're watching sports, whatever. You your money to stand up.

"That's why we reclaim our country, and I'm going to quit talking. I'll be hoarse like Ammon.

"But God bless America!"

Mark Conner, a local entertainer and retired Marine, was asked to lead the group in the National Anthem. Ironically these lyrics come from *Defense of Fort McHenry,* a poem written on September 14, 1814, by the 35-year-old lawyer and amateur poet, Francis Scott Key, after he witnessed the bombardment of Fort McHenry by British Royal Navy ships in Baltimore Harbor.

"O say can you see, by the dawn's early light,

What so proudly we hail'd at the twilight's last gleaming,

Whose broad stripes and bright stars through the perilous fight

O'er the ramparts we watch'd were so gallantly streaming?"

                  … Mark belts out as the crowd joins in.

About this time, Cliven and Carol arrived at the staging area.

As the crowd continued in chorus, the horses filed across the
nearby bridge and one-by-one galloped up a nearby hill to line up
together across the skyline, led by the American flag. Most of the
other horsemen were carrying other flags; many of the states were
represented. The 'DON'T TREAD ON ME' – or Gadsden Flag – was
there, as well. The flag is named after American general and politician
Christopher Gadsden (1724–1805), who designed it in 1775 during
the American Revolution. The Continental Marines used it as an early
motto flag, along with the Moultrie flag in protest to the tyranny of the
British Government.

Today, it's a symbol for modern Americans who believe that America
has swung far from the intentions of the Founding Fathers in the
Constitution and the founding principles of the Bill of Rights. It
is clearly a statement to the Government of The United States as
Gadsden intended it to be.

Among the riders was a riderless horse, saddled with a pair of boots
facing in reverse in the stirrups. This horse symbolizes a 'warrior who
would ride no more.' This symbol honors a fallen military cavalry
officer during his memorial or funeral. That day the riderless horse
was "giving honor to all of America's fallen soldiers," said Cliven,
pointing this out.

As the horses completed their line-up at the top of the hill, a flock of
geese flew over in a V formation. It was likened to a fly-by of military
jets, bringing a conclusion to the performance.

"I think God was giving us a sign of His approval," Cliven told me in all seriousness. "The whole thing couldn't have been rehearsed and been any better."

Approximately 9:00 am, Cliven offered the stage to Sheriff Gillespie; neither man knew for sure what the other was going to say. To stage-right stood several Sheriff officers, across the front of the stage stood camouflage-dressed militiamen, standing as private security. On the stage stood a small podium draped in red, white and blue. A modest sound system had also been set up. And, of course, hundreds of protesters stood patiently awaiting directions for the day. What came next was a surprise to everyone, even the Bundys.

The Sheriff, in his standard tan colored uniform, took the microphone and stood behind the podium; Cliven stood just to the right of him.

Sheriff Gillespie began.

"Good morning." He cleared his throat. "My purpose out here this morning is to continue, from my standpoint, to keep a very emotional issue … safe. With that being said, I believe a press release has already been put forth that the BLM is going to cease this operation.

"The Gold Butte allotment will be reopened to the public. And they will be removing their assets."

The crowd roared with approval. "Immediately!" one yelled.

"Where's the cows?" another screamed from the back of the crowd.

Smiling, the Sheriff, continued.

"What I would hope to sit down with you," he looked at Cliven, "and talk about is how that is facilitated in a safe way, and you and I have had the ability to sit down and talk before on a number of occasions. We may not always agree, but we have been respectful to each other's opinion, and to the process. So, that's why I'm here, to start that with you, number one, to advise you of that, but I was advised when I was coming here, that that (statement) had already been released. I don't know if you or the people here were aware of that.

"The next step is something that I believe you and I should sit down and talk about."

Someone in the crowd yelled the question again: "Where's the cows?"

The Sheriff turned his head and looked at Cliven over his right shoulder. "So, I'll turn that back over to you, I guess… the last few days, and that's what needs to be discussed."

"You're holding them hostage to broker a deal!" someone said. "He wants their property back!" yelled another as the Sheriff steps aside.

Amid the cheers and the clapping due to the Sheriff's announcement, Cliven took the stage. He had his "Sunday go-to-meetings" on: a pressed western shirt and bolo tie, and a Cowboy hat. He began to speak while the crowd continued clapping.

"Good morning, citizens of Clark County, Nevada. Good morning, America. Good morning, world!" cheered Cliven Bundy.

"It's a good day in Bunkerville!" a man in the front cheered.

"It is. It's a beautiful day in Bunkerville," Cliven replied.

"Isn't this a beautiful land we live in, too? What do you think about the Virgin River? It looks pretty nice."

The crowd responded with more clapping.

Cliven looked down at his notes at this point.

"I'm here not to negotiate with the Sheriff, get some legs underneath him and help him along the way if we can, but let me tell you something. I woke up last night, I didn't know what I was going to do, I have a list, this morning, I knew when I woke up, and this is what

242

we, the people, are going to demand this morning.

"The Sheriff has said he's been negotiating with the BLM, and that's really nice. You know he's going to negotiate with 'We the People.' Okay, our first thing we're going to require of him ... I need to get my glasses back off. I'm able to talk a little bit this morning. That's pretty good."

"Another victory for God and the good guys!" someone in the crowd interrupted.

Cliven, turning to his left, directly addressed the sheriff. "Sheriff, this is what "We the People' are asking this morning.

He continued, speaking to the sheriff, "Disarm the park service at Red Rock Park and all other parks that the federal government claim to have jurisdiction over.

"Take your county bulldozers and loaders and tear down that entrance places, where they ticket us, and where the entrance and make us citizens plead and please, you gave them their ... You get the County the equipment out there and tear those things down this morning."

A voice from the crowd interrupts. "Immediately!" "Do your job, Sheriff!" another yelled. "We respect you, Sheriff, we respect your job. Do your job, Sir," a third yelled in agreement.

Amid the cheering Cliven said, "You disarm those park service people."

"Yeah, Sheriff, do your job!" another yelled.

Cliven pressed through the clapping and cheering. "You take a pick-up; but I want those arms. We want those arms picked up... Call Virgin Valley Disposal and go up here to this compound, and we want all of those arms put in that compound today. We want those arms delivered, right here under these flags, in one hour, and media..."

Another voice in the crowd, "Media, document it!"

"Are you here, media?" Cliven inquired, looking across the crowd. "I want you to go to every place that they got a Federal Park Service Station, and you watch those County machines tear down those places today in the next hour, and if you report back to these people, we, the people, in one hour. If they're not done, then we'll decide what we're going to do from this point on. Thank you."

Cliven stepped away from the podium. The Sheriff and his entourage of deputies left the stage and walked toward their patrol cars. Among the cheering crowd: "Freedom for USA!" "And bring his cows back!" "Where's the cows?" "Where's the stolen property?" "Follow the Constitution – that's all we ask."

Cliven quickly stepped back to the podium, "One hour. One hour. We're going to stand here for one hour." He wanted to be sure that Sheriff Gillespie understood his seriousness.

For the next hour, the crowd milled about. They sometimes chanted, and other times shouted out slogans. The enthusiasm and excitement was contagious as they waited.

At one point, Ammon took the microphone again. "I want to make sure everybody's clear that the Sheriff's come talk to me, and I said I'm not the negotiator. I'm not a negotiator, and I would never negotiate something that wasn't mine to negotiate."

The crowd responded to Ammon's statement: "Get 'er done." "We don't need the federal government to protect us." "Disarm them now." "We'll protect ourselves." "One hour!"

Another in the crowd spoke loudly above the clamor, as if he were on the stage giving a speech: "Ladies and gentlemen, you are watching history right now. You are watching history. This is how the people, this Federal Government… The Federal Government does not want our land. We, the people, want our land. God gave me this land, and we're going to freaking keep it."

The cheers of protest continued.

"Do your job, Sheriff! Get rid of the illegal guns at BLM now. They

244

have no permits. They have no rights to carry a weapon. They have no right to wear a badge."

"Get rid of the helicopters, too," another chimed in.

"Got one hour," yet from another.

"We don't need the federal government," still from another.

One of the reporters was doing a stand-up for the studio: "Just heard Cliven Bundy gave them one hour to disarm and take down the fee areas."

He had to stop as the crowd began to chant: "USA! USA!"

As it quiets down he tried to begin again: "What you see, live, the Sheriff has just finished speaking. Cliven Bundy gave him one hour to disarm the BLM. Then the posse rode in. I don't know if you can see it; but the guy who carried the flag to the top of the hill has now planted it up there, standing beside it with his horse. And here's the crowd, down here."

Then the crowd drowned him out again, chanting in unison: "Indivisible, with liberty and justice for all."

Another approached the stage and yelled to Cliven: "They're saying in the mainstream media that this has all been resolved and everything's good to go."

Someone else yelled: "That's what we heard, too. Everybody's headed home."

Cliven quickly took the microphone: "So, media, is that a lie you're putting out to the American people and the world, that we are all dispersed and we're over with this Protest? Media, if that's the kind of thing you're going to put out today when there's all these people, all these people, these people here on this land, America ... If that's what you're putting out, I feel sorry for you, media."

The reporter who had attempted the video report earlier yelled out:

"Mr. Bundy, can you restate what you told the Sheriff?"

Cliven, still behind the podium, answered; "I told the Sheriff he had one hour to bring those guns before us right here from the park service and the BLM and to tear down those (park) entries ... Where they charge us money to go on our land, and where they try to control us. I told him to tear down that booth over there where that boy, a few weeks ago, got killed, with rangers. That's the kind of thing we don't want no more. We don't want to be policed under these people. We're not going to put up with that no more."

The crowd chimed in: "No more!"

But Cliven continued, "They have one hour to take their bulldozers and knock those down. I wonder how the County Commissioners are handling that today?" He smiled.

A crowd member asked, "Are they taking pictures of it?"

"I need a report." Cliven told the crowd. Then asked, "Should we give him five more minutes?"

Crowd members chanted, "Five more minutes. Five minutes. If they don't come, increase the demand, Cliven."

Cliven's announcement interrupted the chants. "All we got to do is open the gate and let them (impounded cattle) back down on the river and their home."

Cliven spent a few minutes giving directions the crowd as to where they should proceed. The people with cars would need to merge onto Interstate 15, then off again onto a private road and park to proceed on foot. The lead cars would need to stop traffic so all the cars could safely merge, and then exit. The horses would need to take an access road the longer way around. About five miles in all total from the stage to the Toquop Wash, a sandy wash bed under the highway north and south bound bridges, where they intended to protest. As the crowd moved off to the wash, Clive, Carol and a few others stayed behind at the Staging area, just in case the Sheriff returned.

He completed his instructions with: "Get her going, cowboys. Let's go get 'er done"[2]

He and Carol remained at the stage that day, never going down to the wash and the site of the Protest.

Toquop Wash. *Saturday, April 12, 2014, approximately 11:00 am*
The cars were streaming off the highway and into a large dusty field to park; the crowd was vibrating with the enthusiasm from the stage. They were ready to get the cattle back and experience the victory for America for which they had hoped and prayed. As they walked the half-mile or so to the wash, the mood quickly changed.

As they began to spill out from the road unto the wash under the southbound bridge, the BLM had erected a barricade of panel fencing with no gate. On the other side were dozens of BLM and National Park Service officers in full military kit, taking a 'stacked' formation[3] (a shooting position used in military operations for offensive battle situations). Immediately, they began to command that the beginnings of the crowd disperse. They had their weapons up in firing position

2 Author's note: One reporter there quoted Cliven as saying 'Get yer guns." It was a misquote, presumably because he could not hear Cliven over the crowd.
3 http://www.military.com/forums/0,15240,79595,00.html
Author's Note: All of the "quotes" are taken from the actual transcript of what was said in each situation.

and did warn that the crowd would be fired upon. They were also, surrounded by 'over watch' spotters and snipers to coordinate a firing plan (according to court testimony of then-Special Agent in Charge Dan Love).

Ammon Bundy, being in that first group to arrive, immediately saw the dangers and called to the first dozens of protester to the side away from the line of fire to gather and pray. In the cell phone video of the group kneeling and praying, you could see the change from enthusiasm of the morning stage event to the serious trepidation with the situation they found themselves in at the wash. During that prayer, and after the prayer concluded, the crowd continued streaming into the wash.

Again, Ammon took charge and instructed the crowd wait and not advance on the barricade until all the crowd and horses had arrived. "Let get some courage and go as a group" Ammon shouted. A few of the militia started to trickle in. Ammon told the militia to disperse and leave the area (at least five times he told them to move away, according to court testimony). "No long guns, no camouflage," Ammon directed. He could see that their presence would be misunderstood, even threaten the federal agents.

Upon Ammon's instruction, the militia moved back, under the northbound bridge and away from the protesters, with some up under the shade of the bridge and over to the sides of the open area of the wash. As the crowd began to gather in mass they began to stretch out in a line across the wash. All the while, BLM agents continued to broadcast their commands over the loud speaker, though sometimes unintelligible from the two-football field distance from the crowd. As the crowd began to form a line across the wash, the media and photographers arrived. Reporter Dennis Michael Lynch, a freelance reporter for Fox News and documentary filmmaker, attempted to approach the barricade. He called out he is unarmed, that he is a reporter and he just wanted to get to hear BLM's side of the of why they are escalating the situation and intervene, if possible, on behalf of America. "This is Americans pointing automatic weapons at Americans, this just shouldn't be."

He advanced forward toward the barricade, stopping half way to lift his shirt and turn his body in a circle, in an attempt to demonstrate that he is unarmed and not a threat.

"We wish for this to end peacefully. We see you have no weapons." The voice over the loud speaker responded.

"I'll put the camera down. Can I approach? I have NO weapon. Are you really going to shoot these people if they move forward? Yes or No?" he cried out to the BLM agents assembled on the other side of the barrier.

"If you shoot me, you shoot me, I have no gun."

"Move back, move back now," came the agent's response.

Lynch pressed forward. "I'm asking you one question, SIR. We can't hear your announcements that far away, we can't hear it that's why I am coming to you."

"You are in violations of a United States District Court Order," came the response over the loud speaker.

"I do not have weapon… I'm from New York. May I approach so this doesn't end in bloodshed?" Lynch requested.

Then he shouted in frustration. "What is wrong with you? COME ON!" His New York accent was strong.

Later in a news interview on The Blaze, Lynch recounted that experience in the Toquop Wash that day.

In his work as an investigative journalist, "I have looked the Mexican Cartel in the face (on the U.S. border), I can tell you that this is the most nerve racking experience in my life. I really did think the people on the Bundy side were going to get hurt, I really did. Not because they wanted to start a fight. I have the proof in my video that these people wanted to go forward politely, in a non-violent way.

"Some of these guys had their M-16s point right at us. Me specifically, because, I was right out there on the front line. A lot had their guns down.

"They told me if I don't stop they'll shoot."

He went on to make the point that no one in the wash that day acted aggressively with their guns by pointing them or even taking them from their holster.

In asking to respond to the charge from Harry Reid that the Bundys were Terrorist, Lynch, responded in reflection; "The scene in Nevada was like a scene in Afghanistan. If there was any act of terrorism, it was perpetuated by the Government."[4]

---

4 The Blaze T.V. Interview https://www.youtube.com/watch?v=ImB0JztPWDo

Whether you think the government should have taken the cattle or not: "In America, we don't take M16 machine guns (sic the M16 is an automatic rifle, not a machine gun) and point them at Americans. That's what was happening in Nevada!"

Throughout the day many additional protesters arrived. Some had driven through the night and caught in the traffic jam that was created by the protester and the on-lookers that stopped on the overpasses. Law Enforcement was pouring into the area as well, units from Las Vegas, Mesquite, and the Nevada Highway Patrol. All the while, many other protesters would still not arrive until days, even weeks, later. Those that did arrive late on the 12th, as the protesters moved to the wash, came upon a scene with no real direction.

One of those late arrivals was Todd Engel, now one of The Bundy 19. Todd and I became friends while in Pahrump; he shared with me what was happening as he arrived. He described a scene of chaos as the traffic was stopped, and backed up for miles. When he arrived at the bridge, he could see a line of Las Vegas Metro deputies lining the median between the north and southbound highway. I asked him why were they there? He answered, "Oh, the 'crying line.' They were there to keep any of the spectators or protesters from crossing over to the opposing lane."

"Why do you call the line of deputies the 'crying line'?"

He smirked. "Because during my trial (the first trial), one Metro Officer after another took the witness stand and told the jury how that each and every officer in that line so feared for their safety that they had tears in their eyes. Sometimes sobbing uncontrollably. A couple of them even started crying again on the stand!"

"Why? I mean, were they under some sort of threat?" I asked.

"No, when you get home, look at the photos of the line. They were just standing there in regular uniforms, doing traffic duty. Bored to tears."

"Then why all the drama on the stand?" I pressed.

"Because they had been coached as to how to best support the

Government's case in its prosecution."

"So, they were lying under oath?" I asked the obvious question.

"I don't doubt they were worried how that day was going to turn out, but sobbing... PLEASE!" Todd answered sarcastically.

"So, how could you see them? Weren't you down in the wash with the others?" I went on.

Todd explained he had arrived late morning after driving straight through from Idaho. Coming upon the crowd, he quickly found a place to park and kitted up. He headed over to the northbound bridge to get an idea of the situation. As he gazed over he could see the line-up of protesters and the horses filing in to the wash. He could see the stacked position of the federal agents targeting the protesters. Also, he noticed only two other militia-looking individuals on the overpass, a few dozen feet further from him. He was standing erect, with the Jersey barrier just waist high in front of him. He was thinking, "These guys are screwed."

"Who?" I asked. "The protesters?"

"No, the BLM. They had put themselves in a tactically inferior position, in a valley. It's like rule number one in tactics: don't defend a valley!" he explained incredulously. "As soon as I rolled up, I could see these guys (the Federal Agents) had no idea what they were doing."

"Were you thinking, 'Great, we got them!'" I asked.

"NO! I was thinking these guys are so stupid that if anything goes wrong, those people in the wash are going to get hurt and, if they do open fire, the rest of us (militia) will need to return fire to protect them. If that happens lots of people were going to die."
I paused, thinking of possible the ramifications.

He continued. "There wasn't much we could do from the bridge, except make some noise. We were so far from the BLM position it would be nearly impossible to hit anyone."

"So, what did you do?" I asked.

"Nothing at first. I wasn't sure what to do. Then I saw a mirror flash from the mountain to the right of the wash. Then another from the BLM trucks below."

"What does that mean?" I asked, not fully understanding what he was describing.

"It means 'over watch!'" He could tell that didn't help to clarify. "It means snipers! It means that they were targeting the men on the bridge."

"But, I thought they were too far?" I persisted.

"Not for snipers. Don't you watch TV?"

I do watch TV but he was presenting a narrative I couldn't wrap my head around. It was hard for me to believe the idea that my government was actually targeting American citizens with deadly force from a position of several hundred yards away. Honestly, I thought he might have been embellishing his story to fit his own narrative for the courtroom. Except later, I realized by the time I met Todd in Pahrump, he had already been to court.

"Okay, explain it to me like I am a six-year-old," I pushed back.

Todd sighed, but continued. "They were targeting me and the other guys on the bridge. From an elevated position (the hill to the right) and from the wash, not that the shooter below could have hit me with an AR or M16. But, that wasn't my concern. All it took was a backfire from a passing car, a stupid idiot in the crowd below, or a BLM agent with a bad decision and all hell would have broken loose. And, from where I was sitting, all the women and children below were going to die! Lots of people were going to die!"

The second trial did unveil that very fear Todd had faced. The jury got to hear what I had heard from Todd was not only true; but also, maybe even, prophetic. Todd Engel was closer to being right than even he realized. The officers below at the barricade had been radioed notice from the over-watch position of the militiamen on the bridge. According to their sworn testimony during the second trial they had targeted the men on the bridge, Eric Parker, Rickey Loveland and Todd Engel, from the wash. They had removed the safety from their weapons and 'taken the slack' out of their triggers waiting for permission to fire from their command.

In that trial's cross examination by the defense, it became clear that they had an extremely difficult time even identifying each of the men. They may have shot at a spectator or one of the men. More likely their bullets would not have found a target at all. But, as Todd pointed out, if one thing had gone wrong it's entirely possible everyone with a gun that day might have opened fire and, as Todd Engel first told me of the danger of the situation back in Pahrump, "Lots of people were going to die!"

Notably, Sheriff Gillespie mentioned the same potential for disaster in an interview with a local media; he detailed the potential for all that could have gone wrong.

"When people talk about Bunkerville, thank goodness they don't talk about it in the same light as they do Ruby Ridge and Waco. If it hadn't been for the level of professionalism and commitment to de-escalation that the Las Vegas Metropolitan Police Department had and continues to have, you might have had something else."[5]

"So, what did you do, Todd?" I asked, becoming impatient with his sarcasm.

"I realized that I might just get shot and I ran up the highway and found a Sheriff's Deputy. I told him that on the bridge, I had mirror flashes and that if somebody doesn't tell those BLM idiots to back down, all hell was going to break loose."

"What did the deputy do?" I asked.

5 https://lasvegassun.com/news/2014/jul/02/sheriff-breaks-silence-says-blm-bundy-share-blame-/

"He immediate got on the radio and raced away in his car."

"Then what?" I responded, looking for the end of his tale.
"I stayed off the bridge and down near the Highway Patrol cars that were dealing with the traffic."

"You didn't go back to the bridge?" I pressed for clarification.

"Nope. I realized I was a target out there and I wanted to stay out of the line of fire. That's where I stayed until the Protest was over. Then, I headed to the Bundy Ranch where I parked my truck and climbed under it for some much-needed sleep. The next morning, I was up and drove back to Idaho."

"Did you even get to meet Cliven?" I wondered curiously.

"I just shook hands with him as he passed through the camping area at the ranch thanking people."

"It doesn't even seem you knew Cliven or any of the Bundys."

"No, I didn't. I got to know them here, in Pahrump," Todd answered.

A couple of days later in the lock-up recreation yard, I asked Todd a question that was nagging at me.

"How long were you at the Bunkerville Standoff?"

His answer shocked me. "About an hour and a half," he answered.

I sat there stunned.

The U.S. Attorney wanted a sentence of 20 years in Federal Prison for Todd Engel because of his role in Bunkerville. At just 49 years old, if the government gets its way, Todd will be 58 years old (with time off for good behavior) when he is released. A steep price to pay for an hour and a half on a bridge in the middle of the Mojave Desert. It turns out that Todd's role was much more than he knew that day.

It was Todd's warning to the sheriff's deputy that forced then Under Sheriff Joe Lombardo (he later was elected Sheriff when Gillespie retired) and Sheriff Deputy Chief Tom Roberts to insert themselves into the Standoff and take command, something Cliven had asked to happen for years. It was Lombardo who denied the request by the BLM officer in the wash to shoot, citing the obvious safety concerns. Uniform video of one the BLM officer shows Sheriff Deputy Chief Tom Roberts ordering the BLM officers to low ready or sling their weapons. "There is no need for long guns or any of that crap." He told them to deescalate the situation. In that same video, as Roberts walked away, the BLM agents mocked him and one even says, "Don't take orders from that officer." Apparently this agent didn't know or ignored who or what authority he had.

Ultimately, under Lombardo's and Roberts' leadership and intervention, the disaster of the Toquop Wash was averted. The radio log of that day shows that Sheriff Deputy Chief Tom Roberts told his officers to "Get our folks up here to interact with these folks instead of these BLM."

Backing off

Down in the wash, the horses finally arrived and combined to form a line behind the protesters who were on foot. Now that they were all together, the protesters moved forward towards the barricade. In Pahrump, Davey told me how, as they slowly walked forward, there was real fear and confusion.

"What do you mean, confusion?" I asked. Obviously, I understood the fear; but, why confusion?"

"Because the BLM was supposed to be gone. When we got to the wash we expected that the BLM to have picked up and left, like the Sheriff said. We were just going to release the cattle and celebrate; but what we walked into nobody was prepared for," he explained.

With nearly every step, the BLM repeated their demands over the loud speaker.

Behind the barricade, the BLM and Park Service agents had a different mood in their ranks. Sealed discovery video leaked to the Public Broadcasting Network (PBS), show Front Line says it all in the following agents' conversations.

"You're my lethal; I want you guys to be ready for a second wave. When I call in second wave, come in."

"Are you f**king people stupid or what?"

"Fat dude right behind the tree has got a long gun. Motherf**ker, you come find me you're gonna have hell to pay." Then he starts laughing.

As Dan Love moved toward the barricade to negotiate with the Bundys, one officer was caught on camera. "Interesting tactic, if it works he's a genius. If not..." he started laughing. "We're gonna..."

Snide Laughter. "Fat A**" slid down."

"It's pretty much a shoot first ask questions later," a second officer replied. "I'm with ya."

"No gun there. He's just holding his back, standing like a sissy." More laughter. "She must not be married."

"It's Code 4, they're not actively assaulting us yet." There's laughter and boasting in their conversations.

Referring to the arrival of Deputy Chief Roberts, "They're gonna get their shoes dirty."

The time stamp on the video also shows that the BLM officers continue to aim their weapons at the protesters, even while the sheriff's deputies are in the line of fire.

The agents demonstrated bravado, at times hubris. The uniform, radio chatter and dash cam video demonstrated a clear banter between Government agents that exposed they were in over their head, beyond their training, and, at the time, a danger to the protesters, sheriff's deputies, and even themselves.

There were decisions on the fly, orders, and then counter orders.

Clearly, you can hear on the radio orders to pull back. Then another voice among the agents at the barricade counters to disregard that order. One officer stated, "If those horses charge us ... to open fire as that will be the only thing that will stop them." Another agent informed the other agents that his uniform camera is on, indicating that they need to be careful what they are saying. The others paused, and then just picked up where they were after hastily considering what he had said. As the video footage rolls on, you can unmistakably hear mockery between male agents who talked about shooting a protester's dog, before shooting the protester himself.

However, later in court under oath, a female agent claims that she was afraid for her life from the protesters. This same agent is shown actually walking down to the barricade. The location was approximately 75 feet in front of their stacking positions, behind the Government SUVs her fellow agents had taken, then turns her back to the cheering crowd of protesters and visibly, not in fear as she claimed under oath, took a selfie.

Dan Love had assembled a group of authoritarians who, as Todd shared with me, were a "who's who" of controversial BLM and NPS officers. Explaining that when, in his court discovery, he first read the names of the officers that were there that day, he recognized many of them as officers who had been the subject of questionable enforcement practice from all over the western states. This is something he follows in the media in rural Idaho where he lives.

And now Dan Love had brought them together in Bunkerville, as his team.

This was all ongoing as the protesters slowly approached the barricade to within about 25 yards and began to sing the Nation Anthem and then, "God Bless America."

Finally, Dan Love emerged from the group of government agents, looking a bit like a frat boy wearing a T-shirt, olive green utility vest, dark sunglasses, sporting a scruffy beard pulled to a point off his chin, and his baseball cap on backyards. He walked down to the barricade and called out to David Bundy, someone he knew on sight due to David's arrest earlier that week. But it's Ammon Bundy who came forward to meet at the barrier. David Bundy came alongside him. There, Dennis Michael Lynch had his camera and proceeded to captures the entire exchange between them.

Ammon told Love, "You guys need to leave," and pointed with his hand like he was directing traffic. Then again, "You need to leave."

"I am telling you, you need to de-escalate the situation." Love countered, waving with his right hand. Then he pressed, "I am imploring upon you your responsibility to de-escalate the situation."

"No, no they're staying here…" pointing to the protesters, "…until they're gone," next pointing to the agents just up the road. That's what we're doing," Ammon stated emphatically.

In the background, the crowd started chanting, "Go Home, Go Home," as they pressed forward toward the barrier. Then, over the public-address system, an agent yelled, "Stop that, stop that!" as some of the crowd began to grab the fence.

One of the by-standers said, "You need to tell those officers to quit pointing their guns at us." Love turned to look over his shoulder. "Lower your guns, low ready!" The officers ignored Love's commands. He walked away towards the BLM officers at the trucks.

This conversation seemed to lead nowhere.

Love returned sometime later, speaking very quickly now, and told the brothers, "I am currently in negotiation with your family to find a peaceful resolution to this. Don't escalate. Just give us time to work things out with Metro back here," as he motioned toward their command center.

"No, No, No, I understand what you are doing. And you'll have that time to leave." Ammon told Love.

Love pressed on. "I want you to push them back off the gate right now (referring to the crowd). Let me work with you, and you, and you. Come in here with me." He pointed at Ammon and David Bundy.

Ammon said, "No, we're not going in there." He started to move away from the fence. "We're staying right here." Ammon informed Love.

Love quickly assured them, "You have my word that no one is going to take you into custody." Then he said, "Okay, if you want to stay right here that's good, they're getting your dad up top." He pointed up to the bridge. "You need to back them up, for peace and safety, I can't get them to lower their guns until they back off."

None of Dan Love's representations of Cliven's participation in the stand down negotiations were true. Cliven never left the stage that day, nor received any phone calls from anyone from law enforcement to come to the command center as stated by Love.

As asked by Love in their conversation, Ammon and David convinced the crowd to back up about 25 yards away from the barricade.

Sheriff Deputy Chief Roberts, still in his standard tan colored uniform (not in swat gear and apparently in shiny shoes), came to the barricade along with some of his deputies and retrieved the Bundy brothers, Ammon and David, back to the barricade fence. Ammon once again affirmed the Bundy view of the Sheriff having full authority. He said to the Sheriff, "You have the authority here. We will do what you tell us to do. As long as it doesn't compromise our mission here."

Roberts asked the Bundy brothers to climb over the fence and come back away from it to discuss the peaceful resolution to the rising tensions. Reporter Dennis Michael Lynch climbed over and followed along. David Bundy summarized the resulting negotiation to me at Pahrump. "They (Love) said they wanted five days to leave. We told them NO, you need to leave today. They said they needed one day. We told them NO, you need to leave now. They wanted at least an hour. We settled on 30 minutes."

As they waited for the BLM to depart back at the barricade, Ammon took off his hat and humbly asked Roberts, "Would you stay here?" From the video you can see the stress and concern on Ammon's face. He made the request again.

Empathetically, Roberts responded, "Sure," almost in a falsetto squeak.

The Straw that Broke …
Finally, at 1:34 pm, Deputy Sheriff Chief Roberts gave the command to the BLM and NPS rangers to back away from the protesters. "Nice and orderly. I don't think anybody is going to shoot at ya or anything."

An accord was reached and the BLM and NPS rangers, still assembled in a stacking formation, began to walk backwards up the road toward the cattle compound. Clearly, they were making a show of their retreat, demonstrating that they may be fired upon at any moment. The BLM's SUVs also backed up just ahead or beside of the rangers as they continue to walk backwards. All the while the handful of sheriff's deputies stood casually between the protesters and the BLM and Park Service agents, casually speaking with a few of the protesters.

Dan Love's parting words to the Bundys were "to make sure you have your Dad come down and 'Pull the Pin' and let the cattle out." Once again, he referred to the pin that holds the gate on the cattle pen closed.

The Glory of Relief
With the retreat of the government agents, the crowd began to cheer and enthusiastically wave the flags they hold. The men are shaking hands and whooping it up with many protesters dancing about. The children there are excitedly jumping and dancing, as well. The celebration came to a crescendo when Ammon walked to the barricade and, first asking permission of Deputy Chief Roberts, pulled out his pocket knife and cut the zip ties that fasten the BLM's closure sign from the fence. Then, he turned to the crowd and thrust the sign into the air in victory and gave a shout.

Up at the bridge area someone hung a hand painted sign over the bridge so it was seen below, "The West has been Won Again." The protesters and spectators there could see the convoy of 117 government SUVs coming down the dirt road. Many of the protesters gathered at the location where they'd merge onto the now flowing highway, and mocked and ridiculed them as the SUVs sped away northeast towards Mesquite.

I asked Todd with a sly grin, "Were you one of those?"

"I sure was." he told me. "Looking back, it wasn't my finest hour. And believe me I later regretted it."

"Oh?"

"Yeah, the prosecution played that video of me over and over for the jury during my trial."

"So, basically, you were convicted for being arrogant jerk." I put an exclamation mark on Todd's confession.

"Maybe so. Maybe so," Todd supposed, shaking his head, his face showing regret.

Back at Bundy headquarters, Cliven got a call from Ammon about the standoff resolution. There was another big celebration growing on the banks of the Virgin River. The protesters there started jumping in the water hoot'n and holler'n, and splashing about. Cliven and Carol joined them.

Cliven received yet another call from Ammon. "Hey dad. Why don't you come up here and pull the pin? Let the cattle out?"

"Nah, I don't need to be the one." Cliven responded. "Let some ol' lady do it.

"Just let 'em go. They'll be home." Thankfully for him, Cliven isn't real big on ceremony.

"Pulling the Pin"
Down in the wash, four sheriff's vehicles and Sheriff Lombardo, himself, had arrived to escort the Bundy brothers and the horseback riders up to the compound to release the cattle just to keep the peace. To the Bundys' surprise a couple of the deputies helped take the fence panels down and released the cows. Despite Love and U.S. Attorney Dan Bogden's (according to Dan Love's testimony) plans the night before, no one (of the target outlaws) '*Pulled the Pin*.' The cowboys

drove the animals quietly down the wash, past a quiet and solemn crowd, back on to their range. They were "home," just as Cliven said.

Todd Engel stood along the highway and watched the 117 government vehicles leave the compound that day. According to court testimony by Incident Commander Daniel P. Love, there were 145 Bureau of Land Management and National Park Service agents in those vehicles, as well as the support personnel involved in the operation.

There were also 52 additional agents in full tactical gear from the FBI and Los Angeles SWAT teams. This information was a surprise to The Bundy 19, finding out 43 months AFTER the standoff. Somehow the government was able to keep secret the FBI's presence and their purpose until November 2017 with two trials completed and days before Cliven's trial was to begin, even after numerous requests and prosecution denials for disclosure by The Bundy 19 defense teams. It was only by accident that the revelation was made by a BLM agent who inadvertently mentioned the FBI command trailer in the compound, their surveillance equipment trained on the Bundy household, and their liaison in the Command Center, running the 'live feed' display for the command team during the agent's testimony. That brought the total of government agents to nearly <u>197</u> to roundup Cliven Bundy's cattle. Though even this number does not account for the dozens of other Government law enforcement in attendance.

Aftermath of The Protest
In the days following the "~~Standoff~~" Protest, the Bundys assessed the cost to the animals. They uncovered several cows and at least one bull shot and buried in a shallow grave. Cliven wondered aloud to me one day as we leaned against the fence in Pahrump how many animals were sold.

I asked, "Why? I thought none of them actually made it to the auction yard."

"Well we don't really know. Some of them cows that was released had sales yard numbered stickers on them," Cliven said.

I immediately knew what he meant. As animals are unloaded down the chute at the sales yard, the auction staff will slap numbered stickers on their backs to keep inventory as to what seller the animals belong. Later I witnessed the video of the cows' release and I could easily see that very stickers Cliven mentioned.

"How did that happen?" I asked Cliven.

I knew that there were only a couple reasons those cows would have the stickers on them. *First*, because someone bought cattle at the sales yard and transported them to the Bundy Ranch. Though, this scenario is just not likely. Or *second*, some of Cliven's cattle made it as far as the corrals of an auction yard somewhere and then were turned away by the State Veterinarian or Brand Inspector, or maybe the sales yard management. The government's contract cowboys would have been required to load them back up and return them to the government compound.

I asked Cliven if that's what had happened. "Dunno," he replied. "I tried to get the Nevada State Brand Inspectors records for inspections on my cattle. But they wanted $1200 for the copies. Before I could pull that kind of money together, I was put in here."

"Do you think some of the cattle were sold?" I questioned.

"Don't know that either. Maybe... we did have near 27 orphaned babies after the BLM roundup."

"Do you think they sold the cows WITHOUT their babies?" I asked, somewhat stunned.

"Could of, or they killed the mommas and buried them out on the ranch somewhere and we just haven't found 'em yet. All I know is we had babies looking for mommas and no mommas looking for babies."

"What happened to the baby calves?"

"We bottled fed them. Most all of 'em made it," he answered as we walked back into the G2 unit as our recreation time ended. "They're home, have been for more than three years. That's all that matters."

Cliven raised his hands above his head to be patted down prior to our reentry in to the noisy, chaotic human warehouse of this privately-run, contract prison.

Chapter 11

– THE SPIN –

Changing the Narrative to Fit Your Agenda

In the days and weeks following, the media was interested in the events of the "Standoff" (as it was now being portrayed across the headlines of the world news).

"I remember one journalist calling the house and want'n a interview," Cliven recalled as we were sitting at those icy metal tables in Pahrump. "I think they were from France. I asked 'em, 'What do you want to interview me for?' She told me, 'Half the world loves you; half the world hates you. And everyone wants to know what you're doing.' I jus' had a hard time understandin' all the attention!"

Cliven and the family decided that all the media attention was fortuitous and would bring attention to the issues of the Federal Government's overreach, not just property rights and the abuses to neighboring ranchers; but, abuse to the Constitution, state sovereignty and freedoms - for ALL citizens. They began to accept interview requests from media worldwide.

This author has read hundreds of articles and watched many hours of reporting on television. It is crystal-clear that virtually every media source approached Cliven with its own agenda hoping he would fulfill it for them.

Conservative media sources wanted Cliven to become the 'Poster Boy' for their narrative, their agenda, for small government and against overspending. Liberal media portrayed Cliven as a militia wacko, forming an army against the benevolent government that just wanted to protect the desert tortoise. The environmental lobby went crazy, demonizing Cliven as a hater of Mother Earth, and the conspiracists were convinced that there is a 'much bigger plot" afoot against Cliven and all of the American people.

In all of that agenda mongering, Cliven's simple message was lost.

For Cliven, it was not a "Standoff." It was a protest against the sheriff who wouldn't defend him against the overreach of the Feds; though the Sheriff eventually did protect him.

For Cliven, he was just standing up for his property rights.

He was not a 'welfare rancher,' as some portrayed him.

For Cliven, the Protest was his duty, not an act of violence.

For Cliven, his statement, "I'll do whatever it takes," was one of determination, not a threat of violence as so many presumed it meant. Cliven Bundy didn't want anyone hurt nor has he ever encouraged violence. But, for the public, he has now been miscast as a whole bunch of something he's not.

As you get to know the man, you will find him intelligent, funny, and fun loving. He is a man of conviction and willing and determined to do whatever it takes to stand for what he believes, prepared even to go to prison for the remainder of his life.

Cliven Bundy: Racist?

With his protest, Cliven quickly gained enemies. Those enemies' agendas were driving various competing narratives, and, for a time, it seemed the conservative media narrative was at the forefront of the world stage led by Sean Hannity. These enemies began to surround the Bundy family.

Back in Pahrump, Cliven asked me a curious question, one I only understand now: "If I give you my story, will you tell it as I give it? Or, are you going to tell it with your own agend'ee?"

"I don't understand. If it's your story, then I'll tell your story," I'd replied.

At this stage, I was removed from the narratives, competing agendas, and my own personal bias. I only knew the man who sat before me, with virtually no knowledge of what others were saying.

Now I understand what Cliven meant and how I was uniquely placed in his life to tell his story from his perspective.

I know now that Cliven was responding to the 'frenemies' that surrounded him in those early days, those who intended to portray him poorly – or even convict him – as the CI in his ranks nearly did.

Not long after the BLM ceased their round-up operation and pulled out that day in April, Cliven was encouraged to meet with the remaining protesters remaining, some even still streaming in, at the ranch in the days following April 12, 2014. Cliven was asked to share his views on various issues; it was often caught on cell phone video.

Here is the transcript of his comments regarding race (edited lightly):

> "And so what I'm testifyin' to ya, the I was in the Watts riot. I seen the beginning fire and I seen that last fire. What I seen is civil disturbance. People are not happy. People are thinkin' they don't have their freedoms, they don't have these things, and they didn't have 'em. We've progressed to quite a bit from that day until now, and we sure don't want to go back. We sure don't want these colored people to have to go back to that point. We sure don't want these Mexican people to go back to that point. We can make a difference right now by taking care of some of these bureaucracies, and do it in a peaceful way.
>
> Let me talk to ya about the Mexicans. These are just things that I know about them from the neighbor ... I wanna tell ya one more thing I know about the Negro. When I went to go through Las Vegas, North Las Vegas, and I would see these little government houses, and in front of that government house the door was usually open and the older people and the kids, and there was at least a half dozen people sittin' on the porch. They didn't have nothin' to do. They didn't have nothin' for their kids to do. They didn't have nothin' for their young girls to do, and because they were basically on government subsidy, and so now what do they do? They

abort their young children, they put their young men in jail because they never learned how to pick cotton. And I've often wondered, are they better off as slaves pickin' cotton and havin' a family life and doing things, or are they better off under government subsidy?"

Yeah, they didn't get no more freedom. They got less freedom, they had less family life and their happiness, you can see in their faces, they weren't happy sittin' on that concrete sidewalks. Down there they could probably growin' their turnips. So that's all government, that's not freedom.

Now let me talk about the Spanish people. You know I understand that they come over here against our Constitution and cross our borders; but, they're here and they're people and I've worked beside a lot of 'em. Don't tell me they don't work and don't tell me they don't pay taxes. And don't tell me they don't have better family structures than most of us white people. When you see those Mexican families, they're together, they picnic together, they're spending their time together, and I'll tell you in my way of thinkin', they're awful nice people, and we need to have those people join us and be with us, comin' to our party."

Just four days later, Cliven's comments – taken unmistakably out-of-context – were printed in a New York Times article about Cliven's ongoing media attention. The 'racist comments' were not the focus of the piece, but it was soon to become the headline of the main stream media.

From the New York Times:

"He said he would continue holding a daily news conference; on Saturday, it drew one reporter and one photographer, so Mr. Bundy used the time to officiate at what was in effect a town meeting with supporters, discussing, in a long, loping discourse, the prevalence of abortion, the abuses of welfare and his views on race.

"I want to tell you one more thing I know about the Negro," he said. Mr. Bundy recalled driving past a public-housing project in North Las Vegas, "and in front of that government house the door was usually open and the older people and the kids — and there is always at least a half a dozen people

270

sitting on the porch — they didn't have nothing to do. They didn't have nothing for their kids to do. They didn't have nothing for their young girls to do.

"And because they were basically on government subsidy, so now what do they do?" he asked. "They abort their young children, they put their young men in jail, because they never learned how to pick cotton. And I've often wondered, are they better off as slaves, picking cotton and having a family life and doing things, or are they better off under government subsidy? They didn't get no more freedom. They got less freedom." [1]

In the days to follow, the mainstream media took Cliven's words even further out of the context and began to form a new narrative more suitable to their own agenda. From these manipulated words, the narrative shifted from support to ostracizing Cliven Bundy, painting him as a racist.

The next day the headlines now read:

"Rand Paul Condemns Cliven Bundy's Remarks on Blacks" – NYTIMES

"Cliven Bundy Accidentally Explained What's Wrong With the Republican Party" – NYTIMES

"Can't we all call Bundy's comments 'racist'?" – THE WASHINGTON POST

"Cliven Bundy: Are Black People 'Better Off As Slaves' Than 'Under Government Subsidy?'" – HUFFINGTON POST

"No, Sean Hannity, you can't distance yourself from Cliven Bundy" – THE WASHINGTON POST

It was true the conservative media had now pushed Cliven off the boat and had paddled away as fast as they could. Sean Hannity, chanting the cadence, "It's beyond disturbing, it's beyond disturbing…" Stroke, stroke.

---

1 https://www.nytimes.com/2014/04/24/us/politics/rancher-proudly-breaks-the-law-becoming-a-hero-in-the-west.html

In his April 24, 2014 commentary, Hannity said, "I believe those comments are downright racist, they are repugnant, they are bigoted, and it's beyond disturbing. I find those comments to be deplorable, and I think it's extremely unfortunate that Cliven Bundy holds those views."

Sean Hannity never supported Cliven Bundy again.

You decide if Cliven Bundy is a racist.

But before you do, first consider a couple of points.

First, reread his comments again in full context. He uses the words "Negro," "Mexicans," "colored people" that seem appropriate to a man of the Vietnam era, who has farmed his whole life in very rural Nevada, and actually, has no television. He doesn't keep up with the politically-correct terms that offend so many these days. He uses the terms that he heard and knows from growing up in his childhood.

Second, review his view of the "Mexicans" whom he knows and with whom works along side. These opinions are not aligned with the conservative political media narrative of moochers and welfare abusers.

Were his word choices poor? Maybe. But with an honest read of his comments, you can only take away his grievance is towards the government, not against any people of color.

Ask yourself, "Is he right about the welfare system?" At least one economics professor from George Mason University thinks so. "The undeniable truth is that neither slavery, nor Jim Crow, nor the harshest racism has decimated the black family the way the welfare state has," said Walter Williams.

According to Williams, the number one problem is the weak family structure.

In 1960, just 22 percent of black children were raised in single-parent families.

Fifty years later, more than 70 percent of black children were raised in single-parent families.

According to the 1938 Encyclopedia of the Social Sciences, that year

11 percent of black children were born to unwed mothers. Today about 75 percent of black children are born to unwed mothers. "That can't be a legacy of slavery, it can't be some delayed reaction to slavery."

Professor Williams goes further, "the bottom line is that the black family was stronger the first 100 years after slavery than during what will be the second 100 years. All blacks were poor originally; but now, 30 percent are poor. Two-parent black families are rarely poor. Only 8 percent of black married-couple families live in poverty. Among black families in which both the husband and wife work full time, the poverty rate is under 5 percent. Poverty in black families headed by single women is 37 percent. It's the welfare state that decimated the black family, he concludes." [2]

Professor Walter Williams is also a black man. Or, "colored man," as Cliven might say.

Longbow

Two months after BLM Federal Agents released Cliven Bundy's cattle and retreated from the Standoff against The Bundy 19 and the hundreds of protesters that gathered with them on that ominous day, another Federal Government episode was about to unfold before Cliven Bundy's eyes. The government agents' use of unconventional tactical artillery; their inexhaustible arsenal of weaponry and bag of tricks readily available for them to present to the unsuspecting citizen who gets in their way was put aside for an entirely different tactic. The Feds realized that a video or movie was mightier than the sword, having experienced the powerful backlash from Margaret's video when it went viral. So like Joseph Goebles (Reich Minister of Propaganda of Nazi Germany from 1933 to 1945), the government put forward a plot to undermine the grass-roots movement that had begun there on that small Nevada ranch, by somehow, through film, dis-ingratiating their leader, Cliven, from his own public. This would become known as 'OPERATION Longbow'.

It was mid-June 2014 and Cliven was increasingly frustrated by the

2 http://www.independentsentinel.com/black-professor-says-its-welfare-not-slavery-that-decimated-us-blacks/

media's constant mischaracterizations and event-spinning of April 12th, professing over and over again it was an "armed" stand against Federal Agencies. At the same time showing images of Eric Parker, one of the protesters in the crowd, lying prone on the freeway overpass as he looked down the barrel of his rifle. This was the government's attempt to bolster their narrative rather than people's perspective. This totally upset Cliven. He knew the truth first-hand. So, he started thinking that if there was some way he could get the word out about the Feds overreach of the State's sovereign rights he would find how to refute the government-favored media.

It was this frustration that made the timing just right for Operation Longbow.

There was a knock to the door. "Hi, my name is Charles – Chuck – Johnson." There stood Charles Johnson, a white, middle-aged man with a thick southern accent, silver goatee and slicked-back hair. He continued, "And this is my assistant, Anna Brown." She was a tall blonde with a seemingly direct and forthright attitude. "We represent Longbow Productions. I'm the producer. I find your story fascinating. I would like to share the 'business opportunities' I envision for your family. I do a lot of documentary work and seeing your situation unfolding from a distance has amazed me. Especially all the national momentum you've already got. Can we come inside?"

And that's how it started. (Does this sound like something you've already read … say, about the Redds, maybe?)

Once inside, Anna immediately began to speak. "We want the American citizens to know that for the first time in almost 200 years, normal, average citizens, hardworking Americans, stood up, and they stood up against, you know, the tyrannical government, and they were able to get the government to back down."

She would use that line many times before anyone would catch on to her true loyalties and purposes in working for the alleged, and now notorious, Longbow.

"At first," Cliven recounts, "I dunno, it felt like the spirit of my Father in Heaven was warning me. I guess. There just seemed to be somethin' wrong. I could feel it. And so, at first, I just stayed away from it, and had them checked out. Eventually, I seen their work they were doin' were real good – and although we couldn't confirm their legit or not, couldn't even find their headquarters in Nashville, Tennessee. But their office building looked real professional. And so, Ammon finally convinced me to be part of the documentary Longbow was making right there on our ranch."

Cliven continued. "Mike, I saw my interviews and some of the boys came out real good." A frown overshadowed his face. "But it turned to be an entire fraud." His voice began to take on a serious, melancholy inflection. "They were all FBI undercover agents!"

"Wait" – I retorted. "You mean to tell me that the FBI got ahold of your Longbow videos?"

"No, they were all FBI Agents, Chuck Johnson, Anna Brown, and the entire filming crew making the Longbow documentary videos. All of them were FBI, sent in to …" (now emphasizing) "… trick us into saying somethin' incriminat'n against ourselves! Yeah, it was all a big lie. The Longbow production crew pretended to be helping us in order to put us in trouble and destroy the grass roots movement that's begun."

"Well. Did you say anything you regret while on video?" I inquired.

"Nah, me and the family - we done good. We just told 'em about jurisdiction and how we're sick and tired of the government runnin' us outta our land. But em' other ones (referring to the other video interviews outside the family) that's what come to be the basis of this here government's charge of conspiracy." He started waving his hand out in front of him, as if to show you his house, though we were in lock-up.

"Cliven, when or how did you figure all this out, being duped by the Feds, I mean?"

It was a startling revelation. "We found out from the first trial, when there came in Charles Johnson to sit down right beside the prosecutor being introduced as an FBI Agent, to give testimony (if needed) on behalf of the Federal Government's charge against us Bundy 19, of conspiracy."

"We didn't jus' go to Longbow from the beginnin'," said Cliven. "There's an entire conversat'n that went on or before we all had agreed to use their filmin' services to get the right message out to the public."

It's clear from the Longbow video that Ammon, at first, wasn't sold on the idea at all, telling Chuck Johnson that they had received a lot of interest from various media people regarding making a documentary, and that they wanted to reach a lot of people and couldn't do hundreds of different documentaries. Ammon then says that Chuck would have to get more familiar with the story before he decided to take on the entire project. In this same conversation, Johnson admitted he wanted to document history and he "didn't want to be investigating crimes, as some might."

From the video:

> Ryan asked Anna, "So, who's your audience?"
>
> "I'd like get it out to all America," Anna answered.
>
> Then Ryan says, "I just want to be straight forward with you. There's been a bunch of red flags go up in our minds, that hasn't happened with a lot of other companies."
>
> "What?" Anna's voice is rising.
>
> "Is your address to your main company, a Federal Building in Nashville, Tennessee?"
>
> "No," Anna insists, giving Ryan an address to an office building about a mile from Vanderbilt University.
>
> "So that's not a Federal Building?" Ryan reiterated.
>
> "No. I'm not a liar," Anna countered.
>
> "There's been a lot of red flags in the community about Longbow productions," reiterates Ryan. "It's almost like you're trying to make us incriminate ourselves."

At one point in time, Chick Johnson addressed Ryan about that - insisting that the project was completely legitimate, saying, "I want a truthful documentary. But we have to ask probing questions to appear completely journalistically sound. After all, I'm investing my own money here because I also don't want it to get into the wrong hands."

So Ryan at that point said, "Alright, let's proceed."

At the metal day room table, Cliven continued.

"Why, Johnson asked me lots of questions, to which I told him that ranch has been home for me most all my life, an' explained how on the day of the Standoff, the Feds had my home surrounded, an' how the news spread through social media quickly, fueled by photographs showin' federal agents aimin' sniper rifles from the hilltops.

"Johnson asked me questions about the militias, probin' into whether it was a coordinated effort that had taken place at the Standoff. So, I made it clear that the armed groups, whoever they were, just showed up, and that I had nothin' to do with invit'n 'em. The ranch was out of my control, and the Feds had "total" control of everythin' that happened that day.

"Johnson asked me once, 'People either look at you as a folk hero or some kind of instigator against the Government, because you were the one who must have instigated it, because if you were just doing what was right. Why would you need all those people with guns there?' Now, how would you respond to that?

"'I mean, you know, I gotta face this,' I told Johnson, 'When the militia steps up there, and they do a service for me. Now as far as I can say, all I can say is that I'm thankful for that service.'" Cliven was thinking about his family's protection at the time.

After listening to everything Cliven shared about this matter, it was extraordinary to realize the FBI agents were unable to get him to say anything he wouldn't otherwise have said gladly before a legitimate public radio, newspaper, or television station, with a golden opportunity to get his message in front of the American people. And they were unsuccessful – despite their best efforts – spending nearly a year trying to get Cliven before their cameras, offering money, hotel stays at the luxurious Bellagio Hotel in Las Vegas, and coveted National Finals Rodeo Tickets. Cliven said Johnson and the other undercover FBI agents were just another group of journalists to him. Even when they were finally able to do so, the FBI agents were unable to get him to say anything he wouldn't otherwise have said.

But what was surprising to Cliven, as he shared with me, it never entered the remotest reaches of his mind that this Government would set him up in a false, alleged conspiracy –- after the fact! Yet that's precisely what they did.

The Longbow interviews that were used as Government Trial Discovery to support the "conspiracy" charge, were centered around two men who were both full of their own self-imaginations, playing right into the FBI's entrapment.

The first man was Greg Burleson, who presented a grandiose image himself that would scare anyone. He took the stand and testified that when he gave his interview with Longbow he was "drunk" because the Longbow crew had been providing him drinks, straight shots of hard liquor, to get him "lubricated" before the interview began.

The second man was Eric Parker, of the "infamous sniper" photo, seen as the lone man looking down the barrel of his rifle at the law enforcement all around as he lay prone on the freeway overpass. The media had focused on this photo constantly during the months following the Standoff, using him as proof that a militia group was within the crowds of protesters to ready to shoot people.

In the Longbow video interviews, Parker explained that his motivation for traveling to Nevada was twofold. *First*, he saw the video depicting the BLM tasing Cliven's son and throwing his sister to the ground as part of a broader trend of police brutality. And, *secondly*, when he saw 'free speech zones' coupled with the presence of well-armed Federal Agents, Parker explained, that he and his friends hoped to prevent what they viewed as unlawful arrests or use of force against protesters.

"They got 200 armed men with body armor rolling around," Eric

Parker said. "We need 200 armed men with body armor rolling around" (to support the people from the Government). Far from the coordinated operation that the Government prosecutors would later allege, Parker said the actual confrontation was disorganized and ultimately terrifying.

"I thought we would be there, armed, of course, and stand our ground making sure that the illegal arrests stopped," he says. "I wouldn't have thought in 100 years we would be on a bridge staring down federal agents."

When he took his position on the pavement, the moment when the famous photo was taken, Parker gave testimony that his hands were shaking, literally.

"How do you acquire your target?" Chuck Johnson asked Parker.

"There's no picking the target," answers Parker. "I wasn't chambered, and my finger wasn't on the trigger. Nobody wanted to die."

Eric Parker was arrested in the raid of 2016. In a 10-page account of his conversation with his arresting agents, Parker said he had been contacted by at least two organizations offering to put "armed security at his house to shoot it out with the FBI when they arrived." Parked said he declined because he "does not want to see any violent confrontation with the FBI." Parker was the only Standoff participant who mentioned his brush with the suspicious documentary film crew Longbow. As stated, "A media company called Longbow Productions later interviewed Parker for a documentary about the Bundy situation but the movie has never been released," Parker's arresting agent noted. Parker believes the documentary film crew must be associated with the FBI.

But as it turned out, it was the interviews with Greg Burleson that would ultimately be used to do the greatest harm in supporting the prosecutorial conspiracy charges against the Bundys.

As seen of the video, he was given alcohol before the interview with Chuck Johnson commenced. After getting into a drunken state, Johnson led Burleson down a series of leading questions that played right into his own vain imaginations, about the government conspiracies and legitimately justifying the military action against the government.

It was revealed in open Court that Burleson told the FBI, that he came to the Bundy Ranch in Nevada to "kill federal agents" and "cut their heads off with his axe." Later he told his former FBI handler that he specifically targeted BLM Agents' "center mass" that day at the Standoff.

But most importantly, it was revealed in Court that Greg Burleson was in fact a confidential informant working for the FBI.

Or, at least he used to be.

Webster's Dictionary defines "conspiracy" as a secret plan of an unlawful act.

These Longbow video interviews are what eventually got the Bundys in lockup. It wasn't from what the Bundys said linking them to a conspiracy; but, rather, by what Greg Burleson, CI, and Eric Parker said "after the fact" on Longbow videos that placed them together making the link the Government has used against them.

Remember, Longbow was the FBI and the Federal Government with one end in mind: to get the Bundys in prison and to squelch their grassroots movement of the American people. It wasn't what the Bundys did that landed them in prison. It was the strategically-planned conspiracy using government agents and informants who plotted against the Bundys. The government used these agents in an unprecedented and underhanded means eventually accomplishing their illegal ends: putting The Bundy 19 in prison.

After all, Cliven and the Bundys never met either Burleson or Parker until the day of the Standoff, along with hundreds of others. The nonsense that these two said over a video, regardless of the reasons why they said it, should have nothing to do with Cliven Bundy or the true reasons and meaning behind the protest against Governmental jurisdiction of Nevada State land!

When the Reporters Committee for Freedom of the Press caught wind of the FBI impersonating journalists in Operation Longbow, they expressed their concern to the Director of the FBI and filed a Freedom of Information Act request. In that request, they asked the FBI to reveal how many other times the FBI has pretended to be legitimate journalist in their criminal investigations. The FBI ignored the request. This resulted in the unusual step of the Reporters Committee for Freedom of the Press to file a lawsuit forcing the Department of Justice and FBI to comply with the law. [3] "Journalists across the nation are concerned with the 'chilling effect' that this type of impersonation has on the public when revealing stories to the press. The public needs to be able to trust they are actually talking to the media when they are blowing the whistle on the abuses of government and not to the government themselves, which will use the information against them in retaliation."

Confidential Informants: Who Needs Evidence When You Can Make It Up?

As reviewed before, tried and true practices in Federal investigations are "paid informants," also known as CIs. They have immunity agreements with the Government as witnesses and or as undercover federal "agents." When an average citizen hears these terms, they think of mob bosses, organized crime; "stool pigeons," "snitches," and "rats" that bring down the "big boss" of major crime syndicates.

Most people would really be surprised to know that these illegal and unconstitutional tools of law enforcement are regularly used in practically every single federal case, with few exceptions.

In The Bundy 19 case, undercover FBI CIs pretended to be a documentary film producer, assistant and crew, duping purposely intoxicated people into uncontrolled rantings of bravado and vain imaginations, not to mention the day-to-day lying for the specific – and intentional – purpose of "entrapment;" using unfair advantage to cause harm to innocent citizens whom the Government wishes to control.

And there were others including Ryan Payne, who made boastful statements that were used to put the Bundys all in lockup, where most

3 https://www.washingtontimes.com/news/2017/aug/21/reports-sue-info-fbi-bundy-ranch-infiltration/

all sit right now.

Evidently Ryan Payne had misgivings about his role in putting the Bundys behind bars, and therefore put together an affidavit of sorts to those involved. In that declaration, dated September 19, 2016, he stated that there was never any plan to accomplish any of the objectives he stated there were (in various media accounts), and no "certain capabilities," as he alleged and described to the press. In fact, he states categorically "they did not actually exist." He went on to explain some of his assertions that he made were not even possible, nor was there any "command structure," nor plan to execute by his command and control. There was no planning of any type of leading up the April 12th Standoff. Also, his statements concerning "tactical superiority" or a long-range "marksman" never existed at all… except those that were used by the Federal Agents of the BLM and by the Forest Service Rangers, who would point their AR-15 rifles at innocent men, women and children.

Payne goes on to say that no one gave orders; because, there was no "commander" to give them, nor did anyone agree to follow any orders. Payne explains further that all his nonsensical statements were his way of disseminating a misinformation campaign to "protect the Bundys" from another "Ruby Ridge execution" where a woman holding her baby was shot by an FBI sniper. Payne's plan was to make the Feds believe there was an armed military encampment in Bunkerville, Nevada, not just willing to respond but able to respond to any aggressive show of force by the Federal Government like "Ruby Ridge."

Also, Payne stated that any "government retaliation" against the lawful protesters at their homes across the States could result in a "similar response," meaning that Payne and or others would go after Federal Agents at their personal homes as well, wherever that may be.

Rather apologetically, Payne then noted all his fabrications were misused in order to indict and imprison Cliven Bundy and others by their "mimicking his words;" but, not his intent.

Be that as it may, the Government uses CIs everywhere and whenever they feel it will benefit them. Even at LaVoy's funeral, federal agents infiltrate to gather intelligence, and witnesses are sometimes recruited by the offer of "immunity" from the prosecution for their testimony against "the target," presumably "the big fish." This is considered a fair trade-off in order to bring down major crime bosses and the like. Often, the prosecution gives the "snitch" witness protection from any reprisals that might result from their testimony. That's fine for the movies, theatre, and television shows, but in modern day-to-day Federal investigations, we find that immunity deals are common in every court case.

Remember, here is how it works:

The investigating agency will identify their "target," then they interview someone else in the same business or organization to make the following simulated approach: "We know he/she did it; you just need to tell us HOW."

CIs are a bit different. They are recruited before the potential crime, in order to infiltrate the targeted 'alleged' offender (in this case, the Bundys' Protest), in order to observe any crimes first-hand and report them to their investigating "handler." It is important to note that the CI won't get paid if there is no resultant crime on which to inform. So, it is in their interest to shape the report in such a way that it would be considered a crime. Sometimes they twist the intent or outright lie. After all, they have the complete immunity from prosecution themselves. In many cases, the CIs will do whatever it takes to help the prosecutor secure a conviction because the CI has made a deal that will result in a lower sentence, known as a "downward departure" in his sentencing, sometimes a completely different case in which he's the target.

There are some oddities in regard to The Bundy 19. If there were any "conspiracy" at all, as the Feds alleged, it should have been easily proven. If you stop to think it through, as the Federal Government must have done, if there was a guilty party in The Bundy 19 case, and if conspiracy was indeed happening, Longbow Productions would not have needed to be invented. As well, Ryan Payne wouldn't have had to give his damaging and falsely-given testimony to ensure that the Bundys would end up in lock-up. If a conspiracy did exist on its own merit, then a witness would have been found apart from the use of Confidential Informants. But that is what's so obvious here.

There was no such witness to be found because there was no conspiracy. Even though the Government had between five (5) to eleven (11) CIs among the crowd that fateful day of the Standoff, at the end of the day, the Government found nothing concrete to prove their foolish theory of conspiracy. There wasn't one witness to justify their decision to launch Operation Longbow.

As a matter of fact, there was no one who knew conclusively, beyond any shadow of doubt, that The Bundy 19 and their movement did encompass the criminal element of a "conspiracy" to commit an illegal act. Except the Federal Government. Yet, even knowing all that, nevertheless the government strategically, and with malicious intent, plotted and launched Operation Longbow; the result being to put the Bundy's in lock-up.

It is clear now that it was the government CIs planted in among the protesting crowds at the Standoff brought rifles and guns to sabotage and ruin the righteous movements and intentions of "free speech" against the Government's unconstitutional actions in Nevada. It is also obvious that the Government was trying to frame the rally according to their purposes, twisting it into an armed assault against the government by the use of their hired CIs, like Glenn Beck's "Overton Window" story [4], only this one is for real – with true covert operations planned and launched against the American people on their own homeland. Sounds a little bit like Waco. Who could argue?

In a November 6, 2014 letter to the New York Times, FBI Director James Comey defended the practice of confidential informants, stating: "That technique was proper and appropriate under Justice Department and FBI guidelines at the time. ... Today, the use of such an unusual technique would probably require higher level approvals, but it would still be lawful and, in a rare case, appropriate." Maybe Comey would argue this. Then again, he's not director anymore and under investigation himself.

Whether the practice is illegal or not, it's for the courts to decide. But one thing is clear; it was unethical. As Cliven said during the day of the Standoff, the confidential informants that he became aware of later on were the very instigators who tried to incite the protesters against

---

4 https://en.wikipedia.org/wiki/The_Overton_Window

the Federal agents' orders. One of them, Cliven said, urged the crowd forward in violation of the agents' orders to stand behind a line or get shot.

But thankfully the CIs' attempts to incite the gathering of law-abiding citizens protesting a legitimate constitutional issue with the Federal Government was not successful, although they tried their best to turn it into a riot and a place of bloodshed. That never happened. Instead the Standoff participants were kneeling, praying, waving American flags, and singing patriotic songs of inspiration all to let the government know it was way out-of-line.

Most of the protesters would have been shocked to find out the truth of just how far out of line the Feds had really gone! And I'm sure none of them thought the Feds had intermingled the crowd with CIs who were attempting to instigate a confrontation to bloodshed, to endanger them and their children's lives. But that's exactly what happened.

At the end of both the first and second trials, the jury was "hung" (undecided). Despite this fact, The Bundy 19 were incarcerated in federal prison, detained not only because of mentally unstable CIs' testimonies, but because the Federal Government organized and planned to make an example out of Cliven Bundy and The Bundy 19 no matter what it took. Unfair advantage or not, that is what's at the heart of the matter.

Needless to say, Cliven Bundy and his boys are more than just "cautious" these days. After all the many betrayals, 'frenemies,' frauds and confidential informants lying to them, along with the Government, they're starting to see the world from a more skeptical but clear paradigm of understanding. No one said it was gonna be easy or simple. But life can shock you sometimes, like it has the Bundys.

At risk of repeating myself, I experienced their wariness firsthand while in lock-up at Pahrump. It took quite a while before they would trust me, or open up to me in conversation. And, truthfully, who could blame them? It was common to walk up on them as they were in conversation only to find the exchange immediately die. They would turn to look at me as if I'd interrupted them.

But that's what being guarded and cautious looks like. After all, in the world they've come to know, there's only one thing for certain. Nothing is what it appears to be. That may be truer than it sounds at first.

Then again, if you were sitting down with them in Pahrump, I'd guarantee you'd understand exactly what Cliven and the boys are going through.

Chapter 12

– DANGERS IN LOCK-UP –
Prison Culture and Politics

One of the many volatile dangers in prison life, especially a Detention Center like Pahrump, is the constant transfer and moving of inmates, day and night, creating new shifts in the pecking order of prison politics between races, gangs, and ages. This high turnover breeds serious threats of uncertainty. It's an atmosphere, a vibe, a feeling of vulnerability, and added stress to an already upsetting situation.

One morning, I found myself in that situation with a new bunkie. He was a young Armenian man, about 34 years old. Initially, our interactions were cordial, as prisoners go. But quickly it became apparent he was immature and having trouble fitting in. Like a restless, self-absorbed teenager, he kept climbing up to and down from his upper bunk, repeatedly banging his footlocker and talking loudly across aisles, showing a general disrespect for me and the others in and around his area.

Prison has its own protocol. In that regard, it was my duty – my job, so to speak – as his bunkie to "pull him up," which means to confront him in regard to the issue at hand. I needed to draw his attention to the fact that he needed to show respect for the men who lived around him by bathing more, talking less, and acting more responsible – more aware of others around him. So, I began a process of hinting, insinuating, and suggesting the best I knew how. But he was clueless. It became obvious it was time to confront him and talk with him more directly.

One morning, after a particularly difficult night dealing with his noisy disruptive ways, I decided it was time. Now I know these situations can turn bad, and oftentimes turn physical, which is exactly what I didn't want to happen. There are consequences to that sort of activity including loss of 'good' time, phone privileges, commissary, plus dealing with the physical violence of a beating and/or injury. So, I planned my words carefully, thinking through various scenarios, and measured my willingness to go through with confronting this man.

Someone who has never been to prison might think, "Can't you just move bunks?" The answer is not really; because if you ask the CO (Correctional Officer) to move bunks, then you must give a reason, and if you tell the truth to the CO, then you are labeled a "snitch." Not a good thing. Besides, once you appear weak, you'll be continuously and mercilessly preyed upon. Knowing this, I needed to stand up for myself and those around me as prison protocol dictated.

It was right after breakfast that I approached him and asked if we could talk somewhere.

Agreeing, we walked over to the day room area with its many tables, always under the watchful eye of the 24-hour surveillance cameras, figuring that if anything goes awry, at least it will be on video camera to witness the entire altercation. Anyway, I should be okay; after all, I'm a fit guy who knows how to scrap, even if it's been 25 years. And since my last fight, the worst that could happen is a couple of bruises, right? At least, that's what I said to myself.

There we were in the day room area. I said, "Bunkie, you need to gain some respect for me and those around you."

"Or what?" he replied back defensively.

"Or you need to move bunks," I responded.

Well, that 'set him off' like a firecracker, schizoid child... He started yelling and threatening me.

Calmly, I asked him to come back to the conversation, as by this point he was 10 to 15 feet away from me, carrying on and having a 'fit' like a complete adolescent.

I tried to bring some peace and quiet to the situation. "Look, I just need some respect here, the all night-talking and commotion is NOT okay," I stressed.

"Why don't you ask nicely?" he yelled excitably. Then after a second of thinking, he said, "If you don't like it, you move!" He was still obviously worked up.

We now had the attention of the entire unit and, though I was remaining calm, I sensed this needed to end. Just then, the "shot-caller" for the unit walked up to us and said to take it somewhere else. The "shot-caller" is the detainee who represents a particular racial group. The shot-caller who has the most authority is the one who represents the largest racial group in the prison at that point in time. At this time, it was the Southsiders, a gang out of South Central Los Angeles.

At the same time the shot-caller was indignantly instructing us to take it somewhere else, the CO was opening up the recreation yard for the Unit. So, I thought that it would be a good time to end this one-sided conversation. I headed for the door. But, my bunkie followed me, yelling out, "I'll kick your ass, old man!" Immediately, I spun around on my heels and while looking him straight in the eyes – like Clint Eastwood in a close-up shot – I said, "I can back this up – can you?"

He stepped back, dumbfounded, as the others around could see I was not in the least bit afraid.

Then to my surprise, my bunkie headed straight for the CO at the door, still threatening me, but he told the CO that HE needs to move to another bunk. That effectively labeled him a "snitch" to every man in the unit. Needless to say, my recreation time was highly unsettling as my bunkie pranced around, trying to gain supporters from the different ethnic groups and races in the mix.

I just sat there with my back against the perimeter fence wondering what was going to happen next. Realizing at any time I could be called upon to defend myself. It was a tense time waiting as my bunkie sat around with groups of men, trying to gather support any way possible. Finally, it was becoming more and more evident that he was afraid of me and wanted others to take on his fight. As an Armenian, he had only four other men from his racial background there in the G2 Unit. They were all older fat men, unwilling to fight or even consider it. In a desperate attempt at support my bunkie approached the Southsiders and woven an indicting false tale that my complaint was not against him ... but was against them! Interestingly, the Southsiders had recently taken up playing cards near my bunk; but, they were polite, respectful, and truly no trouble at all, although my bunkie spun his own story to get me in harms' way.

After lunch I was pulled aside by the white shot-caller. He regretted to inform me that the White-Boys would NOT come to my defense against the Southsiders, reasoning that I didn't follow protocol by not first asking permission of the White-Boys calling-out Southsiders. I simply nodded, not wanting their help anyway but wondering since when did my Armenian bunkie become a Southsider? What did I get myself into here? Am I somehow in the middle of a prison gang conflict?

While I was wondering about all this, the CO showed up and pulled me aside to tell me to leave his nice young Armenian man alone, then the CO walked off. I now seemed to be out of the pot, only to be in the fire!

I sat on my bunk most of the day praying and wondering what to do next. My neighbor, hearing what transpired, talked to both the Armenians and to the CO, having verified that indeed the problem lay at my bunkie's feet, and not with me. I decided it was time to have a talk with the Shot-Caller of the Southsiders.

The approach was received but he was in the "power" position, and so I had to hear him out first. After he spoke, I got to respond and explain that in truth my problem was not with the Southsiders or with the card game. My problem was simply with my bunkie. Man to man, I explained why I had confronted him directly, as prison protocol dictated, and as we talked together the shot-caller realized I'd been in prison for a while and was following "how things are done." The conversation ended with a truce plus his commitment that my bunkie would never be disrespectful again. He even offered to change or switch bunkies if I wanted. And lastly, if my bunkie was ever a problem again, just let him know and he'd deal with him – his way.

That night, my bunkie was so quiet I wasn't sure he was even there. The next morning my bunkie was gone, shipped out to another institution. But ever since then, the Southsiders all call me "O.G." (O.G. means 'original gangster' and is considered a term of respect). A couple of days later one of the more hardcore Southsiders, with tattoos around his throat and forehead, apologized to me and to my neighbor if he had disturbed us the night before. He hadn't of course, but it was a way of saying how much they respected us and wouldn't want to offend us in any way.

Later that night, I reflected on the last couple of days, and how glad I was that God brought me through what could have been – and was in fact – a truly dangerous situation and wondered, even though I'd never been in a gang, whether I should consider putting O.G. on my resume? And what about the Bundys? How would they fair and navigate through this living situation?

That evening, it dawned upon me that often prison politics seem to go hand in hand with the Cliven's deep faith, loyalty, and NO SNITCHING. All three are central theological principles of his faith. It was Jesus' "Golden Rule" that respect for others is built upon, "faithfulness" is what Cliven's belief system is rooted in and Jesus would never put anyone in harm's way, and even died for those who were in harm's way – of their own sin! It was astonishing to realize that the principles of Cliven's faith are demonstrated and held in high esteem far behind the barbed-wire fences and prison walls by those we refer to as "criminals." And with that I fell asleep, exhausted from one of the longest days I've ever had in prison lock-up.

Camp Liberty
In the months I was with Cliven, the word got out about the mistreatment of Ammon and Ryan by the Correctional Officers. I had never met Ammon or Ryan nearly the entire two months I was there. They were in the "hole," as the inmates refer to it, aptly named for the psychological depression you go into being separated from all stimulus for months, even years, at a time. Or also known as solitary confinement (administrative segregation) as the prison officials officially title it. The hole has become the de facto punishment for the Federal Prison System, even for the most minor of offenses. It used to be the place where a violent or dangerous prisoner was placed for the safety of the staff or other inmates.

But today, an inmate is sent there for having too many books or hanging his shirt on his bunk for it to dry. And once you are targeted as a 'troublemaker' you can't seem to get a break and will be singled out for extra attention. President Obama condemned this practice and issued an Executive Order to stop the practice except in extreme cases.[1] The Executive Order was ignored by the Department of Prisons and the practice continues today, unabated.

That is the category within which Ammon and Ryan Bundy were placed. They were subjected to extra, unnecessary strip-searches, and their property frequently scrutinized looking for and finding contraband violations. There were simple things – though "violations" – like having an extra pencil or socks with a hole in them. Once their property was examined and violations found, their disciplinary record would be exaggerated with the offense accompanied by entries such as "violent non-compliance with commands" or "contraband on person." They were roughed up in areas where there were no video cameras, like the elevator or courthouse bathrooms.

After a while, it becomes retaliation and power play by those entrenched in the system. If that wasn't bad enough, the disciplinary record was used by the prosecutor as evidence that Ryan and Ammon were a threat to society, claiming "if they can't obey the rules in the Detention Center, how can the court expect them to obey the rules given to them by the court for pretrial release?" And there they remained locked-up, as innocent men in Pahrump. In Ryan's case, *per* his disciplinary record, he was required to be tased in the Detention Center. Todd Engel's record showed he physically attacked a CO. Both allegations were patently false and completely made up. Eventually these items were expunged from their record. Yet the allegations showed up in their respective court proceedings. The damage was done.

In hopes of relief, both Ryan and Ammon began to broadcast phone interviews about their mistreatment while in the Detention Center. Family members made calls to the warden, the local sheriff, and the news media. Nothing was done. In the spring of 2017, a band of supporters gathered outside the Detention Center to bring attention to the mistreatment. In fact, they camped there, refusing to leave until their grievances were heard. They came to call their little camp of 20 people Camp Liberty. Each day they would conduct a "Jericho

1 https://www.washingtonpost.com/opinions/barack-obama-why-we-must-rethink-solitary-confinement/2016/01/25/29a361f2-c384-11e5-8965-0607e0e265ce_story.html?utm_term=.5aa8005456d2

March" around the institution singing and waving flags. They posted an American Flag flying upside down, the universal signal of distress. It was so high in the air, we could see it from the G2 Unit. And, of course, there were lots and lots of prayers. In time, it had a minimal effect, with the new warden conducting an investigation. The warden asked each of the men meet with the prison officials individually.

The Bundy 19 were gathered in the prison chapel as a waiting room of sorts for their interviews. It was the first time in months that they were all together in the same room. Together, the first order of business was to circle, hold hands, and kneel in prayer. After a brief time of shaking hands and greeting one another, Cliven spoke. "I told 'em that we needed to stay united and not let them separate us against one another." The men agreed and they decided to tell the prison official just one message. They didn't recognize their Constitutional authority to hold them, but hold them they did. And, if they wanted to truly address their grievances they would only meet with the local Sheriff together as a group. The prison officials were dumbfounded, never hearing such requests from a group of detainees, and sent them all back to their Units. Only after additional pressure from Camp Liberty, media attention and a phone call campaign to the local Sheriff did officials investigate.

As you can imagine, little came out of the investigation. But, Ryan and Ammon were released out of the "hole" for a brief time anyway.

The Detention Center Responds
Earlier in Chapter One, I described the dark soul or "vibe" of all such institutions. The Detention Center in Pahrump was no different. Though the building was newer, the staff appeared better trained than the other institutions in which I had been, there was still a feeling of oppression about it. That dark soul came to reveal itself when Camp Liberty was first set up.

It started on a Saturday. None of the detainees knew why, at first, all of the phones were shut off. We were ordered to stay in our bunks or cells all day; visiting was canceled; television was cut to the outside world, and mail ceased. Effectively, we had been cut off to the outside world, with no information coming in or going out. Families had come from long distances to the institution for visits only to be turned away with no explanation. The "goon squad" began to roam the halls of the institution. The "goon squad" is what the inmates call the rapid response team that is called out for riots. It's a fully kitted out team of Correctional Officers who put down a prison riot with full force and violence. The detainees were immediately on edge.

After the four days we were required to stay in our bunks, the edge transformed to anger. Inmates started to grumble and speak out; in fact, it was starting to turn into a self-fulfilling prophecy of a pending riot. The unit officer of the G2 Unit stood in front of the men in an attempt to quell the anger. He placed the blame squarely on the Bundys and their protesters outside (Camp Liberty). He wanted anyone to know if we didn't like the treatment that we should take it up with the Bundys. Essentially, by casting blame on the Bundys, he put a hit out on The Bundy 19. Never had any of The Bundy 19 been in more danger then at that moment. Not even in comparison to finding themselves the target of the BLM guns. Prison justice and politics could have moved swiftly on any one of them. Any one of them could have been beaten to death before lights out was called that night.

But, it never happened. The shot callers had seen right through the Prison Official's play to throw The Bundy 19 under the bus and refused to act. Besides, each of The Bundy 19 had gained so much respect from the other detainees for their compassionate and respectful attitude to all the races that it would take much more than the CO's "fronting off" the Bundys as one of the Southsiders told me. Twenty-four hours later the lock down ended and we all returned to our normal routine.

Nevertheless, Camp Liberty remained in place outside the Detention Center for another twenty-six days.

Look at What I Started

"Did you see what happened last night?" Cliven asked me as he plopped down next to me as I sat on my bunk.

Quizzically, I responded, "No, not really."

"Ask some of the fellers here, they all saw it," he responded. "Then apply it to what we have been talking about."

"Ah, ok." I had no idea what he was talking about. Then, Cliven wandered off to use an open phone, one that just became available.

It turns out I did miss something pretty cool for a bunch of guys who are locked up. Not at all what I might have been thinking, as my mind flipped through different scenarios. Was it a fight? Did one of the Bundy boys get into trouble? All just guesses.

As I would never have suspected, there were fireworks last night. There were real, authentic fireworks entertaining the men at the G2 Unit. It all happened after I went to bed. As I'm an early riser, my head hits the pillow by 9:30 or 10:00 pm. Apparently, after I turned in, the protesters from Camp Liberty, who continued camping outside the Detention Center, set off a series of fireworks into the night sky: red, white, and blue sparkling bursts of celebration, of freedom. For over an hour, the men watched the display through the bar-covered windows overlooking the recreation yard. Though obscured by razor wire, chain link fencing, bars, and a crowd of men, each detainee just loved it. We were all aware the protesters were outside, since the Correctional Corporation of America made it evident the first weekend the protesters arrived.

Catching up to Cliven after his phone call, I said, "Okay, I asked everybody. There were a bunch of fireworks from Camp Liberty, and…"

"Did you see what I started? Cliven asks me in all earnestness.

"Well. No… I don't get what your saying." I replied.

Cliven smiled and continued. More than twenty years ago, I said "no" to the Federal Government and I had no idea what I was starting. All these years later, there are thousands of supporters out there across the nation, even in other countries, that believe in what we're doin'. 'Nuff so they come to the desert in Nevada and camp out, giving up part of their lives to stand with us and say, "NO!" and "ENOUGH!" Many are not ranchers, in fact most aren't. But, they care about liberty, so they come. I am just honored."

"But, what about all that don't agree with you?" I quizzed.

"They just need to be educated, some won't be. But, I do this for them, too."

For the first time, I realized just how BIG this was, this stand of Cliven Bundy's. I walked away wondering if, somehow, I had stumbled into history, a history in the making. The could even be the same kind of history made by our Founding Fathers, the Martin Luther King's Freedom Riders and so many others that changed the direction of our nation for the better. Those that did so at great cost to themselves and their families in order for others to live free. I suppose it will be revealed as time puts a punctuation mark on Cliven Bundy's life.

June 14, 2017 FLAG DAY

There stood the new unit manager, a short fat woman sporting a short, buzzed, flattop military haircut, black shiny military-style boots and her men's civilian pants tucked into her boots. She didn't wear a uniform like the others that represented the staff at the Detention Center; but, preferred large billowing men's clothes to go along with an ugly, masculine way about her. She had just taken over the management of the G2 Unit and decided to be the "new sheriff in town" and "lay down the law" about how the unit would be managed. She announced she'd hold a town hall meeting with the G2 Unit. Previously, when we had several town hall meetings, they were two-way conversations between the staff and detainees. Even when the new warden came around, this was the format followed.

But, this person had a different agenda. Instead of the expected protocol, she just started barking orders. Dr. Wetselaar, an old doctor (the oldest incarcerated person in U.S. history at 93-years old) wheeled up to the front of the detainees as we sat on our bunks, partially because he can't hear due to the acoustics in this echo-y cinder block box we all live in, but also because he was mad. His anger was due to an infection he had developed in his left thumb, visibly swollen and red and had developed a yellow streak down its length. He had made numerous complaints and requests for medical attention. As an MD for over 65 years, he knew the ramifications of this yellow streak and was in no mood for their nonsense. So, he pushed his little roller-wheeled chair right up front to the unit manager.

The doctor began to raise his voice, passionately complaining about conditions, lack of medical care and how, though we were in the desert, it was always cold indoors. This clearly angered the unit manager and even seemed to intimidate her. She ordered the Doc (as the detainees called him) back to his bunk. He complied; but, not without yelling, with anger now, "I have been treated better in a Nazi concentration camp!" This could easily have been true as he was briefly imprisoned in such a place as a Dutch resistance fighter during WWII. Her completely inappropriate action raised the ire of the remaining men; some hollered their legitimate complaints, others just yelled in protest. Not one left his bunks or threw anything; no one was in danger, as I had seen many times prior. They were simply expressing their protest of the Doc's treatment.

Her response was to escalate the situation, to exert her authority, and call for more officers in backup even though there were three officers and staff in the unit. She decided to retaliate.

One by one they removed the "offenders," taking each out of the unit while videoing each removal, rolling up all their personal belongings and placing them in trash bags.

First out went the Doc, oxygen machine in tow behind his wheeled chair. Taken next was Todd, who was in a front row bunk and clearly visible to where the staff was standing during the encounter. But, more curiously, out went Melvin Bundy and another older man, Jim, who was 72-years-old.

Why those two? Their bunks were in the back row and in the furthest corner from the staff, so it would have been impossible to distinguish those two from anyone else. Then I remembered. Three days earlier, Jim had verbally protested to this same woman when his personal items were confiscated. She obviously didn't like the protest and used the situation to sweep him up in her display of power. Melvin Bundy went for no other reason than he was a Bundy. Each man was taken to the hole, to be held for investigation for 30 days, a favorite practice, to skirt the rules of the institution. If an officer wants to retaliate against a detainee, they put this person up on charges, then after 30 days the charges are dropped, effectively punishing the detainee without actually needing something to charge the person with. This practice resulted in Dr. Wetselaar being the oldest man in America to be sent to the hole.

June 16, 2017
Dr. Wetselaar had yet to return to the G2 Unit and was presumably still in the hole. Davey Bundy begins to get anxious for the doctor, as he had been caring for and looking out for him. In this care, Davey made sure Doc was warm and tucked in each night, bringing him a warm cup of green tea in the morning, helping him dress. As we sat for breakfast on the cold stainless steel tables, I notice Davey pushing his

food around, obviously preoccupied. This was odd for Davey. He was usually a big eater, finishing his tray and welcoming any other items shared with him.

But today he was "off his feed", as his dad would say.

I ventured an inquiry, "You doing OK?"

Davey didn't even look up. "Yeah, I'm okay... am just sick of this place. Three of my brothers keep getting thrown in the hole over nothing. Now the Doc is in the hole, 'cuz he spoke his mind at a town hall. I am really tired of this." Getting angry and worked up, he said, "I mean, the old man can't even put his socks on by himself!"

Davey stopped and reflected a moment. Cliven and I joined him as those at the table stopped eating and stared down at our food. Then *BOOM*. Every table, every man is startled by what sounds like a gunshot. The entire unit is eerily quiet. There's not a sound as every man there tried to determine what just happened. Looking to my left, I noticed Davey, in utter frustration, had slammed his hand, open palm, down on his empty breakfast milk carton. It was a small, individual serving-size carton, the type your children might get at school. The concussion left no escape path for the air trapped within, except to burst through the sides of the carton. The result? *BOOM*!

After a few seconds the G2 Unit settled back down to normal.

"I need to do something," Davey exclaimed, standing up.

I thought to myself, "In this mood, I hope Davey doesn't do something stupid, like so many I have seen before him ..."

Surprisingly, Davey did something rarely seen in prison. He asked the CO if he could volunteer to go in the hole, too. Not in protest or out of some sort of misguided guilt, but to serve as an in-home care person for Doc. I guess his request was better referred to as an "in cell care" person. I was astonished. Here in front of me I was staring at one of America's "most dangerous domestic terrorists," requesting to live in one of the most physically difficult and physically dangerous places on earth to come to the aid of this elderly man. Honestly, I was a bit ashamed that my level of concern didn't reach as high as Davey's. But his selfless act inspired me. Cliven, in his direct cowboy way, says to Davey, "Do what you think best." Then he picked up all our breakfast trays and wandered off to return them.

At this, I was made fully aware why all the Bundy men's wives are so proud of them. They're men of compassion, men of conviction, standing strong – or as their wives like to say "BundyStrong," referring to their contagious strength that can buoy them in this most difficult time.

Not long after breakfast, Davey and I were called to medical – along with several other men – for routine checkups. There, in the waiting room, was Ms. White, a pleasant African American CO, middle-aged, seemingly wise beyond her years. She was also the CO operating the video camera two days earlier when Dr. Wetselaar and the three others were sent to the hole.

Davey, with the old Doc still on his mind, asked her, "Is Dr. Wetselaar here in medical?" He had realized that it was possible he was being cared for at the same time, instead of punishing him.

She responded to the negative, and then continued on with, "I guess there was quite a commotion the other day. It was good we placed him to protective custody."

This caused Davey's ire to be raised. "Oh, bull. You guys took him and punished him for having the courage to raise his concerns about the treatment here. Those other men, they were friendly to the Doc, protective even. Don't give me your bull!"

She paused for a second. Then she responded, "I wondered. It seemed odd, as I have gotten to know the Doctor. Everybody loves him."

Davey pressed on. "Did you say anything that you thought something was wrong?"

"No, there was an emergency call and I did what I was told."

Davey, having more conviction now, more resolute that I have ever seen in him, stated, "That was the excuse of the Nazi's at Nuremberg. 'I was just following orders.' If they told you to force a bunch of us into a room to gas us, would you just be following orders? Would you go home that night, hug your babies, eat your dinner and say your prayers, consoled by the thoughts that you were just 'following orders'? Would you tell your husband 'we gassed 52, today. It was a busy day.' Would he say you were just following orders?"

Those in the room were silent. I was stunned. I almost stopped him, and then thought better of it.

Finally, she hollowly responded, "Don't be mad at us. We're just doing our jobs. Be mad at the judge."

Davey and the rest of the men sat quietly as she retreated into the clinic with nothing more to say.

Interestingly enough, within the hour of Davey's interaction in medical, two things happened almost simultaneously: The warden visited Dr. Wetselaar in the hole and sat and listened to the Doctor's account of the incident, according to Dr. Wetselaar, all the while shaking her head in disappointment. The other one of the managers came in to G2 Unit to take statements about the incident. All of which were damning to the new unit manager.

That evening, all four men were released from the hole and returned to the G units; two came back to G2 Unit – Dr. Wetselaar and Jim. The other two, Todd and Mel, members of The Bundy 19, were sent to a different unit. Once again dividing the co-defendants from one another, and Mel Bundy from his brother and father.

That night at our dinner table, we were missing a man, a son, and a brother.

My Final Days There
In the days I was with Cliven, it was amazing to see how the Bundy stand injected itself into the entire institution and into the lives of every detainee. Each kept up with the upcoming trial as the television news, local and national newspapers all kept the Bundy story in the

headlines. The men there, the other detainees, followed each turn of events like it was their very own family member, an uncle or a grandfather. After each story, there would be conversations, questions. And, of course, answers from the Bundys. This is a true testimony to their kindness and patience. Clearly, the Bundy family did not fit in with the remainder of the detainees; bank robbers, car jackers, drug dealers, you name it, The Detention Center was an ever-changing collection of society's worst, but Cliven Bundy was their favorite grandfather.

It was amazing how strongly The Bundy 19 held together. The immense pressure on them, the media, the prosecutorial threats and ploys were the most difficult times a person could ever imagine enduring.

It's easy to stand on the sidelines, in the spectator stands and smugly say things like, "If you're innocent, go to trial." Or, "Only the guilty take a plea bargain." But the reality is much different. A defendant in the modern justice system is extremely disadvantaged once they are locked-up. The immense pressure is spirit-breaking as you face an undetermined future and the life of you and your family lies in the balance. In my mind, I predicted that many of The Bundy 19 would succumb to this pressure and take a Plea Deal, trading their true convictions for their freedom and admit to crimes they didn't commit.

But not Cliven Bundy; his determination is resolute. He will do ___*whatever it takes*___ to see our country return to its liberty.

Now that you have read his account and heard his story, ask yourself:

Is Cliven Bundy a Domestic Terrorist? Or an American Patriot?

Before you answer, keep this in mind: The few acts of physical violence that occurred during the Standoff were the tasing of Ammon Bundy, the knocking down of Margaret, Cliven's sister, to the ground, and the stomping on the head of Davey Bundy after he was knocked to the ground.

CLIVEN BUNDY:

Never present at the scene of any confrontation in the Toquop Wash.

Never carried or brandished a weapon.

Never stood in the way of Federal agents.

Never supplied weapons to anyone.

Never directed anyone to assault a Federal agent/officer.

Never directed or advised anyone to do anything illegal during the Standoff or ever.

Never assaulted anyone, ever. He has NO criminal history.

Never asked anyone to come, and when they did, he told them they were their own agent.

Never pointed a gun at a Federal agent nor did he tell anyone else to do.

After being arrested at the Portland Airport in Oregon, the government-held assertions in Cliven's original court appearance in Oregon were summarized by Steven Myhre, acting U.S. Attorney in Las Vegas as the following:

No clear evidence that he *didn't* commit a crime. Cliven must prove a <u>false</u> negative.

The charges are not about grazing rights.

The charges are about violence, pointing guns.

Mr. Bundy does not recognize the Federal Courts, does not recognize Federal Court Orders, and does not recognize jurisdiction of Federal Courts.

Most significantly, Mr. Bundy and his conspirators were able, in a very short period of time, to muster, recruit, and bring gunmen to Nevada to engage in his assault. To "chest-up" with the BLM officers and assault them and raise their weapons at them. That Cliven Bundy usually moves with bodyguards, has armed checkpoints, in and around his property and on public lands, and armed patrols. All in an effort to keep the Federal Government away from him, preventing agents from arresting him and otherwise enforcing the laws as to him. There are no conditions or restrictions that could adequately assure the safety of the community and other persons nor assure his appearance at further court proceedings.

305

The brief for the detention hearing came only five minutes
before Mr. Grefenson (Bundy's attorney in Oregon) left
for court.

Mr. Grefenson asked for a recess to read the government
brief, which was denied.

Mr. Grefenson asked for testimony of witnesses, which was
denied.

Cliven Bundy was remanded into custody.

Cliven Bundy, presumed innocent, held in lock-up beginning in
February 2016, faces the trial of his life, where, if found guilty, he
could very likely spend the remainder of his natural life in Prison,
never, ever seeing his four boys again (Ryan, Ammon, Melvin, or
Davey).

June 21, 2017
I fell asleep late that evening late. I had a lot on my mind. My future,
Cliven's future, and how the fortuitous meeting of this one quiet,
honorable man had changed my life.

It wasn't more than an hour later I was told to "roll-up." And just like
that, my days with Cliven Bundy, the real-deal American Patriot, were over.

It was early, about 3:00 am, and I was packing my bedroll and clothing to return to the officers in Pahrump as I prepared to be taken to Las Vegas for eventual release. I had spent exactly two months with Cliven.

As I was stripping the sheets and blanket off my bed I was startled and looked up to see someone standing close to me. It was Cliven. All the other men were sound asleep. Somehow Cliven knew I was leaving and came to say goodbye. He smiled, we hugged, and quietly pushed away from one another. Cliven didn't say anything, he couldn't; I couldn't either. We both were choked up with tears; we both knew we were now friends for all the days God would give us in our lives. But I also knew the fight was still going on. Cliven, the entire Bundy 19, were and are in my prayers every day, and will not be forgotten. Not now, and not ever.

As I looked back from the van as it headed off towards Las Vegas at early light of dawn, I thanked God for the divine appointment with Cliven and the boys, something I'd take with me for the rest of my life.

Then I sighed, offering a quiet prayer to God.

"God, do a miracle for them ... they're gonna need it."

Author's Epilogue

309

Chapter 13

– MIRACLES DO HAPPEN –
Cliven Bundy Goes Free

Eight months after Cliven and I hugged and said goodbye, Supervising Federal Judge Gloria Navarro declared a mistrial in the criminal trial of Cliven Bundy, Ammon Bundy, Ryan Bundy and Ryan Payne. She stated:

"A universal sense of justice has been violated." — Judge Gloria Navarro. [1]

Judge Navarro dismissed all charges against the four men with prejudice. With that, she immediately released Cliven and the other three from lock-up. Honestly, I never thought I'd see Cliven a free man again. I was stunned, the whole world was stunned, but not Cliven Bundy. During the nearly 700 days of imprisonment as a political prisoner in Pahrump, Nevada, he never wavered in his faith that the truth would set him free. Was it the truth that set him free ... or was it the truth withheld?

Judge Navarro - No Friend to The Bundy 19
In the preceding 12 months, there had been two trials of what the prosecution deemed as the 'low hanging fruit' of defendants. "Tier One"[2] is the category name the prosecutors gave defendants that they believed would be the easiest to convict, setting the basis to find conspiracy charges for the remaining defendants. But, in the first trial the federal prosecutors were only able to secure two real convictions, those of Greg Burleson and Todd Engel, and these convictions were only on some of the charges. The jury either acquitted or were undecided on the remaining defendants, and remaining charges. This was a devastating setback for the prosecutors. Remember, their view was that they had these men dead-to-rights and a conviction of all charges should have been guaranteed. Even with this set back, the prosecutors were not deterred, setting a new trial to retry the Tier One defendants. In the trial and retrial, the conduct and rulings of Judge

---

1 Trial Transcripts, January 8, 2018, USA v. Cliven Bundy
2 USA v. Cliven Bundy et, al – Charging Document, Indictment and Superseding Indictment

Navarro were surprising, to put it mildly.

Motion *in Limine*

Before the trials began, the prosecutors filed several motions limiting (known as *in limine*) the scope of evidence that could be presented during the trial. This is common practice in U.S. courtrooms today. *In limine* (Latin: [ɪn ˈliːmɪˌne]; "at the start", literally, "on the threshold") motions are presented outside the jury presence and set the framework of the trial. There were several *in limine* motions that the prosecution submitted before the Tier One trial, severely limiting the defendants' defense.

1. The first argument before the court stated that there was no justification, nor any circumstance for the defendants to carry or point a weapon at a federal officer. This, of course, would limit any argument using a defense based on the Second Amendment, the right to bear arms, and the Nevada Statutes allowing a citizen to open carry a firearm.

2. The next argument before the court was regarding intent. Here, the prosecution argued that the mindset of the defendants had no bearing on whether a law was broken. It only mattered if they could prove it happened. This line of thinking meant that if the government could prove the Tier One defendants possessed a firearm on April 12, 2014, during the "Standoff," they committed an assault on federal officers. It would not matter whether they pointed the weapons at federal officers or not, irrespective of whether they actually fired upon them. In the case of Todd Engel, under this ruling he would be found guilty of assault even if the officers were not aware of his presence.

3. The third argument, as a legal basis, was prejudicial to the defense. For this trial, assault would be defined as threatening and provoking fear in the intended victim coupled with the ability to carry it out. In this case, the federal law enforcement officers were the alleged intended victims and all they would need to say was they were frightened.

4. The fourth argument revolved around the testimony of Agent-in-Charge Dan Love which, under this argument would not be admissible, nor would the revelation of his misconduct coming to light. Though much of the initial indictment was based on Love's testimony, (the Grand Jury used his testimony to indict all of The Bundy 19), his testimony was now "irrelevant and inadmissible." The defense teams were not allowed to interview him. Defense could not name or even mention him during the trial.

These rules tipped the scales against the defendants as the trial began. All the prosecution needed to do was demonstrate these men:

a) had a firearm and
b) the federal officers were frightened.

By whom or what did not matter under the ruling of this court. With these restrictions, the defendants had no defense under the Constitution, state law or even reason and logic.

As the trial began, the prosecution presented dozens of photos of each man with a firearm. Social media posts were used as evidence that the defendants came to Nevada with intent to kill law enforcement – notice how 'intent' went only one way – and the defendants were not allowed to explain their view of the events. Taking the stand and under oath, each federal officer actually wept to visibly express to the jurors how frightened they were. Even Las Vegas Metro officers took the stand expressing their fear, though they never entered the wash, nor in the line of fire that day. Most disappointing, though, was the testimony of Las Vegas Sheriff Joe Lombardo. If you recall from Chapter 10, his actions quelled the very tense situation in the wash, which ended peacefully. His testimony directly contradicted his public statements from the "Standoff." His accounting was made after actual events, clearly visible from dozens of hours of video, all of which was submitted into evidence.

It was apparent with the first two trials that the "Blue Veil of Silence" was in full effect as law enforcement followed the prosecution's lead in their attempt to obtain a conviction, not necessarily justice.

During the trial the judge referred to the defendants as "co-conspirators", and defense witnesses were admonished that they might themselves be prosecuted as un-indicted co-conspirators if they gave testimony of the events of April 12, 2014. Each witness was referred to an attorney to review their rights prior to giving their testimony. This had a chilling effect on the defense witnesses as, one by one, each refused to testify. At one point during the trial, Judge Navarro threatened to prosecute all the defense lawyers for misconduct. With this threat, the defense lawyers asked for a continuance in the trial, so they could consult their own defense lawyers! With this request, the threat lost steam. Even Defendant Eric Parker was denied his 1st, 6th and 14th Amendment rights to testify on his own behalf when, at the beginning of his testimony, Judge Navarro ordered him off the stand for indicating he was looking towards the government sniper positions on the mesa above the Toquop Wash. Any reference of the government agents' conduct was ruled as irrelevant, inadmissible and was summarily forbidden. This was encompassed in the previous rulings she had made (listed above). When Eric was removed from the stand he sat down and quietly sobbed at the defense table. Finally, in one of the most dramatic moves ever observed in such a high-stakes trial, each of the defense teams refused to present closing statements. Unmistakably the defense teams were telegraphing to the jury that they had nothing to say. Not "nothing else to say", as in no defense, but that the Judge had so hamstrung the defense that there was plainly nothing they were allowed to say. It was a risky, but bold, strategy that ultimately worked.

By the end of the Tier One defendants' second trial, the prosecution was unable to secure any further convictions. The new jury again found in favor of the defense on most of the charges and only one juror could not decide on just one charge. The jury was 'hung" a second time. This was devastating to the prosecution. How could they possibly not have secured the convictions of these "low hanging fruit" Tier One defendants when they had all of the rulings and evidence stacked in their favor? They vowed to carry on, to conduct a _**third**_ trial against the Tier One Defendants.

The third trial for Tier One defendants faced a court scheduling problem. The prosecutors attempted some calculated maneuvering by asking the court to split up The Bundy 19 into three separate trials, arranging the trials to lay ground work in succession against the next tier of defendants. Their two devastating losses with Tier One had clearly placed that plan in jeopardy. The court refused to push back the Tier Two and Tier Three trials any further, instructing the prosecution to retry Tier One after the Tier Three defendants. That meant Tier One defendants would need to sit in prison for at least another 18 months before the prosecution would get another swipe at them. With no assault convictions to build their case upon, it would become very difficult to convict Cliven Bundy of conspiracy to assault a federal officer. Remember, Cliven Bundy was never in the Toquop Wash during the 'Standoff' and he never carried a gun that day.

Who is this person?

For almost two years, friends and relatives of The Bundy 19 mustered every political ally they could find. The patriot community had come together to conduct rallies, fundraising events, letter writing campaigns and petitions. Brianna Bundy, wife of Mel Bundy one of The Bundy 19, attempted to crash a visit at a mutual friend's home by the new Secretary of the Interior, Ryan Zinke, to plea for President Trump to fulfill his promise to look into the matter. Shamefully, Secretary Zinke refused even 5 minutes with her at the private home in Bunkerville. More importantly, the patriot community took to social media to get their message out of the injustice The Bundy 19 were experiencing. It was a message that the main stream media (MSM) refused to report.

It is my opinion the Bundy supporters were viewed as uneducated hicks (or worse), emotionally-driven and not worthy of a story. But, they did have a story, an intensely emotional one. It is hard to fully communicate the pain of the effects that this type of persecution had on a family. The wives and children were alone while facing the prospect of never being united with their husband again, paying the growing mountain of bills, dealing with lawyers, and soothing children traumatized by the stress of the situation. Add to that the strain of harassment from hate-filled and threatening phone calls and social media posts bombarding them day and night. Their fair-weather friends shunned them, other acquaintances offered unsolicited advice about cutting their losses (*e.g.* divorce the loser) and worse. These families were under siege. I believe Brianna Bundy said it best when turned away from speaking to Secretary Zinke; "Don't you understand my kids have been orphaned and I am a widow at the hands of the

Federal Government." They received very little empathy for the situation they faced.

With determination, they took to social media as a platform to voice what was happening to them. Each day, people like Andrea Parker, wife of Eric Parker, Kelli Steward, John Lamb and Vincent Easley – all "Citizen Reporters" – gave daily updates on the trials via Internet radio and Facebook Live. Follow-up reports were done via blogs and Twitter. The stories were picked up by alternative media sources like *ReDoubt News, FreeRange Report* and *Range Magazine*. In time, these sources outpaced the coverage of the MSM who took little interest in the "Bundy antics." In time, the success of alternative reporting became a point of envy by the MSM, as those daily reports had tens of thousands of followers watch at least a day. There were daily, peacefully organized demonstration outside the courthouse that pointed out Judge Navarro's abuses. These campaigns began to get the attention of Attorney General Jeff Sessions and legislators in Idaho, Utah, and Arizona. Each responded with the passage of bills in Idaho and Arizona to support The Bundy 19. The Utah congressional team were catalysts in initiating the OIG investigation into the misconduct of Dan Love. Longtime political figures like Larry Klayman and Roger Stone took up the Bundy cause and, through lobbying, bringing the situation to the attention of President Trump and Attorney General Sessions. I believe all of this activity ultimately had an effect on Judge Navarro.

What brought real intensity was a little noticed August opinion piece in the Las Vegas Review Journal, the local news source in Las Vegas, Nevada.

> "After failing to gain convictions during the first proceeding in April, federal prosecutors got virtually everything they wanted in their retrial of four defendants charged in connection with the 2014 standoff at Cliven Bundy's ranch near Bunkerville.

> U.S. District Judge Gloria Navarro eviscerated the defense team's legal strategy and limited testimony favorable to the accused. Meanwhile, she gave the government wide latitude to tie the four men to extremist groups.

> It's a wonder the trial wasn't moved to San Francisco and the jury pool confined to the Center for Biological Diversity's donor list.

> **In the end, however, the result was familiar — and should send a loud message to the government.**
>
> On Tuesday, a Las Vegas jury handed federal prosecutors yet another embarrassing defeat. Two defendants were cleared of all charges and released Tuesday night. Jurors found the two other men not guilty of the majority of allegations, while deadlocking on a handful of other charges against them. It wasn't even close. The Review-Journal's David Ferrera reported that jurors told defense attorneys the vote was originally 11-1 in favor of acquittal.
>
> A virtual washout for the U.S. attorney's office."[3]
> "… the government should give it up. The case is weak, as the two previous misfires prove. Another trial would be a waste of time and taxpayer treasure.
>
> As for the remaining defendants and their upcoming trials, who would predict a slam dunk for the prosecution at this point? But whether you believe the Bundy protesters are right-wing nuts, misunderstood freedom fighters or something in between, it's hard to dispute that the high-handedness of BLM agents and the overreach of government attorneys has been a gift to the defense and created significant hurdles for the prosecution."

Had I read this accurately? The arguably liberal *Las Vegas Review Journal* editorial board all but called Judge Navarro's courtroom a Kangaroo Court. This pressure must have had its effect. I believe it did.

Judge Gloria Navarro was an entirely different person from the start of Cliven's trial.

The Trial

Cliven Bundy's trial started November 2017. Leading up to his trial, the defense team successfully maneuvered Dan Love into court for an evidentiary hearing. What had changed? No longer could the prosecution defend against the allegations of Love's misconduct. The allegations were proven, and he had been dismissed from his position with the Bureau of Land Management. It was clear from the opening

3 https://www.reviewjournal.com/opinion/editorials/editorial-the-government-loses-again-in-the-bundy-prosecution/ (emphasis Author's)

motions and evidential testimony by Special Agent in Charge Daniel P. Love – and from the additional officers that were involved in the round-up operations in April 2014 –there was much more to the story than most were aware from the previous two trials.

As the trial began, and because of my background, I quickly recognized that I was more knowledgeable on the issues than most in the courtroom. As I listened to the opening statements, the prosecution's witnesses, the cross examinations, and the evidentiary hearings I didn't hear much that was new. Most of what I heard confirmed what I had already written on Cliven's story.

Opening Statements

The prosecution launched their opening statements with a slide show. Each slide told a story of the day of the Standoff, each showed a photo of a man holding a firearm. Assistant U.S. Attorney Steven Myhre spoke with great vigor and authority to set the framework of his case. "This case is about pointing guns at federal officers, it's about threatening them, it's about assaulting them!" he paused. "It's not about anything else." Myhre's opening lasted about 45 minutes, with its objective to convince the jury they had literally stopped a civil war.

Only after the prosecution completed its presentation of evidence did each defendant's lawyer give an opening statement, beginning with Ammon Bundy. It's a well-known legal tactic that allows the defense to tailor an opening statement to the evidence the prosecution presents. The other defendants then followed. Ryan Bundy, representing himself, made a brilliant opening statement, a statement filled with the human side of the conflict. It can be reread as it's the preface of this book.

Cliven's Attorney, Brett Whipple, seized upon the opening statements of the prosecution with not only slides, but videos as well. He exhibited many of the same slides as the prosecution. He had comments such as "Remember this guy? He's a confidential informant placed there by your government. Remember this guy? He also is a confidential informant placed there by your government. Remember this guy? ..."

One by one Mr. Whipple discredited the prosecutions opening allegations. He brought up the image that the prosecution presented of Ammon Bundy as he was being tasered by the BLM officers.

"Remember this picture? The prosecution didn't show you the context … I have the video." Mr. Whipple proceeded to show the entire set of uncomfortable images of Margret Houston being thrown to the ground and the events leading up to Ammon's tasering. Next, he presented the video of David Bundy's arrest and abuse. "Now, through this trial the prosecution is going to show you lies and half-truths. It will be our job to clear that up for you." Mr. Whipple's opening statement was brilliant and effective from the beginning, showing the prosecution as untrustworthy.

The First Witness for the Prosecution
First witness called was Mary Jo Rugwell, an aging bureaucrat, who had trouble making her way to the witness stand. Rugwell was the BLM's district manager for Southern Nevada from April 2008 through August 2012. She testified in regard to Cliven Bundy's "continuous trespass" and how he refused to get a new 10-year permit in 1993 for his Bunkerville allotment of 154,000 acres. She admitted the fact BLM had changed the permit rules when it was determined that the desert tortoise was a threatened species. According to her testimony, the new permit cut Cliven's herd from 152 to 89 head of cattle and limiting his grazing to the months of June through September. Those are the hottest and driest months, and certainly the worst time of the year to graze cows in that Mojave Desert acreage. In her testimony, she described the agency hired a contractor to fly over the area, resulting in a head count of approximately 900 head of cattle. She claimed cattle were a danger to recreational areas, damaging vegetation and cultural resources. She did admit the cattle count was a soft number, because only about 400 head have the Bundy Ranch earmarks or brand.

Ms. Rugwell was also asked about the grazing fees the Bundy's owed. She was shown a slide with calculations on it.

Grazing fees = Approximately $4,000
Cattle Count = Approximately $360,000

She explained that by the time she left her position in 2012, according to their records, Cliven actually owed approximately $4,000 in grazing fees and $360,000 for the contractor they hired to count the cattle on the range, assessing that fee to the Bundy Ranch. That number was a far cry from the $1 Million that is proclaimed by the MSM.

Rugwell continued her testimony by being thoroughly cross-examined by the defense attorneys. She was asked what happened to the now-gone permit holders on the range? She answered that each of them had been "bought out by Clark County." But continued, "Mr. Bundy opted not to sell his."

Attorney Whipple asked Rugwell about the Threat Assessment Report the FBI made on the Bundy family. Whipple was fishing, because until this point the prosecution had denied that there was ever a threat assessment done on the Bundy's. She responded that the family had been categorized as "not a threat." This exchange was vigorously objected to by the prosecution, ending in a side-bar with Judge Navarro. She ordered the Threat Assessment be delivered to her on Monday, November 20th.

Then Mr. Whipple turned to the subject of water rights.

> Whipple: Can you show me where the Bundy water rights are on this map.
> Rugwell: No, I can't.
> Whipple: Can you point to the Bundy Ranch?
> Rugwell: No, I am not sure.
> Whipple: Okay, how about Lake Mead, maybe that will get your orientated.
> Rugwell: I guess I am not all that familiar with the area.

Changing direction slightly ...

> Whipple: You had a meeting with Mr. (Clark County Commissioner) Collins and others?
> Rugwell: Yes.
> Whipple: Do you recall what Mr. Collins said about water rights?
> Rugwell: He said he believed Mr. Bundy should have access to his water rights.
> Whipple: Do you know who owns the water rights on Gold Butte?
> Rugwell: I do not.
> Whipple: There were range improvements of each and every spring?
> Rugwell: I don't know. I can't say that there are range improvements on every spring.

Next Morgan Philpot, Ammon Bundy's attorney, began his cross-examination regarding water rights.

> Philpot: Did you do any research into stock watering rights?
> Rugwell: No I did not.
> Philpot: Are you aware Mr. Bundy had stock watering rights?
> Rugwell: I'd Heard that, but it was not relevant. This was a trespass issue. I never looked into any stock watering rights myself.
> Then AUSA Daniel Schiess, redirects regarding water rights.
> Shiess: You have been asked about stock watering rights. Do you have any information on who owns water rights?
> Rugwell: No, I do not.

From Mary Jo Rugwell's sworn testimony you and the jury could conclude that:

> 1. She never investigated Cliven's water rights ownership in Gold Butte.
> 2. She had no idea where springs were located or who owned water rights in Southern Nevada. She couldn't even find Lake Mead on a map!
> 3. She did not know if Cliven Bundy had water rights or range improvements.

But, in the discovery provided after the October deadline to the defense, by the prosecution, it is described as follows:

> *Among those documents were the attached letters, which were found to include 2008 correspondence from and to Mary Jo Rugwell, then the supervisor of the BLM in Southern Nevada.*

These documents would have been nice for the defense to have to impeach Rugwell's testimony. They were withheld until after Rugwell's testimony concluded. This underlined the defense's concerns of ongoing misconduct by the prosecution.

In the previous two trials, Judge Navarro allowed the jurors to ask questions of a witness. In this trial she continued with the same procedure. About 6 jurors asked questions after Rugwell had been cross-examined.

The more memorable questions from the jury were:

> (1) Where is Dave Bundy now? Witness Rugwell answered that she did not know.
> (2). Did the Bundy cattle cause any damage before Bundy declined payment of his 1993 permit? Witness Rugwell answered **No**.
> (3) Were any desert tortoises on the Bundy Ranch harmed after Mr. Bundy quit paying fees? Witness Rugwell said **Yes**.

From my view in the gallery, the jury was beginning to follow the case from the first witness.

The next witness called by the prosecution was Terry Petrie, an attorney for the Department of Justice and legal counsel for the BLM. Prosecutor Daniel Scheiss had Petrie read a civil deposition given by Cliven Bundy. This was the same deposition I reviewed in Chapter 6. Next, Ryan Bundy's cross examination of witness Petrie was to refresh the witness's memory of his attorney's oath to uphold the Constitution. Ryan Bundy spent about an hour and a half going through the Constitution. The jury seemed to lean in during Ryan's constitutional lesson. In the end, Mr. Petrie thanked Ryan Bundy for the refresher in the Constitution and admitted Ryan was very knowledgeable.

As the trial progressed, Judge Navarro seemed to have softened towards the defendants. There were many closed courtroom sessions with the defense team and prosecutors. Of course, that meant the public and jury were not allowed in the courtroom during those hearings. Some hearings lasted for many hours. The defense teams seemed beleaguered yet remained hopeful. One attorney stated, "I've never seen anything like it in twenty years of practicing law." Another muttering to me, "It was more astounding than you can imagine." Then came the first crack in the log jam.

Judge Navarro, in what seemed like an out-of-the-blue moment, decided to give the defendants pre-trial release. After nearly two years of confinement for Cliven, and numerous motions before the court, she allowed the four men in Tier Two to petition for pre-trial release. That meant each could be released from prison under certain court-ordered conditions and most of them would be home for Christmas.

Each of the remaining Bundy 19 in the other Tiers also began to petition for release. Only one failed to be released.

In another surprising turn of events, Cliven Bundy refused the release! Cliven Bundy had refused pre-trial release. He stated that he wouldn't leave until all The Bundy 19 were released. Additionally, he would not leave until the government dismissed the charges against each of them and admitted they were wrong to charge them in the first place.

That was quite a stand.

The Break in the Log Jam
Through all the ups and downs of chronicling this story, I experienced one of the saddest days in my life.

Let me explain…

I sat in the courtroom of day 15 of the Cliven Bundy trial (at this point that is six calendar weeks in the courtroom). Over the previous weeks, I had made the journey from my Northern Nevada home, staying weeks at a time in Las Vegas, to watch the wheels of justice turn … slowly … painfully slowly.

December 11th; however, was something different.

When we arrived in the courtroom that Monday, I was shocked to see so few people in the gallery – four reporters and only a handful of Bundy supporters. The jury had been called and waited in the jury room; the defendants, their attorneys, and the prosecution were in position and ready for a new week of battle. We all waited quietly for the judge to enter the courtroom followed by the jury.

And we waited.

Nearly an hour we waited.

"All rise," the court clerk called out and Chief Judge Gloria Navarro entered.

As we retook our seats, Judge Navarro began; "I would like to get some clarifications on the mistrial motions. Though these matters are not ripe, I want to give the parties some idea of my concerns." And, with that, she spent the next full hour listing each motion and 14 of her concerns. Of those she listed, there were seven possible "Brady" violations.

The Brady Rule, named after the Court's rulings in Brady v. Maryland, 373 U.S. 83 (1963), requires prosecutors to disclose materially exculpatory evidence in the government's possession to the defense.

"Brady material," that is the evidence the prosecutor is required to disclose under this rule, includes: evidence favorable to the accused, evidence that goes towards negating a defendant's guilt, evidence that would reduce a defendant's potential sentence, or evidence going to the credibility of a witness.

While Brady violations have several remedies; only one of these – and the most drastic – is a mistrial. Typically, a Brady violation is discovered after a trial has concluded and is used to petition the court to rule for a mistrial and to set aside the conviction. In order to win a mistrial, the defense must prove that there is reasonable probability that the outcome of the trial would have been different in order for a mistrial to be granted.

In the Bundy case, Judge Navarro may have been considering a mistrial just as the trial began to gain steam, months away from its conclusion with a jury verdict. Most judges would prefer that the jury make the final verdict, as is in our legal tradition. But, there is yet another reason for Brady violation ruling: the proof that if the evidence were made available, the case would have taken a different light. This appeared to be Judge Navarro's primary concern.

As careful as Judge Navarro was in listing her concerns, she did not give too many specifics. In a previous (and rare) pre-trial order,

Judge Navarro placed certain evidence under seal. Thus, by her own order, she could not be overly specific. Because I had an extensive understanding of the background of this trial I could extrapolate some of the issues at hand that could shed a "different light" on this trial.

Cliven Bundy has always taken the stance that the Federal Government had no jurisdiction to take the action they did in impounding his cattle. Moreover, the government took the extraordinary action during the impound operation to surround his home, set up checkpoints, and threaten and physically abuse his family. He also told me that they had snipers surrounding his home. Ammon Bundy claimed to have seen the snipers' red targeting lasers not only on him but dancing on the bodies of the Bundy children. And, much, much more.

As I wrote in Chapter 2, when I first heard of these things while incarcerated with Cliven and The Bundy 19, I just figured Cliven was embellishing his story. As it turns out, it was much worse than even Cliven knew.

All along, the prosecution just scoffed at, and summarily dismissed, Cliven's claims.

But, on Monday December 11th, we learned from Judge Navarro several things we didn't know before:

SNIPERS: Yes indeed, there were snipers. The Bundys said this for years. The prosecution denied it. But since, the prosecution acquiesced saying only that, although there were some people lying down along the ridges, they were merely "over-watch" people – just guys with binoculars and radios. However, we learned from Special Agent-in-Charge Dan Love (of all people), in his sworn testimony of October 25, 2017, that there were snipers. With guns. The prosecution's answer was that they were simply "practicing" and there was nothing more to it. My question? What were they "practicing" when they aimed their guns at unarmed American citizens? Does it stop being "practice" and become "implementation" only when they pull the trigger?

ORDERS TO CEASE OPERATIONS: It appeared de-escalation was not a personal option for Dan Love. Pete Santilli attempted to get Love to understand that the Bundy Protest was escalating beyond the

Bundys' local family and friends. National and international media had taken an interest in the story and social media was blowing up, with over one million views of the videos that had been posted of Davey's arrest and the assaults on Margaret and Ammon. And, of course, the existence of the Government's so-called "First Amendment" areas created by the BLM to contain the protesters well away from the focus of the Protest, had become explosive issues, as well.

Additionally, Love's Washington D.C. superiors took notice of the protest size, and their inability to control the narrative due to the ever-growing media coverage, so they decided to cease the operation. The BLM director of media relations said that "it was frustrating" to try to get ahead of the story when they were getting so much criticism of hundreds of lawmakers. It's also clear that this order to cease operations was received by Love, as revealed in the October 25, 2017 (and following), testimony – again, under oath – of the BLM agents who ran the Communications Center and the Operations' Agent Dispatch Desk. The agents in the Communication Center in the BLM compound were ordered to start packing up and shredding documents on April 10th. Note: This was two full days before the events of the April 12th "Standoff" that following Saturday. That also seems to be the same day the FBI and the contract cowboys left, leaving only the BLM Law Enforcement element and NPS Rangers under Dan Love's command.

PROSECUTORIAL INVOLVEMENT: We also know, according to the testimony of Dan Love on October 25, 2017, Love had a conference call with the then U.S. Attorney Dan Bogden in Las Vegas. Together, they conspired how they would bring Cliven to justice. If they could get Cliven to be the one to release the cattle – or "Pull the Pin" (which meant to remove the pin on the gate holding the cattle) – then they could charge him with impeding a federal officer in his duties. This would allow them to tie Cliven and his boys into a conspiracy in relationship to all the other charges of weapons and assault of the Bundy 19. They never anticipated Cliven would simply stay at the staging area the entire day.

We know now that the former Acting U.S. Attorney Steve Myhre and his assistant prosecutor Nadia Ahmed, the actual prosecutors in the

Bundy trials, were photographed at the Command Center compound during the round-up operations meeting with the Operation's leadership. The prosecutors became participants – or, at least, witnesses. They conveniently forgot to mention that to the defense.

PROSECUTORIAL INVOLVEMENT II: We know now that Acting U.S. Attorney Steve Myhre was working with the Department of Interiors' OIG office on a weekly basis to "aid" the OIG Inspectors' investigation into the handling of the shredded evidence, Dan Love's "lost" laptop, and his "lost" notebook. It was discovered that Myhre discouraged the investigators from interviewing anyone actually physically related to the act of shredding. On the stand, none – NOT ONE – of the responsible officers remembered who did the actual shredding. They testified that they knew they hadn't, and they didn't remember seeing anyone else do it; but, they knew they were ordered to do it. Of course, the OIG investigators never interviewed any of these Department of Interior workers prior to their testimony. Still, somehow, that huge volume of evidence was shredded – as shown by the photographs of the shred bags. This was further proof that Myhre was a witness, or most likely a participant and architect.

THE BUNDY THREAT: The defense team continually asked for copies of any evaluations from the government regarding the threat, if any, the Bundys might pose. It wasn't until November 2017 that the prosecution coughed them up. Why? Because, once again, Dan Love and the Director of the BLM in Southern Nevada, Mary Jo Rugwell, mentioned them under oath. It turns out that there was not one, but, in fact, *__four__* such Threat Assessments, starting back in 2011, each report showed the Bundy's were a low threat risk. The Government also paid a consultant – of sorts – $60,000 to evaluate the Bundys; no one knows why they were hired or where that report is. The only reason the defense knows about its existence is because they found the receipt in the discovery.

Oops ...

TECHNICAL SURVEILLANCE: Ryan Bundy remembered seeing a camera set up and monitoring the Bundy household during the weeks leading up to April 12, 2014. The prosecution flatly denied the existence of such a camera, its deployment, or its coverage. They also claimed that the FBI was not involved in the roundup operations nor were they onsite. However, Dan Love and another BLM officer testified that at least one camera was there, set up and maintained by the FBI. The FBI also had their own trailer within the compound with a live video and audio feed from the cameras and microphones that they placed around the compound. The defense teams asked for the footage from those cameras and recordings, but the prosecution claimed that no recordings were made, and no one was watching the defendants. Even Judge Navarro seemed to have a hard time with this one – before the denial of surveillance was impeached by yet another Government witness – the Chief of the Communications Center who, testifying that the FBI liaison ran the live feed and that the command element watched it regularly, particularly as the ranks of the protesters began to swell.

WIRETAPPING: More was revealed through the testimony of Region 4 BLM Law Enforcement officer Robert Schilackin. He came in from Colorado to help the Region 3 BLM Law Enforcement officer deliver the message of their intention to enforce the refreshed court orders for removal of the Bundys' cattle from the public lands (which lie under Bundy's grazing and water rights) and solicit from them what resistance to this BLM action the Bundys might mount. In his testimony, Schilackin admitted they had secretly recorded an interview with a Bundy employee. When asked by the defense if he was aware that was a crime, he blew it off saying that it wasn't a crime.

WIRETAPPING II: Officer Schilackin was equally cavalier with his actions and perhaps, with federal and state law, when he testified on cross examination that he had recorded his Region 3 partner's telephone conversation with Ryan Bundy without revealing this fact at the beginning of the call to the parties. This "poisoned" recording was even played in court (first as snippets and then in its full 46 minutes) by both the Government and then the defense. He added that such recordings were "not part of the plan," but such recordings are done so routinely that it was never given a second thought.

In the session without the jury's presence between these two wiretapping admissions, the Judge allowed their use; but, in passing, made mention of possible criminal charges against the officers and that they would be dealt with later – not wanting the current trial to get bogged down on a separate issue.

WIRETAPPING III: Revealed documents showed once again that the government had been listening in on attorney-client phone calls between the defendants and their counsel. The prosecutors wanted the public to believe that their content was "so mundane and innocuous" that it had no bearing on the trial, but the recordings had been reviewed by a special FBI team and marked as privileged in order to shield them from the defense. The prosecution wanted it both ways. If they were so mundane and innocuous, why hide them?

SPECIAL FORCES: All these new revelations included information that not only was the Clark County Sheriff's Department Special Weapons and Tactics (SWAT) Team deployed to the Toquop Wash on April 12, 2014, but earlier the FBI's Hostage Rescue Team, The National Park Service Special Event Tactical Team (SETT), AND the Los Angeles SWAT Team. All were present on site and had been ready to deploy the entire week, though some departed when given the stand-down order on April 10th.

All along, Cliven Bundy said that there were 200-armed, military-type government men and women surrounding his ranch. The prosecution said in their opening argument that there were only about twenty. We now know the official number is 197. The prosecutors' excuse for not disclosing all these other Special Forces Teams was that they were there for "training and practice" and because they were never used. Hence, there was no need to disclose them to the defense teams. Of course, the defense had a completely different view. The defense team should have had the opportunity to interview each of the approximately 45 new witnesses they never knew about.

DEPLOYMENT: Cliven Bundy has continually said that he was surrounded for over a week. He said there were checkpoints and spying on him and his family. The prosecution denied such "crazy" notions. But, again, Judge Navarro's concern was that the organizational chart that was created to explain the communication and reporting authority between the BLM, and all the other agencies deployed there was missing, along with all the maps showing the agents deployment locations, the paperwork and handwritten materials. This was all probably destroyed in the shredder in an effort to cover-up the magnitude of what was involved.

REPORTS: Another of Judge Navarro's concerns was the revelation that some of the Government Criminal Reports, called 302's, were written in November 2017 – NOT in 2014, as one would expect. They were written only after being requested by the defense after the testimony of Dan Love and the other BLM and OIG officers in October 2017.

The only plausible explanation is that the reports were written *years later* to corroborate the fraudulent narrative the prosecution had put forth and to dispute Love's testimony.

Chapter 14

– USING YOUR SECOND AMENDMENT RIGHTS –
While Practicing Your First Amendment Rights

That night, after court adjourned, Cliven and I spoke on the phone. Judge Navarro's biggest worry was the revelation that there was an actual hit list maintained by the Government with Cliven Bundy's name at its top. This list seemed to be an actual shooting list, only revealed by a BLM agent who was trying to cover his backside. This agent became a whistleblower. When I asked Cliven about who it was, he wouldn't answer me directly, only to say that this BLM agent is no longer employed by the government. I wondered who that could be ...

"Well, we got a couple of BLM guys who have turned into whistleblowers, ya see. And all kind of things are coming out."

"Okay, I need to ask, what's this I am hearing about a kill, list? It's all over social media," I asked.

"Well yeah, there has always been a kill list for me. Remember the militia guys in front of the stage with me? They were there to protect my life. I was on the kill list for quite a long time. For two years, I had bodyguards. I have been on it for quite a few years."

He continued. "In my own mind, I don't need a bodyguard. But, there've always been bodyguards around me ... fer two years, I have had 'em."

And according to the sworn testimony given in court, Cliven was right.

"They had a kill list and I was number one on the kill list," (he uncomfortably chuckles). "This thing is more serious than most people want to think about it."

"So," I asked – somewhat stunned, "did they have a list that was like priorities of who to shoot first?"

"No, it's just a book where a guy is keepin' a kill list. Where they mark off guys they already got rid of. I guess they also had a big poster up in there with my picture on it – the BLM office – with a big "X" thru it."

Hidden Evidence

All of this remarkable evidence had been hidden from the defense, putting them at an extreme disadvantage. Not only did the prosecution choose not to reveal these "Brady" documents, but their duplicitous actions kept the defense from subpoenaing dozens of personnel and their reports.

Assistant U.S. Attorney Daniel R. Schiess complained at length about how much work all of this 'last-minute response' to the defense requests had been to their office. (But it was material that the prosecution should have provided years before at the onset of the discovery process! It was material that finally came to light based on the testimony of Government witnesses.)

Schiess whined, "Just last night, the defense filed a 28-page motion for a mistrial. We need time to answer."

The entire day, prosecutors Myhre and Ahmid sat uncharacteristically quiet. As I looked at them I wondered if they were desperate not to dig themselves in deeper.

I mentioned in Chapter 13 that I was sad as I headed home that afternoon. It was an "in my gut" kind of sad. I wondered why I wasn't angry or surprised. I was sad. As I pondered on the events over the last few months, I realized that my government, in the country that I love so much, was actually acting criminally against its people. I had heard about it, denied that it could possibly happen, yet had seen it before, firsthand in my own trials with the government – but never so defiantly, or so callously. I told a friend that night, "I am sad because we depend and respect the judicial system. We rely on its fairness, and I want this fairness for every accused, even the most heinous of criminals. But especially for Cliven Bundy … a simple rancher standing up for OUR rights."

I woke up the following morning anticipating that the MSM would have these startling court revelations plastered across their front pages. To my shock, nothing. None of the details of Judge Navarro's concerns were being reported. Then, I thought about who those reporters were on December 11th in the courtroom. Two reporters were from environmental websites and one was from the Southern Poverty Law Center. Clearly, these details didn't fit their narrative. The fourth reporter was young, from the *Las Vegas Review Journal*, and admitted to never being in a courtroom. No wonder there was no MSM reporting on the details.

Though, the faithful citizen reporters were doing their best to broadcast the court proceedings.

Mistrial Declared

On December 20, 2017, Judge Navarro came to a decision. She declared a mistrial. She gave the parties an opportunity to file their briefs as to why the case should be dismissed – with or without prejudice – and reset the trial for January 8, 2018. At that point, she dismissed the jury, thanking them for their service. Only then did the MSM begin to pick-up on the previous court decisions.

The next day, December 21, Attorney General (AG) Jeff Session launched an investigation into the DOJ's Las Vegas office: "The Attorney General takes this issue very seriously and has personally directed that an expert in the Department's discovery obligations be deployed to examine the case and advise as to next steps," said Ian Prior, a spokesman for the Department of Justice.

On January 3, 2018, Assistant U.S. Attorney Steven Myhre was demoted. In the summer of 2017 when visiting Las Vegas, AG Sessions made remarks that celebrated Acting U.S. Attorney Myhre for his lead role in the prosecution of Cliven Bundy of The Bundy 19. But now Sessions' vote of confidence had wavered, and he brought in a new U.S. Attorney for the Nevada District.

> [Note: U.S. Attorney Bogden resigned his position in the spring of 2017 after Sessions sought the resignations of 46 U.S. Attorneys remaining from President Obama's

administration. Myhre was promoted to Acting U.S. Attorney at that time.]

After the disgraceful performance, mistrial decision, and prosecutorial misconduct of Myhre and his team, Sessions appointed Texas Federal Prosecutor Dayle Elieson to fill the interim top spot in Nevada, replacing Steven Myhre.

Myhre returned to his previous position of Assistant U.S. Attorney. Ironically, one of his new duties is to train and mentor young attorneys in the Department.

A Packed Courtroom

Finally, January 8, 2018, Decision Day arrived. The courtroom was packed. This time the MSM showed up in force. Family and friends of the Bundy's, patriots, and even members of the jury all converged on the court house to hear the judge's decision on the prosecution's request for a new trial, or if she would dismiss all charges against the defendants with prejudice. ("With prejudice" means that charges can never be brought up again on the defendants.)

The air in the courtroom was a mix of tension and celebration. All the defendants on pre-release looked rested and dressed in business attire. Except Cliven; he remained in leg irons, belly chains and in those silly blue scrubs and orange Crocs in which I first met him. He looked tired, thinner, but was smiling that big cowboy grin of his.

As the Judge entered chambers, all were asked to rise. "Be Seated," the court clerk declared as the Judge sat at the head of the courtroom.

Judge Navarro opened with her standard instructions to the public: "All right. So, before we begin, I just wanted to make some preliminary remarks to remind everyone and to set clear the expectations of how court will be conducted this morning. Please remember this is a courtroom; it is not a sporting event. So, it is never appropriate to make any expression of your opinion, whether verbally or through your body language, no matter how much you may agree or disagree with what is being said."

Judge Navarro proceeded with a long and detailed statement on which she had based her decision, citing "willful" failure to turn over voluminous documents that could have helped the defense fight conspiracy and assault charges.

"The court does regrettably believe a mistrial in this case is the most suitable and only remedy," she declared. The judge then listed six types of evidence that she said prosecutors deliberately withheld before trial, including information about the presence of an FBI surveillance camera on a hill overlooking the Bundy ranch and information concerning issues outside the ranch, maps, an FBI log with entries about snipers, threat assessments that indicated the Bundys were not violent, and that the BLM was trying to provoke a conflict by antagonizing the Bundy's and their supporters. It came to nearly 500 pages of Internal Affairs documentation involving lead bureau Special Agent Love. This material, the judge found, would bolster the defense's stance that defendant Ryan Payne put a call out for support because the Bundys feared they were surrounded by snipers, the BLM and NPS Agents, and felt isolated.

The information could also refute the government's indictment that alleged the defendants used deceit to draw supporters by "falsely" contending snipers were surrounding the ranch.

"The failure to turn over such evidence violates due process," Judge Navarro said. Going even further, she pinned the misconduct on both the prosecutions and the investigating agencies:

> *Here in this case, both the prosecution and the investigative agencies are equally responsible for the failure to produce Brady materials to the defense. In the prior mistrial hearing, the Court explained, in detail, that numerous documents, and the information contained in such documents, should have been provided to the defense and the Court finds this conduct especially egregious because the government chose not to provide this evidence, even after the defense specifically requested it. The Court finds the prosecution's representations that it was unaware of the materiality of the Brady evidence is grossly shocking.* [1]

1 Trial Transcripts, January 8, 2018, USA v. Cliven Bundy

Reporter Maxine Bernstein of *The Oregonian*, who closely followed the trials in both Oregon and Nevada, also pointed out:

> Prosecutors had belittled Ryan Bundy's pretrial motion for information on the "mysterious" devices outside the family ranch in 2014 as "fantastical" and a "fishing expedition," the judge noted. The government willfully withheld a March 28, 2014, law enforcement operation order and an FBI report that showed there was an FBI camera trained on the Bundy home for surveillance.
>
> The FBI's SWAT team put the camera up, repaired it and monitored a live feed from it. The U.S. Attorney's Office was aware of this, the judge said, and didn't share information about the camera until the defense heard a witness confirm its presence. "The government falsely represented the camera that was on the Bundy house was incidental, not purposeful," the judge said.
>
> The judge also found prosecutors withheld a March 3, 2015, FBI report that identified a Bureau of Land Management agent in tactical gear and carrying an AR-15 rifle outside the family ranch on April 5 and April 6, 2014.
>
> In addition, she cited an FBI log with entries that said, "snipers were inserted" and on standby outside the Bundy home. Three entries in the log mentioned snipers present, Navarro noted. Prosecutors claimed they were unaware of the log at first because it was kept on a thumb drive in a tactical vehicle.
>
> "The government is still responsible for information from the investigating agency. The FBI chose not to disclose it," Navarro said.
>
> That, coupled with "the government's strong insistence at prior trials that there were no snipers", convinced her the withholding of the sniper evidence was done knowingly.
>
> She also cited at least four threat assessments that indicated the Bundys likely wouldn't use violence, "would get in your face" but not engage in a shootout, and that the Bureau of Land Management was antagonizing the family "trying to provoke a conflict." The threat evaluations were made by the

FBI Behavioral Analysis Unit, the Southern Nevada Counter Terrorism unit, the FBI Nevada Joint Terrorism Task Force, the Gold Butte Cattle Impound Risk Assessment and the Bureau of Land Management law enforcement arm between 2011 and 2015.[2]

In reviewing the legal basis of her dismissal, Judge Navarro reviewed the 9th Circuit Court of Appeals ruling on U.S.A. v. Chapman, stating:

...the Court looks to Chapman, U.S. v. Chapman. And in Chapman, the district court dismissed an Indictment pursuant to its supervisory powers based on discovery violations that involved 650 pages of undisclosed documents that the Court classified as Brady material. The district court in Chapman found that "the Assistant U.S. Attorney acted flagrantly, willfully and in bad faith" and that he had made "affirmative misrepresentations to the Court," that the defendants would be prejudiced by a new trial and that no lesser standard would adequately remedy the harm done after reviewing the totality of the proceedings before it.

The Ninth Circuit held that the Chapman court did not abuse its discretion by dismissing the Indictment pursuant to its supervisory powers.[3]

USA v. Chapman
Now, let's just stop here for one moment.

This case, USA v. Chapman, that Judge Navarro quoted as a ruling for the basis for the dismissal, was an alleged securities fraud case in 2004, in which the Federal Prosecutors office had been accused of prosecutorial misconduct. The district court dismissed an indictment against Daniel Chapman, Sean Flanagan, and Herbert Jacobi (collectively "Defendants") after the prosecution admitted that it had failed to meet its obligations to disclose over 650 pages of documents to the defense, and thus committed a Brady violation. This landmark case was upheld by the 9th Circuit Court of Appeals in 2008.

2 https://www.oregonlive.com/oregon-standoff/2017/12/mistrial_declared_in_cliven_bu.html
3 Trial Transcripts, January 8, 2018, USA v. Cliven Bundy

Here is a very revealing exchange in the Chapman trial between the Assistant U.S. Attorney (AUSA) and the Court (Judge):

> AUSA: Your Honor, if I could just advise the Court in an abundance of caution rather than find the record of what we turned over, we'll make another copy of everything right now and provide it to the defense counsel immediately.

> COURT: Well, but it's supposed to be turned over. It's not a matter of doing it now.

> The judge declared a brief recess and the court reconvened outside the presence of the jury. The following exchange took place:

> AUSA: Your Honor, we cannot find a record of making this information available to defense counsel. We believe, however, that we did, or it was certainly our intention to do so.

> COURT: But your belief isn't good enough. This stuff has to be disclosed to them.

> AUSA: And we've disclosed it now, your Honor.

> COURT: Well, I understand, but that's late. I'm [not] going to say it's to[o] late, but it's late.

> AUSA: Your Honor, we apologize.

> COURT: Okay, I want this stuff – this stuff is going to be produced or I'm going to start striking testimony or worse.

Defense counsel walked the court through various discovery violations up to that point and urged it to impose immediate sanctions.

The next day, Chapman's attorney alerted the court to hundreds of pages of documents that the government had delivered that morning and the previous evening. They totaled some 650 pages and consisted of rap sheets, plea agreements, cooperation agreements, and other information related to numerous government witnesses, including at least three important witnesses whose testimony was already complete.

In response, the AUSA represented that much of the material under discussion had already been disclosed to the defense, but admitted that he could not prove what information had been disclosed because his office had not kept a log of what materials the government had turned over. He assured the district court, however, that he had made his best effort to comply with the government's obligations. The AUSA argued that neither a mistrial nor a dismissal of the indictment was the appropriate remedy. He urged that the court allow defense counsel sufficient time to review the documents and to recall as necessary any witnesses who had already testified.

The district court expressed frustration, lambasting the prosecutor's conduct as "unconscionable." Based on the material contained in Hearing Exhibit 1, the Judge stated, "I don't see any way this trial can go forward. We're in the third week of it, so I say that regrettably." He noted that he was inclined to dismiss the indictment, but deferred ruling on the motion to dismiss until the parties had a chance to brief the issue. The district court then declared a mistrial, dismissed the jury, and ordered briefing on Defendants' motion to dismiss the second superseding indictment. [4]

Doesn't this interchange seem eerily similar to the Bundy case? In the Chapman case there where only 650 pages of potentially exculpatory evidence withheld from the defense. In the Bundy case there were at least 3,000 pages and much more.

But, these two cases have something else in common.

Both cases were tried in the District Court in Nevada, the very same courthouse as Cliven Bundy's case.

The Assistant US Attorney handling the US v. Chapman case?
And the Bundy Case?

Wait for it…

4 https://caselaw.findlaw.com/us-9th-circuit/1384311.html

AUSA Steven W. Myhre, Acting United States Attorney!

The very landmark case that Judge Navarro used to dismiss the Bundy case for prosecutorial misconduct was indicted by the Las Vegas office and argued by the same Assistant U.S. Attorney.

I will allow you to draw your own conclusions as to a pattern.

The Court's Final Order in USA v. Bundy

Judge Navarro concluded her review with THE ORDER:

> *The government is only proposed a new trial as the appropriate remedy for their discovery violations. However, its conduct has caused the integrity of a future trial and any resulting conviction to be even more questionable. Both the defense and the community possess the right to expect a fair process with a reliable conclusion. Therefore, it is the Court's position that none of the alternative sanctions available are as certain to impress the government with the Court's resoluteness in holding prosecutors and their investigative agencies to the ethical standards which regulate the legal profession as a whole.*
>
> *The Court finds that the government's conduct in this case was indeed outrageous, amounting to a due process violation, and that a new trial is not an adequate sanction for this due process violation.*
>
> *Even if the government's conduct did not rise to the level of a due process violation, the Court would nonetheless dismiss under its supervisory powers because there has*

been flagrant misconduct, substantial prejudice, and no lesser remedy is sufficient. Dismissal is necessary as to these four defendants: Ryan Payne, Ryan Bundy, Ammon Bundy, and Cliven Bundy, and dismissal is justified for all three of the enumerated reasons provided by the law:

> *Number one, to properly remedy the constitutional violation; number two, to protect judicial integrity by ensuring that a conviction rests only on appropriate considerations validly before a jury; and number three, to deter future illegal conduct.*

It is herein ordered that the defendants' Motion to Dismiss with prejudice, Number 2883, public version 3057, as well as Document No. 2906, public version 3058, and Document 3082 and 3085, public version 3087 and 3088, are hereby granted.

The Court hereby vacates the detention orders for Cliven Bundy.[5]

A few hours later Cliven Bundy emerged through the front doors
of the Lloyd George U.S. Courthouse as a free man, greeted by an
enthusiastic crowd of friends and family. And, of course, the media.

As Cliven and his wife Carol walked out into a light rain, hundreds of
supporters cheered. A "Not Guilty" sticker had been stuck to his lapel.
Cliven took off his hat and waved it to the crowd and posed for a few
pictures.

"I'm not used to being free, put it that way," he said. "I've been
a political prisoner for right at 700 days today. I come into this
courtroom an innocent man and I'm going to leave as an innocent man."

"My defense is a 15-second defense: I graze my cattle only on Clark County, Nevada, land and I have no contract with the federal government," he said. "This court has no jurisdiction or authority over this matter. And I've put up with this court in America as a political prisoner for two years."

U.S. Attorney Dayle Elieson of Nevada released a short statement after the decision. "We respect the court's ruling and will make a determination about the next appropriate steps."

Kieran Suckling, executive director of the Center for Biological Diversity, who recently had been a lone counter-protester in front of the courthouse stated:

> *Federal prosecutors clearly bungled this case and let the Bundys get away with breaking the law, The Bundys rallied a militia to mount an armed insurrection against the government. The failure of this case will only embolden this violent and racist anti-government movement that wants to take over our public lands.*

Suckling had never set one foot in the courtroom to hear the evidence.

Chapter 15

– THE WHISTLE IS BLOWN –
There IS Someone Ethical at the BLM

On, December 14, 2017, just days after Judge Navarro revealed her "concerns," a breaking story came from an unlikely media outlet in Idaho. *Redoubt News*, a little-known media website, announced that they had an exclusive breaking story about the Bundy trial. The story came from Matt Shea, a member of the Washington House of Representatives, representing the 4th Legislative District. *ReDoubt News* was (and is) a regular outlet for the citizen journalist and they invested their own professional journalists to cover The Bundy 19 case. Just as Cliven had mentioned to me over the phone from lock-up, there indeed was a whistleblower who recently became known to the defense team, but the prosecution had known about this person for quite a while. Since November 27, 2017, the Department of Justice had a memo in their hands, clearly from the onset of Cliven's trial. Of course, they considered the memo inconsequential to share with the defense. I became aware of this "Breaking News" as calls began flooding in from the mainstream media, all wanting to know what this whistleblower information was all about. They were frustrated that this insignificant news website from Northern Idaho had scooped them. I tuned in – like everyone else – to watch the video as it was broadcast live on Facebook.

As the video appeared, there sat Representative Shea at a large plastic table with a microphone in from of him for the hastily broadcast news story. A handsome, well-groomed man with brownish blond hair, he held a set of notes from which he read, as Shari Dovale, the editor of *ReDoubt News*, tried her best to manage the broadcast, darting in out and of the camera's view.

Despite being a hurriedly set-up interview, what was to come over the next hour was stunning as he discussed and read from the memo.

The Memo
The internal memo was addressed to Andrew D. Goldsmith, Associate Deputy Attorney General, National Criminal Discovery Coordinator. The 18-page document was from Special Agent (SA) Larry "Clint"

Wooten from the BLM offices in Boise, Idaho.

In the memo, SA Wooten, identifies himself as the lead investigator of the Bundy cattle impound of 2014.

> *Issue: As a U.S. Department of Interior (DOI), Bureau of Land Management (BLM), Office of Law Enforcement and Security (OLES) Special Agent (SA) and Case Agent/Lead Investigator for the Cliven Bundy/2014 Gold Butte Trespass Cattle Impound Case out of the District of Nevada in Las Vegas (Case 2: 16-cr-0004q-GMN-PAL-United States of America v. Cliven Bundy, et al), I routinely observed, and the investigation revealed a widespread pattern of bad judgment, lack of discipline, incredible bias, unprofessionalism and misconduct, as well as likely policy, ethical, and legal violations among senior and supervisory staff at the BLM's Office of Law Enforcement and Security. The investigation indicated that these issues amongst law enforcement supervisors in our agency made a mockery of our position of special trust and confidence, portrayed extreme unprofessional bias, adversely affected our agency's mission and likely the trial regarding Cliven Bundy and his alleged co-conspirators and ignored the letter and intent of the law. The issues I uncovered in my opinion also likely put our agency and specific law enforcement supervisors in potential legal, civil, and administrative jeopardy.*

SA Wooten continued, describing how he attempted to report his concerns to his supervisor. He stated that he realized his concerns would most likely fall on deaf ears, as he had first-hand knowledge of his supervisor's actual participation in the misconduct. He stating in the memo that his supervisor was "unconcerned," "dismissive," "unsurprised," and "uninterested." He further explained that, though he was placed in charge of the largest and most expansive investigative case in the BLM history, his boss decided to be a co-lead investigator with him, and that agents more senior to him were to be his "helpers." This was against policy, and a deliberate violation of the chain of command so they could influence the outcome of the investigation. The actions were completely inappropriate because those other agents were directly involved with the activities of the round-up planning and implementation. For 34 months he found himself in this unusual situation. Though he was often publicly acknowledged as the lead agent and publicly thanked for his work, he found that his supervisor insisted upon taking charge of specific tasks.

During this timeframe, my supervisor (but subordinate), a BLM ASAC specifically wanted and had the responsibility of liaison and coordinator for interaction with higher agency officials, cooperating/assisting agencies and with the U.S. Attorney's Office. Although the BLM ASAC was generally uninterested in the mundane day to day work, he specifically took on assignments that were potentially questionable and damaging (such as document shredding research, discovery email search documentation and as the affiant for the Dave Bundy iPad Search Warrant) and attended coordination and staff meetings. Sometimes, I felt like he wanted to steer the investigation away from misconduct discovery by refusing to get case assistance, dismissing my concerns and participating in the misconduct himself. In February of 2017, it became clear to me that keeping quite became an unofficial condition of my future employment with the BLM, future awards, promotions, and a good future job reference. [sic]

As the investigation continued, SA Wooten's concerns deepened:

In my opinion, these issues would likely undermine the investigation, cast considerable doubt on the professionalism of our agency and be possibly used to claim investigator bias/unprofessionalism and to impeach and undermine key witness credibility. The ridiculousness of the conduct, unprofessional amateurish carnival atmosphere, openly made statements, and electronic communications tended to mitigate, the defendant's culpability and ·cast a shadow of doubt of inexcusable bias, unprofessionalism and embarrassment on our agency.

He also expressed his concern about the leaked video and audio footage that was aired in a PBS documentary in May of 2017 and subsequent YouTube videos that presented the BLM officers, all potential prosecution witnesses, in a negative light. These are the same officers, and their comments, included in Chapter 10 of this book.

Many times, these open unprofessional and disrespectful comments and name calling (often by law enforcement supervisors who are potential witnesses and investigative team supervisors) reminded me of middle school. At any given time, you could hear subjects of this investigation openly referred to as "ret*rds," "r*d-necks," "Overweight woman with the big jowls," "d*uche bags," "tractor-face," "idiots," "in-br*d," etc., etc., etc. Also, it was common to receive or have electronic communications reported to me during the course of the investigation in which senior investigators and law enforcement supervisors (some are potential witnesses and investigative team members) specifically made fun of suspects and referenced "Cliven Bundy felony...just kind of rolls off the tongue, doesn't it?," dildos; western themed g@y bars, odors of sweat, playing chess with menstru@ting women, Cliven Bundy sh1tting on cold stainless steel, personal lubricant and Ryan Bundy holding a giant pen1s (on April l2, 2014). Extremely bias and degrading fliers were also openly displayed and passed around the office, a booking photo of Cliven Bundy was (and· is) inappropriately, openly, prominently and proudly displayed in the office of a potential trial witness and my supervisor and an altered and degrading suspect photos were put in an office presentation by my supervisor.

Furthermore, I became aware of potentially captured comments in which our own law enforcement officers allegedly bragged about roughing up Dave Bundy, grinding his face into the ground, and Dave Bundy having little bits of gravel stuck in his face (from April 6, 2014). On two occasions, I also overheard a BLM SAC tell a BLM ASAC that another/other BLM employee(s) and potential trial witnesses didn't properly turn in the required discovery material (likely exculpatory evidence). My supervisor even instigated the unprofessional monitoring of jail calls between defendants and their wives, without prosecutor or FBI consent, for the apparent purpose of making fun of post arrest telephone calls between Idaho defendants/FBI targets (not subjects of BLM's investigation).

Another former BLM ASAC indicated to me that former BLM SAC Love was a liability to our agency and the Cliven Bundy Case. I was even told of threats of physical harm that this former BLM SAC made to his subordinate employee and his family.

Also, more and more it was becoming apparent that the numerous statements made by potential trial witnesses and victims (even by good officers under duress), could potentially cast an unfavorable light on the BLM. (See openly available video/audio footage titled "The Bundy Trial 2017 Leaked Fed Body Cam Evidence," or a video posted on You Tube titled "Leaked Body Cams from the Bundy Ranch!" published by Gavin Seim.) Some of these statements included the following: "Jack-up Hage" (Wayne Hage Jr.), "Are you fucXXXX people stupid or what," "Fat dude, right behind the tree has a long gun)," "'MotherFuXXXX, you come find me and you're gonna have hell to pay," "FatAsX slid down," "Pretty much a shoot first, ask questions-later," "No gun there. He's just holding his back standing like a sissy," "She must not be. married," "Shoot his fucXXXX dog first," "We gotta have fucXX:XX fire discipline," and "I'm recording by the way guys, so ..." Additional Note: In this timeframe, a key witness deactivated his body camera. Further Note: It became clear to me a serious public and professional image problem had developed within the BLM Office of Law Enforcement and Security. I felt I needed to work to correct this and mitigate the damage it no doubt had already done."

SA Wooten was also very concerned about the overall operational parameters set by Love.

> *The investigation also indicated that on multiple occasions, former BLM Special Agent in Charge (SAC) Love specifically and purposely ignored U.S. Attorney's Office and BLM civilian management direction and intent as well as Nevada State Official recommendations in order to command the most intrusive, oppressive, large scale, and militaristic trespass cattle impound possible. Additionally, this investigation also indicated excessive use of force, civil rights and policy violations. The investigation indicated that there was little doubt there was an improper cover-up in virtually every matter that a particular BLM SAC participated in or oversaw and that the BLM SAC was immune from discipline and the consequences of his actions.*

As the investigation went on his concerns regarding his supervisor and the investigation deepened. He witnessed time and time again the prejudicial demeanor toward The Bundy 19, their Mormon faith, which influenced office culture. SA Wooten was even asked at one point "You're not a Mormon, are you?" and "I bet you think I am going to hell." He became concerned over the handling of sworn testimony, noting that on more than one occasion officers that could be potential case witnesses were allowed to sit in the supervisor's office during conference calls with the prosecution team. When asked by AUSA Myhre if he was alone in the room, his supervisor would lie and indicate he was, among the knowing smiles of the other officers. This behavior undermined the purity of the case and the memory of the witnesses as to the facts in the case. Essentially, this allowed the witnesses to hear the prosecution's strategy and then modify their testimony to the prosecutor's narrative.

He also became concerned with the management of information given to the prosecution.

> *My supervisor even took photographs in the secure command post area of the Las Vegas FBI Headquarters and even after he was told that no photographs were allowed, he recklessly emailed out the photos of the "Tracking Wall" in which*

Eric Parker and Cliven Bundy had "X's" through their face and body (indicating prejudice and bias). Thereby, making this electronic communication subject to Federal Records Protections, the Litigation Hold, Discovery, and the FOIA.

Now, let's pause for a moment. Remember, the first eleven chapters of this book where written prior to the revelation of the memo. It was always unclear as to why Davey was simply kicked out the doors of the courthouse or why he was never charged after being arrested by the side of the road videoing. As it turns out, they were told (presumably by BLM civilian management) not to take such an overreaching and aggressive stance. The BLM, specifically Dan Love, was told not to make arrests. Yet, they did – violently and apparently with great glee. The FBI did target Cliven; they had a poster of him and others hanging on the wall of the FBI command center (remember the one they claimed was never there), the same FBI command center that the illegal video was fed into without anyone watching. But, there on the wall were pictures of the men with a targeted "X" through their faces.

Just like Cliven told me from prison.

The Cover Up
Up until February 18, 2017, these hijinks within the BLM offices were business as usual. Then, out of the blue, SA Wooten was relieved of his Bundy investigative responsibilities. He was aggressively interrogated by his supervisor about what he had said, who he had told and was this someone to be trusted. He was also told to turn over all of his case notes and calendars. His office safe was broken into, and all the hard files, including several hard drives containing emails and scanned data of his work on the Bundy case, everything he had documented, were confiscated by his supervisor. All were gone, never to be seen again. These items weren't just routine, these items were taken because they reflected serious misconduct and an embarrassment to the BLM office of Law Enforcement, and the Las Vegas prosecution team.

Why the Change in Wind?
Remember from Chapter 8, four days earlier Congressman Jason

Chavetz and Congressman Blake Farenthold sent a letter to the Department of the Interior's Office of Inspector General demanding Dan Love be investigated. They complained that Love appeared to have destroyed evidence subpoenaed by congress. It was now clear the entire law enforcement division of the BLM was in panic mode. And, SA Wooten had turned from celebrated to a threat.

SA Wooten wouldn't settle for this behavior and pressed his supervisor as to why he was removed from the case:

> *My supervisor told me that AUSA Steven Myhre "furiously demanded" that I be removed from the case and mentioned something about us (the BLM, specifically my supervisor) not turning over (or disclosing) discovery related material (which is true), issues I had with the BLM not following its own enabling statute (which is true, I can elaborate on that later), and a personal issue they thought I had with former BLM SAC Dan Love. Note: Prior to taking the assignment as Bundy/Gold Butte Investigation Case Agent/Lead Investigator for the BLM/ DOI I didn't know and had never spoken to former BLM SAC Dan Love. I was new to the agency and I was also specifically directed to lead an unbiased, professional, and independent investigation, which I tried to do, despite supervisory misconduct. Time after time, I was told of former BLM SAC Love's misconduct. I was told by BLM Law Enforcement Supervisors that he had a "Kill Book" as a trophy and in essence bragged about getting three individuals in Utah to commit suicide (see Operation Cerberus Action out of Blanding, Utah and the death of Dr. Redd), the "Failure Rock," Directing Subordinates to Erase Official Government Files in order to impede the efforts of rival civilian BLM employees in preparation for the "Burning Man" Special Event, unlawfully removing evidence, bragging about the number of OIG and internal investigations on him and indicating that he is untouchable, encouraging subordinates not to cooperate with internal and OIG investigation, his harassment of a female Native American subordinate employee where Mr. Love allegedly had a doll that he referenced to by the*

employee's name and called her his drunk little Indian, etc., etc., etc.

Following this, I became convinced that my supervisor failed to properly disclose substantive and exculpatory case and witness bias related issues to the U.S. Attorney's Office. Also, after speaking with the BLM OLES Chief of the Office of Professional Responsibility/Internal Affairs and two former BLM ASAC's, I became convinced that the previous BLM OLES Director Salvatore Lauro not only allowed former BLM SAC Dan Love complete autonomy and discretion, but also likely provided no oversight and even contributed to an atmosphere of cover-ups, harassment and retaliation for anyone that questioned or reported former BLM SAC Dan Love's misconduct.

In time, I also became convinced (based on my supervisor and Mr. Myhre's statements) that although the U.S. Attorney's Office was generally aware of former BLM SAC Dan Love's misconduct and likely civil rights and excessive force issues, the lead prosecutor (currently the Acting Nevada United States Attorney) Steven Myhre adopted an attitude of '"don't ask, don't tell," in reference to BLM Law Enforcement Supervisory Misconduct that was of a substantive, exculpatory and incredible biased nature. Not only did Mr. Myhre in my opinion not want to know or seek out evidence favorable to the accused, he and my supervisor discouraged the reporting of such issues and even likely covered up the misconduct. Furthermore, when I did report the misconduct, ethical, professional, and legal issues, I also became a victim of whistleblower retaliation.

Additionally, AUSA Steven Myhre adopted a few troubling policies in reference to this case. When we became aware that Dave Bundy's seized iPad likely contained remarks from BLM Law Enforcement Officers that is potentially evidence of civil rights violations and excessive use of force, Mr. Myhre and my supervisor not only apparently failed initiate the appropriate follow - on actions, Mr. Myhre apparently failed to notify the Defense Counsel and also decided not to return the iPad back to Dave Bundy, even though the iPad wasn't going to be searched pursuant to a search warrant or used as evidence in trial and Dave Bundy claimed he needed the iPad for his business. Mr. Myhre also adopted a policy of not giving a jury the option or ability to convict on lesser offenses and instead relied on a hard to prove, complicated prosecution theory in order to achieve maximum punishments (which has generally failed to this point).

He also exposed the prosecution's cover-up of the snipers that were 'not there.'

Also, the government relied on factually incorrect talking points and on (or about) February 15, 2017, misrepresented the case facts about government snipers during trial (it is unknown if this misrepresentation was on purpose or accidental, I can explain this in detail). Note: The investigation indicated that there was at least one school trained Federal Sniper equipped with a scoped/magnified optic bolt action precision rifle, another Federal Officer equipped with a scoped/ magnified optic large frame (308 caliber) AR style rifle, and many officers that utilized magnified optics with long range graduated reticles (out to 1, 000 meters- approximately 500 meters on issued rifles depending on environmental conditions) on standard law enforcement issued AR (223 caliber/5.56mm) and that often officers were in "over watch" positions. Additionally, the investigation also indicated the possibility that the FBI and the Las Vegas Metropolitan Police Department had law enforcement snipers/designated marksmen on hand for possible deployment.

He ends his 18-page statement with concern, not for himself but for The Bundy 19.

I ask that your office ensure that Acting United States Attorney Steven Myhre and the rest of the Cliven Bundy/ Gold Butte Nevada Prosecution and Investigative Team is conducting the prosecution in an ethical, appropriate, and professional matter. I also specifically ask that your office provide oversight to Mr. Myhre and his team regarding the affirmative responsibility to seek out evidence-favorable to the accused, not to discourage the reporting of case issues and suspected misconduct, to report/act on suspected civil rights violations and not to retaliate against an agent that does his required duty. I also ask that your office ensure that the Prosecution Team is free of bias and has ethically and correctly turned over exculpatory evidence to the Defense. I ask that as appropriate, prosecution team bias (by Mr. Myhre and possibly by AUSA Daniel Schiess) and factually incorrect talking points (by AUSA Nadia Ahmed and Mr. Myhre) be disclosed and corrected. Note: Mr. Myhre previously referenced to the defendants as a cult and Mr. Schiess said let's get these "shall we say Deplorables." I was also asked "You're not a Mormon are you." (I can explain these and similar issues in-detail.)

I don't make this complaint lightly. I do this with a heavy heart and I hope that at least in some ways I am mistaken. However, I know that is extremely unlikely.

I have studied this memo and as I did, I felt a mixture of satisfaction and anger. It's a strange combination in a man's soul. After reading this I am satisfied that Cliven Bundy is the real deal as I referred to him in Chapter 2. He never once lied to me or embellished any part of his story, all of which was told to me before I ever heard of the Wooten Memo. The first edition of this book was already in print before this memo was released. In my heart, I felt assured if it had been allowed in court it would have exonerated Cliven Bundy. I was also angry: Angry that men and women sworn to protect The Constitution of The United Sates, and who swore an oath to uphold it with their sacred honor, have apparently trespassed so far past that oath its unconscionable.

At the printing of this edition the remaining men still in lock-up have attempted to use this memo – and the apparently-secret _second_ Wooten Memo – to request that their cases be set aside and or dismissed altogether. The second memo has been confirmed by the various defense teams that it does exist. But, it remains secret under court seal and the prosecution will not let it leave the prosecutor's office. Todd Engel's attorney tried to have SA Wooten give a willing sworn deposition before Engel's sentencing, in hopes that his testimony would bring a fuller understanding as to the abuses of the Justice Department and the BLM. Judge Navarro denied that request. Engel has appealed to the 9th Circuit Court of Appeals. The other men in lock-up, and those who pled guilty, continue to hope the Wooten revelation will bring them relief in the courts. But for now, they remain incarcerated, their families toiling forward without them.

The _Las Vegas Review Journal_, frustrated by the cover-up and court seal of all the evidence including both Wooten memos, has also filed a lawsuit to force Judge Navarro to unseal what has gone on in the Bundy case. The _Las Vegas Review Journal_ suit, as well as various multimillion dollar civil cases brought by the exonerated men of The Bundy 19, all are pending.

As they say, 'the wheels of justice move slowly.'

Unfortunately, often those wheels grind the lives of its victims to dust.

Chapter 16

– BACK ON THE RANCH –
Where Does Cliven Bundy STAND Today?

April 12, 2018 was the four-year anniversary of the Protest in Bunkerville, Nevada, now also widely known worldwide as "The Standoff." My editor, Art Ritter, and I spent the day with Cliven and Carol, back home on their ranch, 94 days after Cliven walked out of the Las Vegas court house a free man.

The Bundy Ranch headquarters hugs the banks of the Virgin River. As I walked out onto the flat bottom field on which it sits, I saw off in the distance a familiar figure wrenching on a farm tractor. There he was just smiling away, appearing as happy as I was ever to see him, waving back at me like he didn't want me to miss him in the few yards between us. He was just as I always envisioned he'd be at home; tan and weathered from the elements. When he took his straw cowboy hat off to wipe the sweat from his brow, I noticed the dark tan line across his forehead, marking where his hat rested every working day in the hot sun of Southern Nevada. He had on dirty Levis and an oil-stained shirt. In the knee-high grass I noticed white rubber boots that reached

just below his knees. Galoshes is what I call them. Perfect for work in the fields of a farm. As I approached, he wiped his dirty hand on his oily shirt and extended it out to greet me in a handshake.

"Well, howdy!" He said.

"You grow cattle out here?" I greeted, pointing to the surrounding desert.

In the hour drive to the Bundy Ranch from Las Vegas, I was set back at the bleakness of the Mojave Desert; miles upon miles of dirt, and brush. The only thing to break up the desert was an occasional photovoltaic (solar panel) farm. I just couldn't imagine desiring to live out in such harshness. I couldn't imagine raising a family, a farm, let alone cattle in such an environment.

At my response, he just laughed, "Well sure I do. Let me show you."

We walked back to the small, modest ranch house, the original home his father had built nestled among some cottonwood trees.

"Let me give you the cook's tour."

We walked around the back of the house and he showed me his small cattle feedlot, horse pens and the various pastures around the Bundy Ranch Headquarters. He showed me the ingenious customizations of his cattle loading chutes and feed troughs. I noticed he didn't have a big barn, like most ranches. With large quantities of hay stacked about, it left me wondering if it was because of the desert climate that there was no need for a barn or the costliness of such a structure. We circled back to the front of the house. Cliven said, "This is Carol's car, we need to clean it out a bit, so you can sit." So, we quickly cleaned out the family SUV. Then, together, we crossed the road that winds past the Bundy Ranch and its sign I had seen in so many newspaper articles. We drove on the adjacent dirt road straight up a hill, then another and then another.

Within twenty minutes we were far above the Virgin River Valley where we had just stood. Not once had we stopped to open or close a gate, something I was used to doing in ranch life. Here, we never saw a fence, let alone a gate. For miles and miles we drove, gaining elevation and ever further into the high desert mountains. Cliven stopped at a well-worn vista point, waving his hand across the horizon toward the desert valley where we started.

"See 'em mountains over there?"

"Sure," noticing Interstate 15 about halfway across the valley.

"That's my range," Cliven stated as a matter of fact. "Down there you can see some of my cattle," indicating a small group of cows near the river in the distance, appearing to be roughly ten miles away. Then he pointed south, "see the lake over there?"

"Yep," I replied looking off in the distance – far off in the distance.

"That's Lake Mead."

Suddenly I was lost in thought, recalling how Cliven had told me he farmed along the shore of Lake Mead. "That looks nearly a hundred miles away," I exclaimed.

"Nearer 65," he replied, as he started up the SUV again and started rolling forward.

As we bounced along, I pondered on the enormity of the range on which Cliven grazed his cattle. But, where were his cattle? For better than an hour we'd been driving, and we had just seen that one small group. Finally, we came up on a small corral of Powder River panels, it's gate pinned wide open for the cows to come and go freely. Inside was a water trough, a salt lick and mineral lick and lots of cow pies (cow manure). I thought to myself, "So, there are more cows here, at least according to the evidence."

We traveled the further along dirt mountain roads. At one point we stopped in the middle of the road, and once more Cliven indicated something on our left. "You see on the left side of the road is burned?"

"Well, sure," I said, thinking how could you not? The vista opened up to a vast area, burned for miles.

Off to the right, he pointed again. "You notice it's not burned over here?" On the right side of the road, the brush and surrounding vegetation was chest high.

"I do" I replied.

"Well, that fire was better than 10 years ago. Nah, more like 12 - I have been away for a while" he continued, smiling. "It takes a long, long time for the desert to recuperate after a fire. Once it gets fully grown and productive like this," pointing back to the right, "It almost never gets back once it's burned. What these environmental people don't understand is that we're either growing food or fuel! Food for us to consume or fuel for a fire to consume, which, of course, we spend millions on trying to put out." Cliven shook his head.

"But, this is all brush. There is little grass here for your cows" I responded.

Cliven opened his door, got out, and walked around his SUV. I watched what he was doing, not sure if I was to follow. He spent a couple of minutes going from plant to bush and picked a bouquet of various plants. Then he came around to the passenger side of the vehicle with a handful of grasses, brush, flowers, and even a few succulents, and thrust it forward though my open passenger window. He pointed at each variety of vegetation in his hand and described to me what each was and how the cows would eat it. "You see, my cows don't graze only on grass, they browse on everything out here. See how all the plants are all flat across the top? It's like somebody used a hedge trimmer on them."

"Sure, enough they all have flattop haircuts," I exclaimed, only just noticing the fact.

"That's because my cows come through here and browse off the tops, about chest high."

He was right. Everything was about the height of a full-grown cow's chin.

"What happens when you prune back a plant?" he quizzed me. "Well, new, healthier growth occurs."

Knowing the answer, I asked, "What happens if you don't prune it back?"

"It goes to seed, dries up and dies."

Again, knowing that answer. "Dry feed makes what?"

Pointing at the miles of burned area, "Fuel!"

Knowing I got his point, he dropped the impromptu teaching bouquet on the ground and returned to the driver's side, satisfied that I'd "learn't somp'n" and started up the vehicle again.

We drove for a while longer and came across a small group of cows and calves. "There are some of my cows," pointing up the hill a bit. I was pleasantly surprise at the look of Cliven's animals. Just as he told me in lock-up, there stood Hereford cows and tiger striped (F1) calves. They looked good, too, real good. Fat, slick and content, but a little skittish. The cows stared at us for a moment and, once they realized we meant no harm, went back to browsing. On the other hand, the calves were ready to bolt at any sudden move. They never broke their stare. I remembered how Cliven explained to me months ago how his cattle were a special breed he developed for the unique environ of the desert of Southern Nevada. They had been carefully bred to endure traveling long distances between water supplies, and bred to browse off the forage, not just the grasses of the Mojave. They behaved more like wild animals than the domesticated cows I was used to. I also recalled how – in all the research I had done for this book – the prosecutors, environmentalists, and BLM managers denigrated Cliven's animal husbandry skills:

"His ranching operation — to the extent it can be called that — is unconventional if not bizarre," Assistant U.S. Attorney Charles Gorder wrote of Bundy in a government memo seeking to deny bail to the rancher, then jailed in Oregon.

"There's sort of a metaphor between Bundy and his cows: They've both gone rogue," says Jeff Ruch, executive director of Public Employees for Environmental Responsibility, a nonprofit that represents employees from agencies such as the BLM. "We, at one point, jokingly suggested they should be hunted as game animals."

"This is some of the worst, least-productive grazing land in the country," says Kieran Suckling, executive director of the Center for Biological Diversity

Apparently, like BLM's Southern District Manager, Mary Jo Rugwell, none had ever actually set foot on the Gold Butte range before making such definitive proclamations. Cliven, like so many other ranchers I have met, far better understood the conservation of the land from which they earned their livelihood than any office-dwelling bureaucrat or so called 'environmentalist'.

As we circled back around to the Bundy Ranch headquarters, we traveled along a deep wash where a flash flood had taken out many miles of the pipe Cliven had laid to provide water from the spring cisterns built in the mountains. These range improvements fed several water troughs throughout the range. These troughs provided water not just to the Bundy cattle, but also to the indigenous wildlife. It was incredible the work and effort it must have taken to initially install, maintain, and now replace these systems. At one of his vast watering systems, Cliven told me how it was first put in by the Basque sheepherders who would graze hundreds of thousands of sheep in the area when he was a kid. We looked at underground cisterns, installed in the early 1800's, at least according to the handwritten etching on one. There were old unused and broken-down water troughs that had at least ten different brands on them, including one with the Bundy's brand, a common practice in order to lay claim on such an important range development, dating from the 1800's. There it was, undeniable proof that this was just as Cliven had claimed; the land his ancestors had been grazing since they came to Nevada.

As we got closer to ranch headquarters, Cliven entertained us with

personal stories of hunting with his dad, and ornery cows he tried to gather in this rough, unforgiving country. As I listened to him, I could feel his love for the land and its history.

The more we descended back to the Virgin River, the clearer the distance we had traveled.

"Cliven, how far have we traveled today?" I asked.

"Oh, 'bout 80 miles I guess," looking at the fuel gauge. "We better go to town and get some fuel before we give this back to Carol."

Off to Mesquite we headed.

What concerns Cliven today?
I had scheduled some time to come to the ranch to attend a dismissal of charges celebration. But those celebratory plans were quickly abandoned out of concern for those that continued to languish in lock-up.

"I am not sure what we can do for 'em," says Cliven, as we rumbled down the desert ranch road on our way to the gas station. "Engel and Burleson might have some chance," referring to the post-conviction relief filings both men have in the motion. "But the ones who'd plead guilty … I just don't know what we can do," he shook his head.

These days, Cliven and Carol are not in the happiest of moods. The men left behind in prison weigh heavy on each of them. "The thought of 'em men still living out their days in prison just breaks my heart." Stopping the truck, we looked over the edge of the northbound bridge of Interstate 15 spanning the Toquop Wash, where the famous standoff was held. Cliven described what happened that day. Carefully, he reiterated, clearly, neither he or Carol were at the Toquop Wash on April 12, 2014. But, Cliven did see the evidence and discovery while preparing for his own trial, giving him great insight into the actions of all of the Bundy 19. Interestingly, he only came to know most of them in federal lock-up.

"Right here, this is as far as Todd had walked out on the bridge," indicating a distance of approximately 35 feet. While I was in Pahrump with Todd Engel, almost a year ago, he told me the story where he had just arrived and gotten out of his pickup when a lady had come running up the northbound bridge yelling that the protesters in the wash were being threatened to be shot. Todd had just arrived from driving all night from Idaho and was curious to see what was going on. He stayed for maybe 20 minutes, before he and the other men on the bridge saw the snipers above them on the mesa, targeting the protesters below. Todd also realized he and the other men were also targeted from those same 'overwatch' positions. Todd sprinted back up to the closest Sheriffs' deputy to plea for the Sheriff to intervene before the men, women, and children, below in the wash, were slaughtered. That Sheriffs' deputy did heed Todd's concern, notifying his command of the precarious situation that was playing out.

Todd remained off the bridge and out of target range for the remainder of the Protest, helping the Nevada Highway Patrol as they attempted to direct traffic and the crowds. Once it was over, and the federal agents left, Todd got in his pickup and headed to get some much-needed sleep. The next day, he drove back to Northern Idaho. Todd learned a few years later how close he had become to losing his life that day. On the day of the standoff, the BLM Rangers had taken their safeties off and requested permission to fire upon the men on the bridge, only to be ordered to stand down by the Sheriff's department as they took control and ordered federal agents to leave the area.

Representing himself at trial, Todd was one of two men to be found guilty in the first trial (Tier One) in 2017. After spending the sum total of one and a half hours at the Protest, the Federal Prosecutor argued that Todd should be sentenced to 20 years in prison. Judge Navarro sentenced him to 14 years, stating that Engel "Just didn't get it," effectively giving him a life sentence. At the Standoff, he spent most of his time with the highway patrol, which did corroborate his version of events during his trial. He never took his gun out of the low ready position, leaving it strapped to his chest or lowered, and pointed it at no one.

Gregory Burleson was another latecomer to the Protest that day. As we looked over the I-15 overpass, Cliven showed me the route and position Greg took down into the Toquop Wash. "Burleson didn't follow the road down like 'em other protesters," said Cliven, recounting the day while sitting behind the wheel of SUV. "He had climbed over the Jersey Barrier and took a more direct route into the wash from the bridge. When he got down in the wash, Ammon told Burleson to get back to the northbound bridge." Ammon had assessed the danger at hand and had ordered anyone with a rifle to retreat back and away from the center of the confrontation in which they now found themselves. Greg Burleson did exactly as he was told: He got out of the confrontation and knelt down, away from the Southern I-15 overpass and where the Federal Agents had taken up the position to fire upon the crowd.

Burleson received a 68-year sentence for his participation that day. "He wasn't found guilty because of what he *did*!" Cliven later editorialized. "He was found guilty for what he *said* after the FBI got him drunk and then interviewed him while pretend'n to be reporters," referring to the undercover operation 'Longbow Productions.'

Then there are the men who were forced into guilty pleas; Jerry Deleamus, Pete Santilli, Eric Parker, Scott Drexler and others who were tried along with Engel and Burleson. Had all the evidence been available to the defendants and their courtroom jurors, they would have made very different decisions. Each of The Bundy 19 was under tremendous pressure, life-altering pressure, that's impossible to understand unless you have personally gone through it. The federal government creates this intense pressure to achieve their 97% conviction rate. It's why nearly everyone who comes into contact with the federal justice system goes to prison, with most drawing long sentences. Americans just assume that if someone is targeted by federal prosecutors, some terrible crime must have been committed, and they are just really good at convicting the guilty. In reality, the federal government practices pressure and manipulation to get the accused to plead guilty, leaving the remaining few to go to trial. Added to this prosecutorial pressure, when the accused maintain their innocence and choose to go to trial, they receive the ire of the prosecutors for challenging them. If they are then found guilty, the federal courts dole out ungodly long sentences like Burleson's and Engel's. They call it the "trial penalty". At the end of the day, U.S. Attorneys often care more about "collecting scalps" then dispensing equal justice.

This is Cliven's deepest desire today: to see each man released and exonerated. After 650 days in prison, Cliven refused to accept the pre-trial release for himself offered by Judge Navarro until every one of The Bundy 19 was released. It was only after all the charges were dismissed against him that he was he forced to leave those men behind still in lock-up – 50 days later. "This thing isn't over. The fight I have today is to see each of 'em men home with their families and all the charges dropped." Shaking his head resolutely, "How can I be happy, how can I celebrate my own release, when so many who came to STAND with me are still in prison? How can I not still STAND with them now?"

After fueling up the SUV in Mesquite, we headed back to the Bundy Ranch Headquarters. When we finally pulled into the headquarters, Carol greeted us at the door. "You men hungry?" she asked with a knowing smile. She welcomed us into their small, but impeccably kept home. As I sat in their modest living room, I had two thoughts.

So much for Cliven being a wealthy man as the media portrayed him, he was supposed to be a millionaire according to the main stream media. My next thought; how did they raise 14 kids in this tiny house? It was a rhetorical question, and I kept it to myself. Carol offered me a cold drink and asked me to sit in Cliven's chair. Cliven was washing up. There, on the wall, was the original oil painting "Pray for America" done by Jon McNaughton. It was of Cliven Bundy sitting horseback in prayer, the very same picture as on the front of this book. I smiled, not knowing that the artist had given the original to him. Then, I had my chance to wash up and we sat together at the big family table laughing and eating Bundy beef, fresh veggies and homemade bread.

At the printing of this book, Cliven has spent the summer putting hay up and attending to the ranch he dearly loves. He had been away so long that there was plenty of work to do. On occasion he speaks to audiences who have an interest in his story. But, mostly he just wants to love God, his family, farm, and raise cattle. He reminded me at the table that evening, "All I'd ever wanted was to be left alone, to live my life. All of this has been thrusted on me. If the government hadn't forced themselves on me, you wouldn't a' heard of the name of Cliven Bundy."

On August 3, 2018, the U.S. Justice Department filed a notice of appeal seeking to preserve its "right" to seek a reversal of the case's dismissal by Judge Gloria Navarro of the U.S. District Court for the District of Nevada of the indictment which named Cliven Bundy, two of his sons – Ammon and Ryan, and Ryan Payne.

Cliven Bundy and his family **remain in criminal jeopardy**. If the Ninth Circuit Court of Appeals in San Francisco sides with the prosecution and overturns Judge Navarro's dismissal, Cliven Bundy may be placed back in custody and a new trial could begin.

If convicted, he will spend the rest of his life in prison.

How can _YOU_ help?

Begin a letter-writing campaign, first to the President,
asking for a pardon for all of the Bundy 19. Send
letters to Attorney General's office and your
congressional representative to cease the further
prosecution of the Bundy's. A visit to their local
congressional office will help show just how serious
this is.

Included with your letter, send them a copy of this
book. Ask them to read it.

Get the word out.
You can do this by purchasing additional copies of this
book and placing them in the hands of those interested.
Ask them to join you in getting the word out about the
abuses of our government. Get extra books for your
library, local bookstores, wherever possible in order to
get this book read. And the truth out there.

Invite Mike to come and speak to your group and share
this story.

For further information on the above or to make your comments about
this book here: _**ClivenBundy.net**_

For more of the author's books, go to **MikeStickler.online.**

Photograph Credits

Courtesy of the Bundy Ranch
Page: vi, 28, 32, 33, 34, 36, 45, 52, 60, 86, 92, 94, 124, 126, 133, 147, 294, 304

Public Record:
Multnomah County, Oregon booking photo Cliven Bundy, Page 15, Round-up Cattle Compound Court Records USA v. Cliven Bundy, Page 225, 246, 252, 305

Jim Urquhart—Reuters
Pages, 24, 46, 239, 245, 247, 267

John Locher, Associate Press
Page 68, 195

Getty Images
Page 204

Associated Press
Page 245, 342

KAnne Designs
Pages 359, 364, 365, 369

CPSIA information can be obtained
at www.ICGtesting.com
Printed in the USA
BVHW04s0943150918
527566BV00020B/284/P